D1000651

COMPENDIUM

OF THE

IMPENDING CRISIS

OF

THE SOUTH.

BY

HINTON ROWAN HELPER,

OF NORTH CAROLINA.

COMPENDIUM

OF THE

IMPENDING CRISIS

OF

THE SOUTH.

BY

HINTON ROWAN HELPER,

OF NORTH CAROLINA.

COUNTRYMEN! I sue for simple justice at your hands,
Naught else I ask, nor less will have;
Act right, therefore, and yield my claim,
Or, by the great God that made all things,
I'll fight, till from my bones my flesh be hack'd!—*Shakspeare*.

The liberal deviseth liberal things,
And by liberal things shall he stand.—*Isaiah*.

MNEMOSYNE PUBLISHING CO., INC.
MIAMI, FLORIDA
1969

Originally Published in New York 1860

𝔗𝔲

CASSIUS M. CLAY,

OF KENTUCKY,

FRANCIS P. BLAIR, Jr.,

OF MISSOURI,

BENJAMIN S. HEDRICK,

OF NORTH CAROLINA,

AND TO THE

NON-SLAVEHOLDING WHITES OF THE SOUTH, GENERALLY,

WHETHER AT HOME OR ABROAD,

THIS WORK IS MOST CORDIALLY DEDICATED

BY THEIR

SINCERE FRIEND AND FELLOW-CITIZEN,

THE AUTHOR.

First Mnemosyne reprinting 1969

**Reprinted from a copy in the
Fisk University Library Negro Collection.**

Copyright © 1969   Mnemosyne Publishing Co., Inc.   Miami, Florida

Library of Congress Catalog Card Number:

75-83966

Printed in the United States of America

PREFACE.

———•◦•———

If my countrymen, particularly my countrymen of the South, still more particularly those of them who are non-slaveholders, shall peruse this work, they will learn that no narrow and partial doctrines of political or social economy, no prejudices of early education, have induced me to write it. If, in any part of it, I have actually deflected from the tone of true patriotism and nationality, I am unable to perceive the fault. What I have committed to paper is but a fair reflex of the honest and long-settled convictions of my heart.

In writing this book it has been no part of my purpose to cast unmerited opprobrium upon slaveholders, or to display any special friendliness or sympathy for the blacks. I have considered my subject more particularly with reference to its economic aspects as regards the whites—not with reference, except in a very slight degree, to its humanitarian or religious aspects. To the latter side of the question, Northern writers have already done full and timely justice. The genius of the North has also most ably and eloquently discussed the subject in the form of novels. New England wives have written the most popular anti-slavery literature of the day. Against this I have nothing to say; it is all well enough for women to give the fictions of slavery; men should give the facts.

I trust that my friends and fellow-citizens of the South will read this book—nay, proud as any Southerner though I am, I entreat, I beg of them to do so. And as the work, considered with reference to its author's nativity, is a novelty—the South being my birth-place and my home, and my ancestry having resided there for more than a century—so I indulge the hope that its reception by my fellow-Southrons will also be novel; that is to say, that they will receive it, as it is offered, in a reasonable and friendly spirit, and that they will read it and reflect upon it as an honest and faithful endeavor to treat a subject of vast import, without rancor or prejudice, by one who naturally comes within the pale of their own sympathies.

An irrepressibly active desire to do something to elevate the South to an honorable and powerful position among the enlightened quarters of the globe, has been the great leading principle that has actuated me in the preparation of the present volume; and so well convinced am I that the plan which I have proposed is the only really practicable one for achieving the desired end, that I earnestly hope to see it prosecuted with energy and zeal, until the Flag of Freedom shall wave triumphantly alike over the valleys of Virginia and the mounds of Mississippi.

H. R. H.

June 21, 1859.

CONTENTS, ALPHABETICALLY ARRANGED.

CHAPTER I.

COMPARISONS BETWEEN THE FREE AND THE SLAVE STATES.

Comparisons are at the bottom of all philosophy. It is by comparisons that we ascertain the difference which exists between things, and it is by comparisons, also, that we ascertain the general features of things, and it is by comparisons that we reach general propositions. Without comparisons we never can generalize. Without comparisons we never could go beyond the knowledge of isolated, disconnected facts.—AGASSIZ.

It is not our intention in this chapter to enter into an elaborate ethnographical essay, to establish peculiarities of difference, mental, moral, or physical, in the great family of man. Neither is it our design to launch into a philosophical disquisition on the laws and principles of light and darkness, with a view of educing any additional evidence of the fact, that as a general rule, the rays of the sun are more fructifying and congenial than the shades of night. Nor yet is it our purpose, by writing a formal treatise on ethics, to draw a broad line of distinction between right and wrong, to point out the propriety of morality and its advantages over immorality, nor to waste time in pressing a universally admitted truism—that virtue is preferable to vice. Self-evident truths require no argumentative demonstration.

What we mean to do is simply this: to take a survey of the relative position and importance of the several states of this confederacy, from the adoption of the national compact; and when, of two sections of the country starting under the same auspices, and with equal natural advantages, we find the one rising to a degree of almost unexampled power and eminence, and the other sinking into a state of comparative imbecility and obscurity, it is our determination to trace out the causes which have led to the elevation of the former, and the depression of the latter, and to use our most earnest and honest endeavors to utterly extirpate whatever opposes the progress and prosperity of any portion of the Union.

This survey we have already made; we have also instituted impartial comparisons between the cardinal sections of the country, north, south, east, and west; and as a true-hearted southerner, whose ancestors have resided in North Carolina between one and two hundred years, and as one who would rather have his native clime excel than be excelled, we feel constrained to confess that we are deeply abashed and chagrined at the disclosures of the comparisons thus instituted. At the time of the

7

adoption of the Constitution in 1789, we commenced an even race with
the North. All things considered, if either the North or the South had
the advantage, it was the latter. In proof of this, let us introduce a few
statistics, beginning with the states of

NEW YORK AND VIRGINIA.

In 1790, when the first census was taken, New York contained 340,120
inhabitants ; at the same time the population of Virginia was 748,308,
being more than twice the number of New York. Just sixty years afterward, as we learn from the census of 1850, New York had a population
of 3,097,394 ; while that of Virginia was only 1,421,661, being less than
half the number of New York! In 1791, the exports of New York
amounted to $2,505,465 ; the exports of Virginia amounted to $3,130,865.
In 1852, the exports of New York amounted to $87,484,456; the exports
of Virginia, during the same year, amounted to only $2,724,657. In 1790,
the imports of New York and Virginia were about equal; in 1853, the
imports of New York amounted to the enormous sum of $178,270,999 :
while those of Virginia, for the same period, amounted to the comparatively pitiful aggregate of only $399,004. In 1850, the products of
manufactures, mining and the mechanics arts in New York amounted to
$237,597,249 ; those of Virginia amounted to only $29,705,387. At the
taking of the last census, the value of real and personal property in Virginia, including negroes, was $391,646,438 ; that of New York, exclusive
of any monetary valuation of human beings, was $1,080,309,216.

In August, 1856, the real and personal estate assessed in the City of
New York amounted in valuation to $511,740,491, showing that New
York City alone is worth far more than the whole State of Virginia.

What says one of Virginia's own sons? He still lives; hear him
speak. Says Gov. Wise:

" It may be painful, but nevertheless, profitable, to recur occasionally to the history of the past ; to listen to the admonitions of experience, and learn lessons of
wisdom from the efforts and actions of those who have preceded us in the drama
of human life. The records of former days show that at a period not very remote,
Virginia stood preëminently the first commercial State in the Union ; when her
commerce exceeded in amount that of all the New England States combined ;
when the city of Norfolk owned more than one hundred trading ships, and her
direct foreign trade exceeded that of the city of New York, now the centre of
trade and the great emporium of North America. At the period of the war of
independence, the commerce of Virginia was four times larger than that of New
York."

The cash value of all the farms, farming implements and machinery
in Virginia, in 1850, was $223,423,315 ; the value of the same in New
York, in the same year, was $576,631,568. In about the same ratio does
the value of the agricultural products and live stock of New York
exceed the value of the agricultural products and live stock of Virginia.
But we will pursue this humiliating comparison no further. With feel-

ings mingled with indignation and disgust, we turn from the picture, and will now pay our respects to

MASSACHUSETTS AND NORTH CAROLINA.

In 1790, Massachusetts contained 378,717 inhabitants; in the same year North Carolina contained 393,751; in 1850, the population of Massachusetts was 994,514, all freemen; while that of North Carolina was only 869,039, of whom 288,548 were slaves. Massachusetts has an area of only 7,800 square miles; the area of North Carolina is 50,704 square miles, which, though less than Virginia, is considerably larger than the State of New York. Massachusetts and North Carolina each have a harbor, Boston and Beaufort, which harbors, with the States that back them, are, by nature, possessed of about equal capacities and advantages for commercial and manufacturing enterprise. Boston has grown to be the second commercial city in the Union; her ships, freighted with the useful and unique inventions and manufactures of her ingenious artisans and mechanics, and bearing upon their stalwart arms the majestic flag of our country, glide triumphantly through the winds and over the waves of every ocean. She has done, and is now doing, great honor to herself, her State and the nation, and her name and fame are spoken with reverence in the remotest regions of the earth.

How is it with Beaufort, in North Carolina, whose harbor is said to be the safest and most commodious anywhere to be found on the Atlantic coast south of the harbor of New York, and but little inferior to that? Has anybody ever heard of her? Do the masts of her ships ever cast a shadow on foreign waters? Upon what distant or benighted shore have her merchants and mariners ever hoisted our national ensign, or spread the arts of civilization and peaceful industry? What changes worthy of note have taken place in the physical features of her superficies since "the evening and the morning were the third day?" But we will make no further attempt to draw a comparison between the populous, wealthy, and renowned city of Boston and the obscure, despicable little village of Beaufort, which, notwithstanding "the placid bosom of its deep and well-protected harbor," has no place in the annals or records of the country, and has scarcely ever been heard of fifty miles from home.

In 1853, the exports of Massachusetts amounted to $16,895,304, and her imports to $41,367,956; during the same time, and indeed during all the time, from the period of the formation of the government up to the year 1853, inclusive, the exports and imports of North Carolina were so utterly insignificant that we are ashamed to record them. In 1850, the products of manufactures, mining and the mechanic arts in Massachusetts, amounted to $151,137,145; those of North Carolina, to only $9,111,245. In 1856, the products of these industrial pursuits in Massachusetts had increased to something over $288,000,000, a sum more than *twice* the value of the entire cotton crop of all the Southern States! In 1850, the cash value of all the farms, farming implements and machinery in Massachusetts, was $112,285,931; the value of the same in North Carolina, in the same year, was only $71,823,298. In 1850, the value of all the real and personal estate in Massachusetts, without recognizing property in man, or setting a monetary price on the head of a single citizen, white or black, amounted to $573,342,286; the value of the same in North Carolina, including negroes, amounted to only $226,800,472. In 1856, the real and personal estate assessed in the city of Boston amounted in valuation to within a fraction of $250,000,000, showing conclusively that so far as dollars and cents are concerned, that single city could buy the whole State of North Carolina, and by right of purchase, if sanctioned by the Constitution of the United States, and by State Constitutions, hold her as a province. In 1850, there were in Massachusetts 1,861 native white and free colored persons over twenty years of age who could not read and write; in the same year, the same class of persons in North Carolina numbered 80,063; while her 288,548 slaves were, by legislative enactments, kept in a state of absolute ignorance and unconditional subordination.

Hoping, however, and believing, that a large majority of the most respectable and patriotic citizens of North Carolina have resolved, or will soon resolve, with unyielding purpose, to cast aside the great obstacle that impedes their progress, and bring into action a new policy which will lead them from poverty and ignorance to wealth and intellectual greatness, and which will shield them not only from the rebukes of their own consciences, but also from the just reproaches of the civilized world, we will, for the present, in deference to their feelings, forbear the further enumeration of these degrading disparities, and turn our attention to

PENNSYLVANIA AND SOUTH CAROLINA.

An old gentleman, now residing in Charleston, told us, but a short while since, that he had a distinct recollection of the time when Charleston imported foreign fabrics for the Philadelphia trade, and when, on a certain occasion, his mother went into a store on Market street to select a silk dress for herself, the merchant, unable to please her fancy, persuaded her to postpone the selection for a few days, or until the arrival of a new stock of superb styles and fashions which he had recently purchased in the metropolis of South Carolina. This was all very proper. Charleston had a spacious harbor, a central position, and a mild climate; and from priority of settlement and business connections, to say nothing of other advantages, she enjoyed greater facilities for commercial transactions than Philadelphia. She had a right to get

custom wherever she could find it, and in securing so valuable a custo-
mer as the Quaker City, she exhibited no small degree of laudable enterprise. But why did she not maintain her supremacy? If the answer
to this query is not already in the reader's mind, it will suggest itself
before he peruses the whole of this work. For the present, suffice it to
say, that the cause of her shameful insignificance and decline is essentially the same that has thrown every other southern city and State in
the rear of progress, and rendered them tributary, in a commercial and
manufacturing point of view, almost entirely tributary, to the more
sagacious and enterprising States and cities of the North.

A most unfortunate day was that for the Palmetto State, and indeed
for the whole South, when the course of trade was changed, and she
found herself the retailer of foreign and domestic goods, imported and
vended by wholesale merchants at the North. Philadelphia ladies no
longer look to the South for late fashions, and fine silks and satins; no
Quaker dame now wears drab apparel of Charleston importation. Like
all other centres of trade in our disreputable part of the confederacy,
the commercial emporium of South Carolina is sick and impoverished;
her silver cord has been loosed; her golden bowl has been broken; and
her unhappy people, without proper or profitable employment, poor in
pocket, and few in number, go mourning or loafing about the streets.
Her annual importations are actually less now than they were a century
ago, when South Carolina was the second commercial province on the
continent, Virginia being the first.

In 1760, as we learn from Mr. Benton's "Thirty Years' View,"
the foreign imports into Charleston were $2,662,000; in 1855, they
amounted to only $1,750,000! In 1854, the imports into Philadelphia,
which, in foreign trade, ranks at present but fourth among the commercial cities of the Union, were $21,963,021. In 1850, the products of
manufactures, mining, and the mechanic arts, in Pennsylvania, amounted
to $155,044,910; the products of the same in South Carolina, amounted
to only $7,063,513.

As shown by the census report of 1850, which was prepared under
the superintendence of a native of South Carolina, who certainly will
not be suspected of injustice to his own section of the country—the
Southern States—the cash value of all the farms, farming implements,
and machinery in Pennsylvania, was $422,598,640; the value of the
same in South Carolina, in the same year, was only $86,518,038. From
a compendium of the same census, we learn that the value of all the
real and personal property in Pennsylvania, actual property, no slaves,
amounted to $729,144,998; the value of the same in South Carolina, in-
cluding the estimated—we were about to say fictitious—value of 384,925
negroes, amounted to only $288,257,694. We have not been able to
obtain the figures necessary to show the exact value of the real and per

sonal estate in Philadelphia, but the amount is estimated to be not less than $300,000,000; and as, in 1859, there were 408,762 free inhabitants in the single city of Philadelphia, against 283,544 of the same class in the whole State of South Carolina, it is quite evident that the former is more powerful than the latter, and far ahead of her in all the elements of genuine and permanent superiority. In Pennsylvania, in 1850, the annual income of public schools amounted to $1,348,249; the same in South Carolina, in the same year, amounted to only $200,600; in the former State there were 393 libraries other than private, in the latter only 26; in Pennsylvania 310 newspapers and periodicals were published, circulating 84,898,672 copies annually; in South Carolina only 46 newspapers and periodicals were published, circulating but 7,145,930 copies per annum.

The incontrovertible facts we have thus far presented are, we think, amply sufficient, both in number and magnitude, to bring conviction to the mind of every candid reader, that there is something wrong, socially, politically and morally wrong, in the policy under which the South has so long loitered and languished. Else, how is it that the North, under the operations of a policy directly the opposite of ours, has surpassed us in almost everything great and good, and left us standing before the world, an object of merited reprehension and derision?

For one, we are heartily ashamed of the inexcusable weakness, inertia and dilapidation everywhere so manifest throughout our native section; but the blame properly attaches itself to an usurping minority of the people, and we are determined that it shall rest where it belongs. More on this subject, however, after a brief but general survey of the inequalities and disparities that exist between those two grand divisions of the country, which, without reference to the situation that any part of their territory bears to the cardinal points, are every day becoming more familiarly known by the appropriate appellation of

THE FREE AND THE SLAVE STATES.

It is a fact well known to every intelligent Southerner that we are compelled to go to the North for almost every article of utility and adornment, from matches, shoepegs and paintings up to cotton-mills, steamships and statuary; that we have no foreign trade, no princely merchants, nor respectable artists; that, in comparison with the free states, we contribute nothing to the literature, polite arts and inventions of the age; that, for want of profitable employment at home, large numbers of our native population find themselves necessitated to emigrate to the West, whilst the free states retain not only the larger proportion of those born within their own limits, but induce, annually, hundreds of thousands of foreigners to settle and remain amongst them; that almost everything produced at the North meets with ready sale, while, at the same time, there is no demand, even among our own citizens, for the productions of Southern industry; that, owing to the absence of a proper system of business amongst us, the North becomes, in one way or another, the proprietor and dispenser of all our floating wealth, and that we are dependent on Northern capitalists for the means necessary to build our railroads, canals and other public improvements; that if we want to visit a foreign country, even though it may lie directly south of us, we find no convenient way of getting there except by taking passage through a Northern port; and that nearly all the profits arising from the exchange of commodities, from insurance and shipping offices, and from the thousand and one industrial pursuits of the country, accrue to the North, and are there invested in the erection of those magnificent cities and stupendous works of art which dazzle the eyes of the South, and attest the superiority of free institutions!

The North is the Mecca of our merchants, and to it they must and do make two pilgrimages per annum—one in the spring and one in the fall. All our commercial, mechanical, manufactural, and literary supplies come from there. We want Bibles, brooms, buckets and books, and we go to the North; we want pens, ink, paper, wafers and envelopes, and we go to the North; we want shoes, hats, handkerchiefs, umbrellas and pocket knives, and we go to the North; we want furniture, crockery, glassware and pianos, and we go to the North; we want toys, primers, school-books, fashionable apparel, machinery, medicines, tomb-stones, and a thousand other things, and we go to the North for them all. Instead of keeping our money in circulation at home, by patronizing our own mechanics, manufacturers, and laborers, we send it all away to the North, and there it remains; it never falls into our hands again.

In one way or another we are more or less subservient to the North every day of our lives. In infancy we are swaddled in Northern muslin; in childhood we are humored with Northern gewgaws; in youth we are instructed out of Northern books; at the age of maturity we sow our "wild oats" on Northern soil; in middle-life we exhaust our wealth, energies and talents in the dishonorable vocation of entailing our dependence on our children and on our children's children, and, to the neglect of our own interests and the interests of those around us, in giving aid and succor to every department of Northern power; in the decline of life we remedy our eye-sight with Northern spectacles, and support our infirmities with Northern canes; in old age we are drugged with Northern physic; and, finally, when we die, our inanimate bodies, shrouded in Northern cambric, are stretched upon the bier, borne to the grave in a Northern carriage, entombed with a **Northern spade, and** memorized with a Northern slab!

But it can hardly be necessary to say more in illustration of this unmanly and unnational dependence, which is so glaring that it cannot fail to be apparent to even the most careless and superficial observer. All the world sees, or ought to see, that in a commercial, mechanical, manufactural, financial, and literary point of view, we are as helpless as babes; that, in comparison with the Free States, our agricultural resources have been greatly exaggerated, misunderstood and mismanaged; and that, instead of cultivating among ourselves a wise policy, of mutual assistance and coöperation with respect to individuals, and of self-reliance with respect to the South at large, instead of giving countenance and encouragement to the industrial enterprises projected among us, and instead of building up, aggrandizing and beautifying our own States, cities and towns, we have been spending our substance at the North, and are daily augmenting and strengthening the very power which now has us so completely under its thumb.

It thus appears, in view of the preceding statistical facts and arguments, that the South, at one time the superior of the North in almost all the ennobling pursuits and conditions of life, has fallen far behind her competitor, and now ranks more as the dependency of a mother country than as the equal confederate of free and independent States. Following the order of our task, the next duty that devolves upon us is to trace out the causes which have conspired to bring about this important change, and to place on record the reasons, as we understand them,

WHY THE NORTH HAS SURPASSED THE SOUTH.

And now that we have come to the very heart and soul of our subject, we feel no disposition to mince matters, but mean to speak plainly and to the point, without any equivocation, mental reservation, or secret evasion whatever. The son of a venerated parent, who, while he lived, was a considerate and merciful slaveholder, a native of the South, born and bred in North Carolina, of a family whose home has been in the valley of the Yadkin for nearly a century and a half, a Southerner by instinct and by all the influences of thought, habits and kindred, and with the desire and fixed purpose to reside permanently within the limits of the South, and with the expectation of dying there also—we feel that we have the right to express our opinion, however humble or unimportant it may be, on any and every question that affects the public good; and, so help us God, "sink or swim, live or die, survive or perish," we are determined to exercise that right with manly firmness, and without fear, favor or affection.

And now to the point. In our opinion, an opinion which has been formed from data obtained by assiduous researches, and comparisons, from laborious investigation, logical reasoning, and earnest reflection, the causes which have impeded the progress and prosperity of the South, which have dwindled our commerce and other similar pursuits, into the most contemptible insignificance; sunk a large majority of our people in galling poverty and ignorance, rendered a small minority conceited and tyrannical, and driven the rest away from their homes; entailed upon us a humiliating dependence on the Free States; disgraced us in the recesses of our own souls, and brought us under reproach in the eyes of all civilized and enlightened nations—may all be traced to one common source, and there find solution in the most hateful and horrible word, that was ever incorporated into the vocabulary of human economy —*Slavery*.

Reared amidst the institution of slavery, believing it to be wrong both in principle and in practice, and having seen and felt its evil influences upon individuals, communities and states, we deem it a duty, no less than a privilege, to enter our protest against it, and, as a Southern man, to use all constitutional means and our most strenuous efforts to overturn and abolish it.

Our repugnance to slavery springs from no one-sided idea, or sickly sentimentality. We have not been hasty in making up our mind on the subject; we have jumped at no conclusions; we have acted with perfect calmness and deliberation; we have carefully considered, and examined the reasons for and against the institution, and have also taken into account the probable consequences of our decision. The more we investigate the matter, the deeper becomes the conviction that we are right; and with this to impel and sustain us, we pursue our labor with love, with hope, and with constantly renewing vigor.

That we shall encounter opposition we consider as certain; perhaps we may even be subjected to insult and violence. From the cruel and conceited defenders of slavery we could look for nothing less. But we shall shrink from no responsibility, and do nothing unbecoming a man; we know how to repel indignity, and if assaulted, shall not fail to make the blow recoil upon the aggressor's head. The road we have to travel may be a rough one, but no impediment shall cause us to falter in our course. The line of our duty is clearly defined, and it is our intention to follow it faithfully, or die in the attempt.

But, thanks to heaven, we have no ominous forebodings of the result of the contest now pending between Liberty and Slavery in this confederacy. Though neither a prophet nor the son of a prophet, our vision is sufficiently penetrative to divine the future so far as to be able to see that the "peculiar institution" has but a short and, as heretofore, inglorious existence before it. Time, the righter of every wrong, is ripening events for the desired consummation of our labors and the fulfillment of our cherished hopes. Each revolving year brings nearer the inevitable crisis. The sooner it comes the better; may heaven, through our humble efforts, hasten its advent.

The first and most sacred duty of every Southerner, who has the honor and the interest of his country at heart, is to declare himself an unquali-fied and uncompromising opponent of slavery. No conditional or half-way declaration will avail; no mere threatening demonstration will succeed. With those who desire to be instrumental in bringing about the triumph of liberty over slavery, there should be neither evasion, vacillation, nor equivocation. We should listen to no modifying terms 'r compromises that may be proposed by the proprietors of the unprofit-able and ungodly institution. Nothing short of the complete abolition of slavery can save the South from falling into the vortex of utter ruin. Too long have we yielded a submissive obedience to the tyrannical domi-nation of an inflated oligarchy; too long have we tolerated their arrogance and self-conceit; too long have we submitted to their unjust and savage exactions. Let us now wrest from them the sceptre of power, estab-lish liberty and equal rights throughout the land, and henceforth and forever guard our legislative halls from the pollutions and usurpa-tions of pro-slavery demagogues.

We have stated, in a cursory manner, the reasons, as we understand them, why the North has surpassed the South, and have endeavored to show, we think successfully, that the highest future welfare of the South can be attained only by the speedy abolition of slavery. We will not, however, rest the case exclusively on our own arguments, but will again appeal to incontrovertible facts and statistics to sustain us in our conclu-sions. But before we do so, we desire to fortify ourself against a charge that is too frequently made by careless and superficial readers. We allude to the objections so often urged against the use of tabular state-ments and statistical facts. It is worthy of note, however, that those objections never come from thorough scholars or profound thinkers. Among the majority of mankind, the science of statistics is only begin-ning to be appreciated; when well understood, it will be recognized as one of the most important branches of knowledge, and, as a matter of course, be introduced and taught as an indispensable element of practical education in all our principal institutions of learning. One of the most vigorous and popular transatlantic writers of the day, Wm. C. Taylor, LL.D., of Dublin, says:

" The cultivation of statistics must be the source of all future improvement in the science of political economy, because it is to the table of the statistician that the economist must look for his facts; and all speculations not founded upon facts, though they may be admired and applauded when first propounded, will, in the end, assuredly be forgotten. Statistical science may almost be regarded as the creation of this age. The word statistics was invented in the middle of the last century by a German professor,* to express a summary view of the physical, moral, and social condition of States ; he justly remarked, that a numerical statement of the extent, density of population, imports, exports, revenues, etc., of a country, more perfectly explained its social condition than general statements, however graphic or however accurate. When such statements began to be collected, and exhibited in a popular form, it was soon discovered that the political and economical sciences were likely

---

* Achenwall, a native of Elbing, Prussia. Born 1719, died 1792.

to gain the position of physical sciences; that is to say, they were about to obtain records of observation, which would test the accuracy of recognized principles, and lead to the discovery of new modes of action. But the great object of this new science is to lead to the knowledge of human nature; that is, to ascertain the general course of operation of man's mental and moral faculties, and to furnish us with a correct standard of judgment, by enabling us to determine the average amount of the past as a guide to the average probabilities of the future. This science is yet in its infancy, but has already produced the most beneficial effects. The accuracy of the tables of life have rendered the calculations of rates of insurance a matter of much greater certainty than they were heretofore; the system of keeping the public accounts has been simplified and improved; and finally, the experimental sciences of medicine and political economy, have been fixed on a firmer foundation than could be anticipated in the last century. Even in private life this science is likely to prove of immense advantage, by directing attention to the collection and registration of facts, and thus preventing the formation of hasty judgments and erroneous conclusions."

The compiler, or rather the superintendent of the seventh United States census, Prof. De Bow, a gentleman of more than ordinary industry and practical learning, who, in his excellent Review, has, from time to time, displayed much commendable zeal in his efforts to develop the industrial resources of the Southern and Southwestern States, and who is, perhaps, the greatest statistician in the country, says:

"Statistics are far from being the barren array of figures ingeniously and laboriously combined into columns and tables, which many persons are apt to suppose them. They constitute rather the ledger of a nation, in which, like the merchant in his books, the citizen can read, at one view, all of the results of a year or of a period of years, as compared with other periods, and deduce the profit or the loss which has been made, in morals, education, wealth or power."

The present John Jay, of New York (it is hoped that the city may never be without a John Jay), in a most ingenious and masterly presentation of "The Statistics of American Agriculture," recently made in the form of an address before the American Geographical and Statistical Society, says:

"In England, the labors of the Statistical Society, whose elaborate and most valuable publications enrich our library, through the courtesy of the British government, have aroused the attention of the people and of Parliament to the truth, that the science of politics finds in the statistical element its most solid foundation."

Impressed with a sense of the propriety of introducing, in this as well as in the succeeding chapters of our work, a number of tabular statements exhibiting the comparative growth and prosperity of the free and slave States, we have deemed it eminently proper to adduce the testimony of these distinguished authors in support of the claims which official facts and accurate statistics lay to our consideration. And here we may remark, that the statistics which we propose to offer, like those already given, have been obtained from official sources, and may, therefore, be relied on as correct. The object we have in view in making a free use of facts and figures, if not already apparent, will soon be understood. It is not so much in its moral and religious aspects that we propose to discuss the question of slavery, as in its social and political character and influences. To say nothing of the sin and the shame of slavery, we believe it is a most expensive and unprofitable institution; and if our brethren of the South will but throw aside their unfounded prejudices and preconceived opinions, and give us a fair and patient hearing, we feel confident that we can bring them to the same conclusion. Indeed, we believe we shall be enabled—not alone by our own contributions, but with the aid of incontestable facts and arguments which we shall introduce from other sources—to convince all true-hearted, candid and intelligent Southerners, who may chance to read our book (and we hope their name may be legion), that slavery, and nothing but slavery, has retarded the progress and prosperity of our portion of the Union; depopulated and impoverished our cities by forcing the more industrious and enterprising natives of the soil to emigrate to the free States; brought our domain under a sparse and inert population by preventing foreign immigration; made us tributary to the North, and reduced us to the humiliating condition of mere provincial subjects in fact, though not in name. We believe, moreover, that every patriotic Southerner thus convinced will feel it a duty he owes to himself, to his country, and to his God, to become a thorough, inflexible, practical Abolitionist. So mote it be!

Now to our figures. Few persons have an adequate idea of the important part the cardinal numbers are now playing in the cause of liberty. They are working wonders in the South. Intelligent business men, from the Chesapeake to the Rio Grande, are beginning to see that slavery, even in a mercenary point of view, is impolitic, because it is unprofitable. Those unique, mysterious little Arabic sentinels on the watch-towers of political economy, 1, 2, 3, 4, 5, 6, 7, 8, 9, 0, have joined forces, allied themselves to the powers of freedom, and are hemming in and combating slavery with the most signal success. If let alone, we have no doubt the digits themselves would soon terminate the existence of human slavery; but we do not mean to let them alone; they must not have all the honor of annihilating the monstrous iniquity. We want to become an auxiliary in the good work, and facilitate it. The liberation of six millions of non-slaveholding whites from the second degree of slavery, and of three millions of miserable kidnapped negroes from the first degree, cannot be accomplished too soon. That it was not accomplished many years ago is our misfortune. It now behooves us to take a bold and determined stand in defence of the alienable rights of ourselves and of our fellow men, and to avenge the multiplicity of wrongs, social and political, which we have suffered at the hands of a most selfish and domineering oligarchy. It is madness to delay. We cannot be too hasty in carrying out our designs. Precipitance in this matter is an utter impossibility. Now is the time for action; let us work.

By taking a sort of inventory of the agricultural products of the free and slave States in 1850, we now propose to correct a most extraordinary and mischievous error into which the people of the South have unconsciously fallen. Agriculture, it is well known, is the sole boast of the South ; and, strange to say, many pro-slavery Southerners who, in our latitude, pass for intelligent men, are so puffed up with the idea of our importance in this respect, that they speak of the North as a sterile region, unfit for cultivation, and quite dependent on the South for the necessaries of life ! Such gross, rampant ignorance deserves no audience. We can prove that the North produces greater quantities of breadstuffs than the South. Figures shall show the facts. Properly, the South has nothing left to boast of ; the North has surpassed her in everything, and is going further and further ahead of her every day. We ask the reader's careful attention to the following tables, which we have prepared at no little cost of time and trouble, and which, when duly considered in connection with the foregoing and subsequent portions of our work, will, we believe, carry conviction to the mind that the downward tendency of the South can be arrested only by the abolition of slavery.

TABLE 1.

AGRICULTURAL PRODUCTS OF THE FREE STATES—1850.

STATES.	Wheat, bushels.	Oats, bushels.	Indian Corn, bushels.	Potatoes, (I. and S.) bushels.	Rye, bushels.	Barley, bushels.
California.............	17,228	......	12,236	10,292	......	9,712
Connecticut	41,762	1,258,738	1,935,043	2,689,805	600,893	19,099
Illinois...	9,414,575	10,087,241	57,646,984	2,672.294	83,364	110,795
Indiana...	6,214,458	5,655,014	52,964,363	2,285,048	78,792	45,483
Iowa.................	1,530,581	1,524,345	8,656,799	282,363	19,916	25,093
Maine..	296,259	2,181,037	1,750,056	3,436,040	102,916	151,731
Massachusetts.. ...	31,211	1,165,146	2,345,490	3,585,384	481,021	112,385
Michigan..............	4,925,889	2,866,056	5,641,420	2,361,074	105,871	75,249
New Hampshire.......	185,658	973,381	1,573,670	4,307,919	183,117	70,256
New Jersey.	1,601,190	3,378,063	8,759,704	3,715,251	1,255,578	6,492
New York	13,121,498	26,552,814	17,858,400	15,403,997	4,148,182	3,585,059
Ohio	14,487,351	13,472,742	59,078,695	5,245,760	425,918	354,358
Pennsylvania..........	15,367,691	21,538,156	19,835,214	6,032,904	4,805,160	165,584
Rhode Island..	49	215.232	539,201	651,029	26,409	18,875
Vermont	535,955	2,307,734	2,032,396	4,951,014	176,283	42,150
Wisconsin	4,286,131	3,414,672	1,988,979	1,402,956	81,253	209,692
	72,157,486	96,590,371	242,618,650	59,033,170	12,574,623	5,002,013

TABLE 2.

AGRICULTURAL PRODUCTS OF THE SLAVE STATES — 1850.

STATES.	Wheat, bushels.	Oats, bushels.	Indian Corn, bushels.	Potatoes, (I. and S.) bushels.	Rye, bushels.	Barley, bushels.
Alabama............ ..	294,044	2,965,696	28,754,048	5,721,205	17,261	3,958
Arkansas.............	199,639	656,183	8,893,939	981,981	8,047	177
Delaware	482,511	604,518	3,145,542	305,985	8,066	56
Florida	1,027	66,586	1,996,809	765,054	1,152	
Georgia	1,088,534	3,820,044	30,080,099	7,213,807	53,750	11,501
Kentucky	2,142,822	8,201,311	58,672,591	2,490,666	415,073	95,343
Louisiana	417	89,637	10,266,373	1,524,085	475	
Maryland	4,494,680	2,242,151	10,749,858	973,932	226,014	745
Mississippi	137,990	1,503,288	22,446,552	5,003.277	9,606	228
Missouri	2,981,652	5,278,079	36,214,537	1,274,511	44,268	9,631
North Carolina	2,130,102	4,052,078	27,941,051	5,716,027	229,563	2,735
South Carolina	1,066,277	2,322,155	16,271,454	4,473,960	43,790	4,583
Tennessee.............	1,619,386	7,703,086	52,276,223	3,845,560	89,137	2,737
Texas................	41,729	199,017	6,028,876	1,426,808	3,108	4,776
Virginia..............	11,212,616	10,179,144	35,254,319	3,130,567	458,930	25,437
	27,904,476	49,882,979	348,992,282	44,847,420	1,608,240	161,907

TABLE 3.

AGRICULTURAL PRODUCTS OF THE FREE STATES — 1850.

STATES.	Buckwheat, bushels.	Beans & Peas, bushels.	Clov. & Grass Seeds, bush.	Flaxseed, bushels.	Value of Garden Products.	Value (chard P
California	......	2,292	......	......	$75,275	$ 1,700
Connecticut...	229,297	19,090	30,469	708	196,874	175,118
Illinois	184,509	82,814	17,807	10,787	127,494	446,049
Indiana	149,740	35,773	30,271	36,888	72,864	324,940
Iowa	52,516	4,475	2,438	1,959	8,848	8,434
Maine........	104,523	205,541	18,311	580	122,387	342,865
Massachusetts	105,895	43,709	6,087	72	600,020	463,995
Michigan	472,917	74,254	26,274	519	14,788	132,650
N. Hampshire.	65,265	70,856	8,900	189	56,810	248,560
New Jersey...	878,984	14,174	91,331	16,525	475,242	607,268
New York	3,188,955	741,546	184,715	57,963	912,047	1,761,950
Ohio	638,060	60,168	140,501	188,880	214,004	695,921
Pennsylvania.	2,193,692	55,281	178,943	41,728	688,714	723,380
Rhode Island..	1,245	6,846	5,036	......	98,298	63,994
Vermont......	209,819	104,649	15,696	989	18,853	315,255
Wisconsin	79,878	20,657	5,486	1,191	32,142	4,823
	8,550,245	1,542,295	762,265	358,923	$3,714,605	$6,332,914

TABLE 4.

AGRICULTURAL PRODUCTS OF THE SLAVE STATES — 1850.

STATES.	Buckwheat, bushels.	Beans & Peas, bushels.	Clov. & Grass Seeds, bush.	Flaxseed, bushels.	Value of Garden Products.	Value of Orchard Prod'ts.
Alabama	848	892,701	685	69	$84,821	$15,408
Arkansas	175	285,788	526	321	17,150	40,141
Delaware.....	8,615	4,120	3,928	.904	12,714	46,574
Florida.......	55	135,359	2	......	8,721	1,280
Georgia	250	1,142,011	560	622	76,500	92,776
Kentucky	16,097	202,574	24,711	75,801	303,120	106,230
Louisiana	3	161,732	99	......	148,329	22,259
Maryland.....	103,671	12,816	17,778	2,446	200,869	164,051
Mississippi....	1,121	1,072,757	617	26	46,250	50,405
Missouri......	23,641	46,017	4,965	13,696	99,454	514,711
N. Carolina...	16,704	1,584,252	1,851	38,196	39,462	84,348
S. Carolina ...	288	1,026,900	406	55	47,286	35,108
Tennessee	19,427	369,321	14,214	18,904	97,183	52,894
Texas	59	179,351	10	26	12,354	12,505
Virginia	214,898	521,579	53,155	52,318	183,047	177,187
	405,357	7,687,227	123,517	203,484	$1,877,260	$1,355,827

RECAPITULATION—FREE STATES.

Wheat	72,157,486 bushels	@	1 50	$108,236,229
Oats	96,590,371 "	"	40	38,636,148
Indian Corn	242,618,650 "	"	60	145,571,190
Potatoes (I. & S.)	59,033,170 "	"	38	22,432,604
Rye	12,574,623 "	"	1 00	12,574,623
Barley	5,002,013 "	"	90	4,501,811
Buckwheat	8,550,245 "	"	50	4,275,122
Beans and Peas	1,542,295 "	"	1 75	2,699,015
Clover and Grass Seeds	762,265 "	"	3 00	2,286,795
Flax Seeds	358,923 "	"	1 25	448,647
Garden Products				3,714,605
Orchard Products				6,332,914

    Total .... 499,190,041 bushels, valued as above, at .. $351,709,703

RECAPITULATION—SLAVE STATES.

Wheat	27,904,476 bushels	@	1 50	$41,856,714
Oats	49,882,799 "	"	40	19,953,191
Indian Corn	348,992,282 "	"	60	209,395,369
Potatoes (I. & S.)	44,847,420 "	"	38	17,042,019
Rye	1,608,240 "	"	1 00	1,608,240
Barley	161,907 "	"	90	145,716
Buckwheat	405,357 "	"	50	202,678
Beans and Peas	7,637,227 "	"	1 75	13,365,147
Clover and Grass Seeds	123,517 "	"	3 00	370,551
Flax Seeds	203,484 "	"	1 25	254,355
Garden Products				1,377,260
Orchard Products				1,355,827

    Total .... 481,766,889 bushels, valued as above, at .. $306,927,067

TOTAL DIFFERENCE—BUSHEL–MEASURE PRODUCTS.

	Bushels.		Value.
Free States	499,190,041		$351,709,703
Slave States	481,766,889		306,927,067

Balance in bushels....... 17,423,152   Difference in value......... $44,782,636

So much for the boasted agricultural superiority of the South! Mark well the balance in bushels, and the difference in value! Is either in favor of the South? No! Are both in favor of the North? Yes! Here we have unquestionable proof that of all the bushel-measure products of the nation, the free States produce far more than one-half; and it is worthy of particular mention, that *the excess of Northern products is of the most valuable kind.* The account shows a balance against the South, in favor of the North, of *seventeen million four hundred and twenty-three thousand one hundred and fifty-two bushels*, and a difference in value of *forty-four million seven hundred and eighty-two thousand six hundred and thirty-six dollars.* Please bear these facts in mind, for, in order to show positively how the free and slave States do stand upon the great and important subject of rural economy, we intend to take an account of all the other products of the soil, of the live-stock upon farms, of the animals slaughtered, and, in fact, of every item of husbandry of the two sections ; and if, in bringing our tabular exercises to a close, we find slavery gaining upon freedom—a thing it has never yet been known to do—we shall, as a matter of course, see that the above amount is transferred to the credit of the side to which it of right belongs.

In making up these tables we have two objects in view ; the first is to open the eyes of the non-slaveholders of the South, to the system of deception, that has been so long practised upon them, and the second is to show slaveholders themselves—we have reference only to those who are not too perverse, or ignorant, to perceive naked truths—that free labor is far more respectable, profitable, and productive, than slave labor. In the South, unfortunately, no kind of labor is either free or respectable. Every white man who is under the necessity of earning his bread, by the sweat of his brow, or by manual labor, in any capacity, no matter how unassuming in deportment, or exemplary in morals, is treated as if he were a loathsome beast, and shunned with disdain. His soul may be the very seat of honor and integrity, yet without slaves—himself a slave —he is accounted as nobody, and would be deemed intolerably presumptuous, if he dared to open his mouth, even so wide as to give faint utterance to a three-lettered monosyllable, like yea or nay, in the presence of an august knight of the whip and the lash.

There are few Southerners who will not be astonished at the disclosures of these statistical comparisons, between the free and the slave States. That the astonishment of the more intelligent and patriotic non-slaveholders will be mingled with indignation, is no more than we anticipate. We confess our own surprise, and deep chagrin, at the result of our investigations. Until we examined into the matter, we thought and hoped the South was really ahead of the North in *one* particular, that of agriculture ; but our thoughts have been changed, and our hopes frustrated, for instead of finding ourselves the possessors of a single advantage, we behold our dear native South stripped of every laurel, and sinking deeper and deeper in the depths of poverty and shame ; while, at the same time, we see the North, our successful rival, extracting and absorbing the few elements of wealth yet remaining among us, and rising higher and higher in the scale of fame, fortune, and invulnerable power. Thus our disappointment gives way to a feeling of intense mortification, and our soul involuntarily, but justly, we believe, cries out for retribution against the treacherous slaveholding legislators, who have so basely and unpatriotically neglected the interests of their poor white constituents and bargained away the rights of posterity. Notwithstanding the fact that the white non-slaveholders of the South are in the majority, as six to one, they have never yet had any uncontrolled part or lot in framing the laws under which they live. There is no legislation except for the benefit of slavery, and slaveholders. As a general rule, poor white persons are regarded with less esteem and attention than negroes, and though the condition of the latter is wretched beyond description, vast numbers of the former are infinitely worse off. A cunningly devised mockery of freedom is guaranteed to them, and that is all. To all intents and purposes they are disfranchised, and outlawed, and the only privilege extended to them, is a shallow and circumscribed participation in the political movements that usher slaveholders into office.

We have not breathed away nine and twenty years in the South, without becoming acquainted with the demagogical manœuverings of the oligarchy. Their intrigues and tricks of legerdemain are as familiar to us as household words; in vain might the world be ransacked for a more precious junto of flatterers and cajolers. It is amusing to ignorance, amazing to credulity, and insulting to intelligence, to hear them in their blustering efforts to mystify and pervert the sacred principles of liberty, and turn the curse of slavery into a blessing. To the illiterate poor whites—made poor and ignorant by the system of slavery—they hold out the idea that slavery is the very bulwark of our liberties, and the foundation of American independence! For hours at a time, day after day, will they expatiate upon the inexpressible beauties and excellences of this great *free* and *independent* nation; and finally with the most extravagant gesticulations and rhetorical flourishes, conclude their nonsensical ravings, by attributing all the glory and prosperity of the country, from Maine to Texas, and from Georgia to California, to the "invaluable institutions of the South!" On the part of the intelligent listener, who cherishes a high regard for truth and justice, it requires no small degree of patience and forbearance to rest quietly under the incoherent, truth-murdering declamations of these subtle-tongued champions of slavery.

The lords of the lash are not only absolute masters of the blacks, who are bought and sold, and driven about like so many cattle, but they are also the oracles and arbiters of all non-slaveholding whites, whose freedom is merely nominal, and whose unparalleled illiteracy and degradation is purposely and fiendishly perpetuated. How little the "poor white trash," the great majority of the Southern people, know of the real condition of the country, is, indeed, sadly astonishing. The truth is, they know nothing of public measures, and little of private affairs, except what their imperious masters, the slave-drivers, condescend to tell, and that is but precious little, and even that little, always garbled and one-sided, is never told except in public harangues; for the haughty cavaliers of shackles and handcuffs will not degrade themselves by holding private converse with those who have neither dimes nor hereditary rights in human flesh.

Whenever it pleases, and to the extent it pleases, a slaveholder to become communicative, poor whites may hear with fear and trembling, but not speak. They must be as mum as dumb brutes, and stand in awe of their august superiors, or be crushed with stern rebukes, cruel oppressions, or downright violence. If they dare to think for themselves, their thoughts must be forever concealed. The expression of any sentiment at all conflicting with the gospel of slavery, dooms them at once in the community in which they live, and then, whether willing or unwilling, they are obliged to become heroes, martyrs, or exiles. They may thirst for knowledge, but there is no Moses among them to smite it out of the rocks of Horeb. The black veil, through whose almost impenetrable meshes light seldom gleams, has long been pendant over their eyes, and there, with fiendish jealousy, slaveholding official sedulously guard it. Non-slaveholders are not only kept in ignorance of what is transpiring at the North, but they are continually misinformed of what is going on even in the South. Never were the poorer classes of a people, and those classes so largely in the majority, and all inhabiting the same country, so basely duped, so adroitly swindled or so unpardonably outraged.

It is expected that the stupid and sequacious masses, the white victims of slavery, will believe, and, as a general thing, they do believe, whatever the slaveholders tell them; and thus it is that they are cajoled into the notion that they are the freest, happiest, and most intelligent people in the world, and are taught to look with prejudice and disapprobation upon every new principle or progressive movement. Thus it is, that the South, woefully inert and inventionless, has lagged behind the North, and is now weltering in the cesspool of ignorance and degradation.

We have already intimated that the opinion is prevalent throughout the South that the free States are quite sterile and unproductive, and that they are mainly dependent on us for breadstuffs and other provisions. So far as the cereals, fruits, garden vegetables and esculent roots are concerned, we have, in the preceding tables, shown the utter falsity of this opinion; and we now propose to show that it is equally erroneous in other particulars, and very far from the truth in the general reckoning. We can prove, and we intend to prove, from facts in our possession, that the hay crop of the free States is worth considerably more in dollars and cents than all the cotton, tobacco, rice, hay and hemp produced in the fifteen slave States. This statement may strike some of our readers with amazement, and others may, for the moment, regard it as quite incredible; but it is true, nevertheless, and we shall soon proceed to confirm it. The single free State of New York produces more than *three times* the quantity of hay that is produced in all the slave States. Ohio produces a larger number of tons than all the Southern and Southwestern States, and so does Pennsylvania. Vermont, little and unpretending as she is, does the same thing, with the exception of Virginia. Look at the facts as presented in the tables, and let your own eyes, physical and intellectual, confirm you in the truth.

2

And yet, forsooth, the slaveholding oligarchy would whip us into the belief that agriculture is not one of the leading and lucrative pursuits of the free States, that the soil there is an uninterrupted barren waste, and that our Northern brethren, having the advantage in nothing except wealth, population, inland and foreign commerce, manufactures, mechanism, inventions, literature, the arts and sciences, and their concomitant branches of profitable industry—miserable objects of charity!—are dependent on us for the necessaries of life.

Next to Virginia, Maryland is the greatest Southern hay-producing State; and yet, it is the opinion of several of the most extensive hay and grain dealers in Baltimore, with whom we have conversed on the subject, that the domestic crop is scarcely equal to one-third the demand, and that the balance required for home consumption, about two-thirds, is chiefly brought from New York, Pennsylvania and Massachusetts. At this rate, Maryland receives and consumes not less than three hundred and fifteen thousand tons of Northern hay every year; and this, as we are informed by the dealers above-mentioned, at an average cost to the last purchaser, by the time it is stowed in the mow, of at least twenty-five dollars per ton; it would thus appear that this most popular and valuable provender, one of the staple commodities of the North, commands a market in a single slave State, to the amount of seven million eight hundred and seventy-five thousand dollars per annum.

In this same State of Maryland, less than one million of dollars' worth of cotton finds a market, the whole number of bales sold here in 1850 amounting to only twenty-three thousand three hundred and twenty-five, valued at seven hundred and forty-six thousand four hundred dollars. Briefly, then, and in round numbers, we may state the case thus: Maryland buys annually seven millions of dollars' worth of hay from the North, and one million of dollars' worth of cotton from the South. Let slaveholders and their fawning defenders read, ponder and compare.

The exact quantities of Northern hay, rye, and buckwheat flour, Irish potatoes, fruits, clover and grass seeds, and other products of the soil, received and consumed in all the slaveholding States, we have no means of ascertaining; but for all practical purposes, we can arrive sufficiently near to the amount by inference from the above data, and from what we see with our eyes and hear with our ears wherever we go. Food from the North for man or for beast, or for both, is for sale in every market in the South. Even in the most insignificant little villages in the interior of the slave States, where books, newspapers and other mediums of intelligence are unknown, where the poor whites and the negroes are alike bowed down in heathenish ignorance and barbarism, and where the news is received but once a week, and then only in a Northern-built stage-coach, drawn by horses in Northern harness, in charge of a driver dressed *cap-a-pie* in Northern habiliments, and with a Northern whip in his hand—the agricultural products of the North, either crude, prepared, pickled or preserved, are ever to be found.

Mortifying as the acknowledgment of the fact is to us, it is our unbiased opinion—an opinion which will, we believe, be indorsed by every intelligent person who goes into a careful examination and comparison of all the facts in the case—that the profits arising to the North from the sale of provender and provisions to the South, are far greater than those arising to the South from the sale of cotton, tobacco and breadstuffs to the North. It follows, then, that the agricultural interests of the North being not only equal but actually superior to those of the South, the hundreds of millions of dollars which the commerce and manufactures of the former annually yield, is just so much clear and independent gain over the latter. It follows, also, from a corresponding train or system of deduction, and with all the foregoing facts in view, that the difference between freedom and slavery is simply the difference between sense and nonsense, wisdom and folly, good and evil, right and wrong.

Any observant American, from whatever point of the compass he may hail, who will take the trouble to pass though the Southern markets, both great and small, as we have done, and inquire where this article, that and the other came from, will be utterly astonished at the variety and quantity of Northern agricultural productions kept for sale. And this state of things is growing worse and worse every year. Exclusively agricultural as the South is in her industrial pursuits, she is barely able to support her sparse and degenerate population. Her men and her domestic animals, both dwarfed into shabby objects of commiseration under the blighting effects of slavery, are constantly feeding on the multifarious products of Northern soil. And if the whole truth must be told, we may here add, that these products, like all other articles of merchandise purchased at the North, are generally bought on credit, and, in a great number of instances, by far too many, never paid for—not, as a general rule, because the purchasers are dishonest or unwilling to pay, but because they are impoverished and depressed by the retrogressive and deadening operations of slavery, that most unprofitable and pernicious institution under which they live.

To show how well we are sustained in our remarks on hay and other special products of the soil, as well as to give circulation to other facts of equal significance, we quote a single passage from an address by Paul C. Cameron, before the Agricultural Society of Orange County, North Carolina. This production is, in the main, so powerfully conceived, so correct and plausible in its statements and conclusions, and so well calculated, though, perhaps, not intended, to arouse the old North State to a sense of her natural greatness and acquired shame, that we could wish

to see it published in pamphlet form, and circulated throughout the
length and breadth of that unfortunate and degraded heritage of slavery.
Mr. Cameron says :

"I know not when I have been more humiliated, as a North Carolina farmer,
than when, a few weeks ago, at a railroad depot at the very doors of our State
capital, I saw wagons drawn by Kentucky mules, loading with Northern hay, for
the supply not only of the town, but to be taken to the country. Such a sight at the
capital of a State whose population is almost exclusively devoted to agriculture, is
a most humiliating exhibition. Let us cease to use everything, as far as it is practicable, that is not the product of our own soil and workshops—not an axe, or a
broom, or bucket, from Connecticut. By every consideration of self-preservation,
we are called to make better efforts to expel the Northern grocer from the State
with his butter, and the Ohio and Kentucky horse, mule and hog driver, from our
county at least. It is a reproach on us as farmers, and no little deduction from
our wealth, that we suffer the population of our towns and villages to supply themselves with butter from another Orange County in New York."

We have promised to prove that the hay crop of the free States is
worth considerably more than all the cotton, tobacco, rice, hay and hemp
produced in the fifteen slave States. The compilers of the last census,
as we learn from Prof. De Bow, the able and courteous superintendent,
in making up the hay-tables, allowed two thousand two hundred and
forty pounds to the ton. The price per ton at which we should estimate
its value has puzzled us to some extent. Dealers in the article at Baltimore think it will average twenty-five dollars, in their market. Four
or five months ago they sold it at thirty dollars per ton. At the very
time we write, though there is less activity in the article than usual, we
learn, from an examination of sundry prices-current and commercial
journals, that hay is selling in Savannah at $33 per ton; in Mobile and
New Orleans at $26; in Charleston at $25; in Louisville at $24; and
in Cincinnati at $23. The average of these prices is *twenty-six dollars
sixteen and two-third cents;* and we suppose it would be fair to employ
the figures which would indicate this amount, the net value of a single
ton, in calculating the total market value of the entire crop. Were we
to do this—and, with the foregoing facts in view, we submit to intelligent men whether we would not be justifiable in doing it—the hay crop
of the free States, 12,690,982 tons, in 1850, would amount in valuation
to the enormous sum of $331,081,695—more than four times the value
of all the cotton produced in the United States during the same period!

But we shall not make the calculation at what we have found to be
the average value per ton throughout the country. What rate, then,
shall be agreed upon as a basis of comparison between the value of the
hay crop of the North and that of the South, and as a means of testing
the truth of our declaration—that the former exceeds the aggregate
value of all the cotton, tobacco, rice, hay and hemp produced in the fifteen slave States? Suppose we take $13 08½—just half the average
value—as the multiplier in this arithmetical exercise. This we can well
afford to do; indeed, we might reduce the amount per ton to much less

than half the average value, and still have a large margin left for tri umphant demonstration. It is not our purpose, however, to make an overwhelming display of the incomparable greatness of the free States.

In estimating the value of the various agricultural products of the two great sections of the country, we have been guided by prices emanating from the Bureau of Agriculture in Washington ; and in a catalogue of those prices now before us, we perceive that the average value of hay throughout the nation is supposed to be not more than half a cent per pound—$11 20 per ton—which, as we have seen above, is considerably less than half the present market value;—and this, too, in the face of the fact that prices generally rule higher than they do just now. It will be admitted on all sides, however, that the prices fixed upon by the Bureau of Agriculture, taken as a whole, are as fair for one section of the country as for the other, and that we cannot blamelessly deviate from them in one particular without deviating from them in another. Eleven dollars and twenty cents ($11 20) per ton shall therefore be the price; and, not-withstanding these greatly reduced figures, we now renew, with an addendum, our declaration and promise, that—*We can prove, and we shall now proceed to prove, that the annual hay crop of the free States is worth considerably more in dollars and cents than all the cotton, tobacco, rice, hay, hemp, and cane sugar annually produced in the fifteen slave States.*

HAY CROP OF THE FREE STATES--1850.

12,690,982 tons @ $11 20...............................$142,138,998

SUNDRY PRODUCTS OF THE SLAVE STATES—1850.

Cotton..............	2,445,779 bales	@ $32 00.....	....$78,264,928
Tobacco...........	185,023,906 lbs.	" 10..........	.18,502,390
Rice (rough)	215,313,497 lbs.	" 4..........	.8,612,539
Hay................	1,137,784 tons	" 11 20..........	.12,743,180
Hemp...............	34,673 tons	" 112 00..........	.3,883,376
Cane Sugar........	237,133,000 lbs.	" 7..........	.16,599,310

Total....$138,605,723

RECAPITULATION.

Hay crop of the free States $142,138,998
Sundry products of the slave States................... 138,605,723

Balance in favor of the free States......$3,533,275

There is the account; look at it, and let it stand in attestation of the exalted virtues and surpassing powers of freedom. Scan it well, Mes-sieurs lords of the lash, and learn from it new lessons of the utter ineffi-ciency, and despicable imbecility of slavery. Examine it minutely, liberty-loving patriots of the North, and behold in it additional evidences of the beauty, grandeur, and superexcellence of free institutions. Trea-sure it up in your minds, outraged friends and non-slaveholders of the

South, and let the recollection of it arouse you to an inflexible determination to extirpate the monstrous enemy that stalks abroad in your land, and to recover the inalienable rights and liberties, which have been filched from you by an unscrupulous oligarchy.

In deference to truth, decency and good sense, it is to be hoped that the enemies of free institutions will never more have the effrontery to open their mouths in extolling the agricultural achievements of slave labor. Especially is it desirable, that, as a simple act of justice to a grossly deceived populace, they may cease their stale and senseless harangues on the importance of cotton. The value of cotton to the South, to the North, to the nation, and to the world, has been so grossly exaggerated, and so extensive have been the evils which have resulted in consequence of the extraordinary misrepresentations concerning it, that we should feel constrained to reproach ourself for remissness of duty, if we failed to make an attempt to explode the popular error. The figures above show what it is, and what it is not. Recur to them, and learn the facts.

So hyperbolically has the importance of cotton been magnified by certain pro-slavery politicians of the South, that the person who would give credence to all their fustian and bombast, would be under the necessity of believing that the very existence of almost everything, in the heaven above, in the earth beneath, and in the water under the earth, depended on it. The truth is, however, that the cotton crop is of but comparatively little value to the South. New England and Old England, by their superior enterprise and sagacity, turn it chiefly to their own advantage. It is carried in their ships, spun in their factories, woven in their looms, insured in their offices, returned again in their own vessels, and, with double freight and cost of manufacturing added, purchased by the South at a high premium. Of all the parties engaged or interested in its transportation and manufacture, the South is the only one that does not make a profit. Nor does she, as a general thing, make a decent profit by producing it.

We are credibly informed that many of the farmers in the immediate vicinity of Baltimore, where we now write, have turned their attention exclusively to hay, and that from one acre they frequently gather two tons, for which they receive *fifty dollars.* Let us now inquire how many dollars may be expected from an acre planted in cotton. Mr. Cameron, from whose able address before the Agricultural Society of Orange County, North Carolina, we have already gleaned some interesting particulars, informs us, that the cotton planters in his part of the country, "have contented themselves with a crop yielding only *ten or twelve dollars per acre,*" and that "the summing up of a large surface gives but a living result." An intelligent resident of the Palmetto State, writing in De Bow's Review, not long since, advances the opinion that the cotton planters of South Carolina are not realizing more than *one per cent.* on the amount of capital they have invested. While in Virginia, very recently, an elderly slaveholder, whose religious walk and conversation had recommended and promoted him to an eldership in the Presbyterian church, and who supports himself and family by raising negroes and tobacco, told us that, for the last eight or ten years, aside from the increase of his human chattels, he felt quite confident *he had not cleared as much even as one per cent. per annum* on the amount of his investment. The real and personal property of this aged *Christian* consists chiefly in a large tract of land and about thirty negroes, most of whom, according to his own confession, are more expensive than profitable. The proceeds arising from the sale of the tobacco they produce, are all absorbed in the purchase of meat and bread for home consumption, and when the crop is stunted by drought, frost, or otherwise cut short, one of the negroes must be sold to raise funds for the support of the others. Such are the agricultural achievements of slave labor; such are the results of "the sum of all villainies." The diabolical institution subsists on its own flesh. At one time children are sold to procure food for the parents, at another, parents are sold to procure food for the children. Within its pestilential atmosphere, nothing succeeds; progress and prosperity are unknown; inanition and slothfulness ensue; everything becomes dull, dismal and unprofitable; wretchedness and desolation stand or lie in bold relief throughout the land; an aspect of most melancholy inactivity and dilapidation broods over every city and town; ignorance and prejudice sit enthroned over the minds of the people; usurping despots wield the sceptre of power; everywhere, and in everything, between Delaware Bay and the Gulf of Mexico, are the multitudinous evils of slavery apparent.

The soil itself soon sickens and dies beneath the unnatural tread of the slave. Hear what the Hon. C. C. Clay, of Alabama, has to say upon the subject. His testimony is eminently suggestive, well-timed, and truthful; and we heartily commend it to the careful consideration of every spirited Southron who loves his country, and desires to see it rescued from the fatal grasp of "the mother of harlots." Says he:

"I can show you, with sorrow, in the older portions of Alabama, and in my native county of Madison, the sad memorials of the artless and exhausting culture of cotton. Our small planters, after taking the cream off their lands, unable to restore them by rest, manures, or otherwise, are going further West and South, in search of other virgin lands, which they may and will despoil and impoverish in like manner. Our wealthier planters, with greater means and no more skill, are buying out their poorer neighbors, extending their plantations, and adding to their slave force. The wealthy few, who are able to live on smaller profits, and to give their blasted fields some rest, are thus pushing off the many who are merely independent. Of the $20,000,000 annually realized from the sales of the cotton crop of Alabama, nearly all not expended in supporting the producers, is re-invested in land and negroes. Thus the white population has decreased and the slave increased almost *pari passu* in several counties of our State. In 1825, Madison county cast about 3,000 votes; now, she cannot cast exceeding 2,300. In traversing that county, one will discover numerous farm-houses, once the abode of industrious and intelligent freemen, now occupied by slaves, or tenantless, deserted and dilapidated ; he will observe fields, once fertile, now unfenced, abandoned and covered with those evil harbingers, fox-tail and broomsedge ; he will see the moss growing on the moldering walls of once thrifty villages, and will find ' one only master grasps the whole domain,' that once furnished happy homes for a dozen white families. Indeed, a country in its infancy, where fifty years ago scarce a forest tree had been felled by the axe of the pioneer, is already exhibiting the painful signs of senility and decay, apparent in Virginia and the Carolinas.''

Some one has said that "an honest confession is good for the soul," and if the adage be true, as we have no doubt it is, we think Mr. C. C. Clay is entitled to a quiet conscience on one score at least. In the extract quoted above, he gives us a graphic description of the ruinous operations and influences of Slavery in the Southwest ; and we, as a native of Carolina, and a traveller through Virginia, are ready to bear testimony to the fitness of his remarks when he referred to those States as examples of senility and decay. With equal propriety, however, he might have stopped nearer home for a subject of comparison. Either of the States bordering upon Alabama, or, indeed, any other slave States, would have answered his purpose quite as well as Virginia and the Carolinas. Wherever slavery exists there he may find parallels to the destruction that is sweeping with such deadly influence over his own unfortunate State.

As for examples of vigorous, industrious and thrifty communities, they can be found anywhere beyond the Upas-shadow of slavery—nowhere else. New York and Massachusetts, which, by nature, are confessedly far inferior to Virginia and the Carolinas, have by the more liberal and equitable policy which they have pursued, in substituting liberty for slavery, attained a degree of eminence and prosperity altogether unknown in the slave States.

Amidst all the hyperbole and cajolery of slave-driving politicians who, as we have already seen, are " the books, the arts, the academies, that show, contain and govern all the South," we are rejoiced to see that Mr. Clay, Mr. Cameron, and a few others, have had the boldness and honesty to step forward and proclaim the truth. All such frank admissions are to be hailed as good omens for the South. Nothing good can come from any attempt to conceal the unconcealable evidences of poverty and desolation everywhere trailing in the wake of slavery. Let the truth be told on all occasions, of the North as well as of the South, and the people will soon begin to discover the egregiousness of their errors, to draw just comparisons, to inquire into cause and effect, and to adopt the more utile measures, manners and customs of their wiser contemporaries.

In willfully traducing and decrying everything North of Mason and Dixon's line, and in excessively magnifying the importance of everything South of it, the oligarchy have, in the eyes of all liberal and intelligent men, only made an exhibition of their uncommon folly and dishonesty. For a long time, it is true, they have succeeded in deceiving the people, in keeping them humbled in the murky sloughs of poverty and ignorance, and in instilling into their untutored minds passions and prejudices expressly calculated to strengthen and protect the accursed institution of slavery ; but, thanks to heaven, their inglorious reign is fast drawing to a close ; with irresistible brilliancy, and in spite of the interdict of tyrants, light from the pure fountain of knowledge is now streaming over the dark places of our land, and, ere long—mark our words—there will ascend from Delaware, and from Texas, and from all the intermediate States, a huzza for Freedom and for Equal Rights, that will utterly confound the friends of despotism, set at defiance the authority of usurpers, and carry consternation to the heart of every slavery-propagandist.

To undeceive the people of the South, to bring them to a knowledge of the inferior and disreputable position which they occupy as a component part of the Union, and to give prominence and popularity to those plans which, if adopted, will elevate us to an equality, socially,. morally, intellectually, industrially, politically, and financially, with the most flourishing and refined nation in the world, and, if possible, to place us in the van of even that, is the object of this work. Slaveholders, either from ignorance or from a willful disposition to propagate error, contend that the South has nothing to be ashamed of, that slavery has proved a blessing to her, and that her superiority over the North in an agricultural point of view, makes amends for all her short-comings in other respects. On the other hand, we contend that many years of continual blushing and severe penance would not suffice to cancel or annul the shame and disgrace that justly attaches to the South in consequence of slavery—the direst evil that e'er befell the land—that the South bears nothing like even a respectable approximation to the North in navigation, commerce or manufactures, and that, contrary to the opinion entertained by ninety-nine hundredths of her people, she is far behind the free States in the only thing of which she has ever dared to boast—agriculture. We submit the question to the arbitration of figures, which, it is said, do not lie. With regard to the bushel-measure products of the soil, of which we have already taken an inventory, we have seen that there is a balance against the South in favor of the North of *seventeen million four hundred and twenty-three thousand one hundred and fifty-two bushels*, and a difference in the value of the same, also in favor of the North, of *forty-four million seven hundred and eighty-two thousand six hundred and thirty-six dollars*. It is certainly a most novel kind of agricultural superiority that the South claims on that score !

Our attention shall now be directed to the twelve principal pound-measure products of the free and of the slave States—*hay, cotton, butter and cheese, tobacco, cane-sugar, wool, rice, hemp, maple sugar, beeswax and honey, flax, and hops*—and in taking an account of them, we shall, in order to show the exact quantity produced in each State, and for the convenience of future reference, pursue the same plan as that adopted in the preceding tables. Whether slavery will appear to better advantage on the scales than it did in the half-bushel, remains to be seen. It is possible that the rickety monster may make a better show on a new track; but if it makes a more ridiculous display, we shall not be surprised. A careful examination of its precedents, has taught us the folly of expecting anything good to issue from it in any manner whatever. It has no disposition to emulate the magnanimity of its betters, and as for a laudable ambition to excel, that is a characteristic altogether foreign to its nature. Languor and inertia are the insalutary viands upon which it delights to satiate its morbid appetite; and "from bad to worse" is the ill-omened motto under which, in all its feeble efforts and achievements, it ekes out a most miserable and deleterious existence.

TABLE 5.

AGRICULTURAL PRODUCTS OF THE FREE STATES — 1850.

STATES.	Hay, tons.	Hemp, tons.	Hops, lbs.	Flax, lbs.	Maple Sugar, lbs.	Tobacco, lbs.
California.....	2,088	.....	......	......	......	1,000
Connecticut...	516,131	.....	554	17,928	50,796	1,267,624
Illinois	601,952	.....	3,551	160,063	248,904	841,394
Indiana.......	403,230	......	92,796	584,469	2,921,192	1,044,620
Iowa	89,055	......	8,242	62,660	78,407	6,041
Maine	755,889	......	40,120	17,081	93,542	
Massachusetts.	651,807	......	121,595	1,162	795,525	138,246
Michigan	404,934	......	10,663	7,152	2,439,794	1,245
N. Hampshire..	598,854	......	257,174	7,652	1,298,863	50
New Jersey ...	435,950	......	2,133	182,965	2,197	310
New York.....	3,728,797	4	2,536,299	940,577	10,357,484	83,189
Ohio	1,443,142	150	63,731	446,932	4,588,209	10,454,449
Pennsylvania .	1,842,970	44	22,088	530,307	2,326,525	912,651
Rhode Island..	74,418	......	277	85	28	
Vermont......	866,153	....	288,023	20,852	6,349,357	
Wisconsin.....	275,662	......	15,930	68,393	610,976	1,268
	12,690,982	198	3,463,176	3,048,278	32,161,799	14,752,087

TABLE 6.

AGRICULTURAL PRODUCTS OF THE SLAVE STATES — 1850.

STATES.	Hay, tons.	Hemp, tons.	Hops, lbs.	Flax, lbs.	Maple Sugar, lbs.	Tobacco, lbs.
Alabama	32,685	.....	276	3,921	643	164,990
Arkansas	3,976	15	157	12,291	9,330	218,936
Delaware	30,159	......	348	17,174	......	
Florida	2,510	......	14	50	......	998,614
Georgia.......	23,449	......	261	5,387	50	423,924
Kentucky	113,747	17,787	4,309	2,100,116	437,405	55,501,196
Louisiana.....	25,752	......	125	......	255	26,878
Maryland.....	157,956	63	1,870	35,686	47,740	21,407,497
Mississippi	12,504	7	473	665	.....	49,960
Missouri	116,925	16,028	4,130	627,160	178,910	17,113,784
North Carolina	145,653	39	9,246	593,796	27,932	11,984,786
South Carolina	20,925	......	26	833	200	74,285
Tennessee	74,091	595	1,032	868,181	158,557	20,148,932
Texas	8,354	....	7	1,048	......	66,897
Virginia.......	369,098	139	11,506	1,000,450	1,227,665	56,803,227
	1,137,784	34,673	33,780	4,768,198	2,088,687	185,023,906

TABLE 6—Continued.

AGRICULTURAL PRODUCTS OF THE SLAVE STATES—1850.

STATES.	Cotton, bales of 400 lbs.	Cane Sugar, hhds. of 1,000 lbs.	Rough Rice, lbs.
Alabama	564,429	87	2,312,252
Arkansas	65,344	......	63,179
Delaware	......	......	......
Florida	45,131	2,750	1,075,090
Georgia	499,091	846	38,950,691
Kentucky	758	10	5,688
Louisiana	178,737	226,001	4,425,349
Maryland	......	......	......
Mississippi,	484,292	8	2,719,856
Missouri	......	.....	700
North Carolina	50,545	......	5,465,868
South Carolina	300,901	77	159,930,613
Tennessee	194,532	3	258,854
Texas	58,072	7,351	88,203
Virginia	3,947	......	17,154
	2,445,779	287,133	215,313,497

TABLE 7.

ANIMAL PRODUCTS OF THE FREE AND THE SLAVE STATES—1850.

ANIMAL PRODUCTS OF THE FREE STATES—1850.				ANIMAL PRODUCTS OF THE SLAVE STATES—1850.			
STATES.	Wool, lbs.	Butter and Cheese, lbs.	Beeswax & Honey, lbs.	STATES.	Wool, lbs.	Butter and Cheese, lbs.	Beeswax & Honey, lbs.
California..	5,520	855		Alabama ..	657,118	4,040,223	897,021
Connecticut	497,454	11,861,396	93,304	Arkansas..	182,595	1,884,327	192,338
Illinois....	2,150,113	13,804,768	869,444	Delaware..	57,768	1,058,495	41,248
Indiana...	2,610,287	13,506,099	935,329	Florida....	23,247	389,513	18,971
Iowa......	373,898	2,381,028	321,711	Georgia...	990,019	4,687,535	732,514
Maine.....	1,364,034	11,678,265	189,618	Kentucky..	2,297,433	10,161,477	1,158,019
Mass......	585,136	15,159,512	59,508	Louisiana..	109,897	685,026	96,701
Michigan .	2,043,283	8,077,390	359,232	Maryland..	477,438	3,810,135	74,802
New Hamp.	1,108,476	10,173,619	117,140	Mississippi.	559,619	4,367,425	397,460
New Jersey	375,396	9,852,966	156,694	Missouri...	1,627,164	8,037,931	1,328,972
New York.	10,071,301	129,507,507	1,755,830	N. Carolina	970,738	4,242,211	512,289
Ohio	10,196,371	55,268,921	804,275	S. Carolina	487,283	2,986,820	216,281
Penn......	4,481,570	42,388,452	839,509	Tennessee.	1,364,378	8,317,266	1,036,572
Rhode Is...	129,692	1,312,178	6,347	Texas.....	131,917	2,440,199	380,825
Vermont ..	3,400,717	20,858,814	249,422	Virginia...	2,860,765	11,525,651	880,767
Wisconsin..	253,963	4,034,033	181,005				
	39,647,211	349,860,783	6,888,868		12,797,329	68,634,224	7,964,760

RECAPITULATION—FREE STATES.

Hay	28,427,799,680 lbs.	@	1-2 c.		$142,138,998
Hemp	443,520	"	"	5 "	22,176
Hops	3,463,176	"	"	15 "	519,476
Flax	3,048,278	"	"	10 "	304,827
Maple Sugar	32,161,799	"	"	8 "	2,572,943
Tobacco	14,752,087	"	"	10 "	1,475,208
Wool	39,647,211	"	"	35 "	13,876,523
Butter and Cheese	349,860,783	"	"	15 "	52,479,117
Beeswax and Honey	6,888,368	"	"	15 "	1,033,255

Total............28,878,064,902 lbs., valued as above, $214,422,523

RECAPITULATION—SLAVE STATES.

Hay	2,548,636,160 lbs.	@	1-2 c.		$12,743,180
Hemp	77,667,520	"	"	5 "	3,883,376
Hops	33,780	"	"	15 "	5,067
Flax	4,766,198	"	"	10 "	476,619
Maple Sugar	2,088,687	"	"	8 "	167,094
Tobacco	185,023,906	"	"	10 "	18,502,390
Wool	12,797,329	"	"	35 "	4,479,065
Butter and Cheese	68,634,224	"	"	15 "	10,295,133
Beeswax and Honey	7,964,760	"	"	15 "	1,194,714
Cotton	978,311,600	"	"	8 "	78,264,928
Cane Sugar	237,133,000	"	"	7 "	16,599,310
Rice (rough)	215,313,497	"	"	4 "	8,612,539

Total.........4,338,370,661 lbs., valued as above, at $155,223,415

TOTAL DIFFERENCE—POUND-MEASURE PRODUCTS.

	Pounds.	Value.
Free States	28,878,064,902	$214,422,523
Slave States	4,338,370,661	155,223,415

Balance in pounds.......24,539,694,241   Difference in value, $59,199,108

Both quantity and value again in favor of the North! Behold also the enormousness of the difference! In this comparison with the South, neither hundreds, thousands, nor millions, according to the regular method of computation, are sufficient to exhibit the excess of the pound-measure products of the North. Recourse must be had to an almost inconceivable number; billions must be called into play; and there are the figures telling us, with unmistakable emphasis and distinctness, that, in this department of agriculture, as in every other, the North is vastly the superior of the South—the figures showing a total balance in favor of the former of *twenty-four billion five hundred and thirty-nine million six hundred and ninety-four thousand two hundred and forty-one pounds*, valued at *fifty-nine million one hundred and ninety-nine thousand one hundred and eight dollars.* And yet the North, as we are unblushingly told by the fire-eating politicians of the South, is a poor, God-forsaken country, bleak, inhospitable, and unproductive!

What next? Is it necessary to adduce other facts in order to prove that the rural wealth of the free States is far greater than that of the slave States? Shall we make a further demonstration of the fertility of northern soil, or bring forward new evidences of the inefficient and desolating system of terra-culture in the South? Will nothing less than " confirmations strong as proofs of holy writ," suffice to convince the South that she is standing in her own light, and ruining both body and soul by the retention of slavery? Whatever duty and expedience require to be done, we are willing to do. Additional proofs are at hand. Slaveholders and slave-breeders shall be convinced, confuted, convicted, and converted. They shall, in their hearts and consciences, if not with their tongues and pens, bear testimony to the triumphant achievements of Free Labor. In the two tables which immediately follow these remarks, they shall see how much more vigorous and fruitful the soil is when under the prudent management of free white husbandmen, than it is when under the rude and nature-murdering tillage of enslaved negroes; and in two subsequent tables they shall find that the live stock, slaughtered animals, farms, and farming implements and machinery, in the free States, are worth at least *one thousand million of dollars* more than the market value of the same in the slave States! In the face, however, of all these most significant and incontrovertible facts, the oligarchy have the unparalleled audacity to tell us that the South is the greatest agricultural country in the world, and that the North is a dreary waste, unfit for cultivation, and quite dependent on us for the necessaries of life. How preposterously false all such babble is, the following tables will show :

TABLE 8.

ACTUAL CROPS PER ACRE ON THE AVERAGE IN THE FREE AND IN THE SLAVE STATES--1850.

STATES.	Wheat, bush.	Oats, bushels.	Rye, bushels.	Indian Corn, bushels.	Irish Potatoes, bushels.	STATES.	Wheat, bush.	Oats, bushels.	Rye, bushels.	Indian Corn, bushels.	Irish Potatoes, bushels.
Connecticut	..	21	..	40	85	Alabama ..	5	12	..	15	60
Illinois ...	11	29	14	33	115	Arkansas...	..	18	..	22	....
Indiana....	12	20	18	33	100	Delaware..	11	20	..	20	....
Iowa......	14	36	..	32	100	Florida....	15	..	..	..	175
Maine.....	10	..	..	27	120	Georgia ...	5	18	7	16	125
Mass.......	16	26	13	31	170	Kentucky..	8	18	11	24	130
Michigan ..	10	26	..	32	140	Louisiana..	..	..	..	16	....
New Hamp.	11	30	..	30	220	Maryland..	13	21	18	23	75
New Jersey	11	26	..	33	...	Mississippi.	9	12	..	18	105
New York..	12	25	17	27	100	Missouri...	11	26	..	34	110
Ohio......	12	21	25	36	...	N. Carolina	7	10	15	17	65
Penn......	15	..	..	20	75	S. Carolina	8	12	..	11	70
Rhode Is...	..	30	..	..	100	Tennessee.	7	19	7	21	120
Vermont...	13	..	20	32	178	Texas.....	15	..	..	20	250
Wisconsin .	14	35	..	30	...	Virginia...	7	13	5	18	75
	161	325	107	436	1,503		121	199	63	275	1,360

RECAPITULATION OF ACTUAL CROPS PER ACRE ON THE AVERAGE—1850.

FREE STATES.		SLAVE STATES.	
Wheat............12 bushels per acre.		Wheat............. 9 bushels per acre.	
Oats..............27 " "		Oats..............17 " "
Rye...............18 " "		Rye...............11 " "
Indian Corn.......31 " "		Indian Corn........20 " "
Irish Potatoes.....125 " "		Irish Potatoes....113 " "

What an obvious contrast between the vigor of Liberty and the impotence of Slavery? What an unanswerable argument in favor of free labor! Add up the two columns of figures above, and what is the result? Two hundred and thirteen bushels as the products of five acres in the North, and only one hundred and seventy bushels as the products of five acres in the South. Look at each item separately, and you will find that the average crop per acre of every article enumerated is greater in the free States than it is in the slave States. Examine the table at large, and you will perceive that while Massachusetts produces sixteen bushels of wheat to the acre, Virginia produces only seven; that Pennsylvania produces fifteen and Georgia only five: that while Iowa produces thirty-six bushels of oats to the acre, Mississippi produces only twelve ; that Rhode Island produces thirty, and North Carolina only ten ; that while Ohio produces twenty-five bushels of rye to the acre, Kentucky produces only eleven ; that Vermont produces twenty, and Tennessee only seven : that while Connecticut produces forty bushels of Indian corn to the acre, Texas produces only twenty ; that New Jersey produces thirty-three, and South Carolina only eleven ; that while New Hampshire produces two hundred and twenty bushels of Irish potatoes to the acre, Maryland produces only seventy-five ; that Michigan produces one hundred and forty, and Alabama only sixty. Now for other beauties of slavery in another table.

TABLE 9.

VALUE OF FARMS AND DOMESTIC ANIMALS IN THE FREE AND IN THE SLAVE STATES—1850.

| | VALUE OF FARMS AND DOMESTIC ANIMALS IN THE FREE STATES—1850. | | | | VALUE OF FARMS AND DOMESTIC ANIMALS IN THE SLAVE STATES—1850. | | |
States.	Value of Live Stock.	Value of Animals Slaughtered.	Cash Value of Farms, Farming Imp., and Machinery.	States.	Value of Live Stock.	Value of Animals Slaughtered.	Cash Value of Farms, Farming Imp., and Machinery
Cal....	$3,351,058	$107,173	$3,977,524	Ala....	$21,690,112	$4,823,485	$69,448,887
Conn..	7,467,490	2,202,266	74,618,963	Ark...	6,647,969	1,163,313	16,866,541
Illinois	24,209,258	4,972,286	102,538,851	Del....	1,849,281	373,665	19,390,310
Ind. ..	22,478,555	6,567,935	143,089,617	Florida	2,880,058	514,685	6,981,904
Iowa..	3,689,275	821,164	17,880,436	Ga....	25,728,416	6,839,762	101,647,595
Maine.	9,705,726	1,646,773	57,146,305	Ky....	29,661,436	6,462,598	160,190,299
Mass..	9,647,710	2,500,924	112,285,931	La. ...	11,152,275	1,458,990	87,391,336
Mich..	8,008,734	1,328,327	54,763,817	Md....	7,997,634	1,954,800	89,641,988
N. H...	8,871,901	1,522,873	57,560,122	Miss...	19,403,662	3,636,582	60,501,561
N. J...	10,679,291	2,638,552	124,663,014	Mo....	19,887,580	3,367,106	67,207,068
N. Y....	73,570,499	13,573,883	576,631,568	N. C...	17,717,647	5,767,866	71,823,298
Ohio..	44,121,741	7,439,243	371,509,188	S. C...	15,060,015	3,502,637	86,568,088
Penn..	41,500,053	8,219,848	422,598,640	Tenn..	29,978,016	6,401,765	103,211,422
R. I...	1,582,637	667,486	17,568,008	Texas.	10,412,927	1,116,187	18,701,712
Vt.....	12,643,228	1,861,336	66,106,509	Va....	33,656,659	7,502,986	223,423,315
Wis. ..	4,897,885	920,178	30,170,181				
	$286,376,541	$56,990,237	$2,233,058,619		$253,723,687	$54,388,377	$1,183,995,274

RECAPITULATION—FREE STATES.

Value of live Stock...$286,376,541
Value of Animals slaughtered.................................... 56,990,237
Value of Farms, Farming-Implements and Machinery...............2,233,058,619

    Total..$2,576,425,397

RECAPITULATION—SLAVE STATES.

Value of Live Stock...$253,723,687
Value of Animals slaughtered..................................... 54,388,377
Value of Farms, Farming-Implements and Machinery...............1,183,995,274

    Total..$1,492,107,338

DIFFERENCE IN VALUE—FARMS AND DOMESTIC ANIMALS.

Free States..$2,576,425,397
Slave States... 1,492,107,338

    Balance in favor of the Free States...................$1,084,318,059

By adding to this last balance in favor cf the free States the differences in value which we found in their favor in our account of the bushel-and-pound-measure products, we shall have a very correct idea of the extent to which the undivided agricultural interests of the free States preponderate over those of the slave States. Let us add the differences together, and see what will be the result.

BALANCES—ALL IN FAVOR OF THE NORTH.

Difference in the value of bushel-measure products................ $44,782,636
Difference in the value of pound-measure products................ 59,199,108
Difference in the value of farms and domestic animals............. 1,084,318,059

Balance in favor of the Free States....................$1,188,299,803

No figures of rhetoric can add emphasis or significance to these figures of arithmetic. They demonstrate conclusively the great moral triumph of Liberty over Slavery. They show unequivocally, in spite of all the blarney and boasting of slaveholding politicians, that the entire value of all the agricultural interests of the free States is very nearly twice as great as the entire value of all the agricultural interests of the slave States—the value of those interests in the former being twenty-five hundred million of dollars, that of those in the latter only fourteen hundred million, leaving a balance in favor of the free States of *one billion one hundred and eighty-eight million two hundred and ninety-nine thousand eight hundred and three dollars !* That is what we call a full, fair and complete vindication of Free Labor. Would we not be correct in calling it a total eclipse of the Black Orb ?

It will be observed that we have omitted the Territories and the District of Columbia in all the preceding tables. We did this purposely. Our object was to draw an equitable comparison between the value of free and slave labor in the thirty-one sovereign States, where the two systems, comparatively unaffected by the wrangling of politicians, and, as a matter of course, free from the interference of the general government, have had the fullest opportunities to exert their influence, to exhibit their virtues, and to commend themselves to the sober judgment of enlightened and discriminating minds. Had we counted the Territories on the side of the North, and the District of Columbia on the side of the South, the result would have been still greater in behalf of free labor. Though "the sum of all villainies" has but a mere nominal existence in Delaware and Maryland, we have invariably counted those States on the side of the South ; and the consequence is, that, in many particulars, the hopeless fortunes of slavery have been propped up and sustained by an imposing array of figures which of right ought to be regarded as the property of freedom. But we like to be generous to an unfortunate foe, and would utterly disdain the use of any unfair means of attack or defence.

We shall take no undue advantage of slavery. It shall have a fair trial, and be judged according to its deserts. Already has it been weighed in the balance, and found wanting; it has been measured in the half-bushel, and found wanting; it has been apprized in the field, and found wanting. Whatever redeeming traits or qualities it may possess, if any, shall be brought to light by subjecting it to other tests.

It was our desire and intention to furnish a correct table of the gallon-measure products of the several States of the Union; but we have not been successful in our attempts to procure the necessary statistics. Enough is known, however, to satisfy us that the value of the milk, wine, ardent spirits, malt liquors, fluids, oils, and molasses, annually produced and sold in the free States, is at least fifty million of dollars greater than the value of the same articles annually produced and sold in the slave States. Of sweet milk alone, it is estimated that the monthly sales in three Northern cities, New York, Philadelphia and Boston, amount to a larger sum than the marketable value of all the rosin, tar, pitch, and turpentine, annually produced in the Southern States.

Our efforts to obtain reliable information respecting another very important branch of profitable industry, the lumber business, have also proved unavailing; and we are left to conjecture as to the amount of revenue annually derived from it in the two grand divisions of our country. The person whose curiosity prompts him to take an account of the immense piles of Northern lumber now lying on the wharves and houseless lots in Baltimore, Richmond, and other slaveholding cities, will not, we imagine, form a very flattering opinion of the products of Southern forests. Let it be remembered that nearly all the clippers, steamers, and small craft, are built at the North; that large cargoes of Eastern lumber are exported to foreign countries; that nine-tenths of the wooden-ware used in the Southern States is manufactured in New England; that, in outrageous disregard of the natural rights and claims of Southern mechanics, the markets of the South are forever filled with Northern furniture, vehicles, axe-helves, walking-canes, yard-sticks, clothes-pins and pen-holders; that the extraordinary number of factories, steam-engines, forges and machine-shops in the free States, require an extraordinary quantity of cord-wood: that a large majority of the magnificent edifices and other structures, both private and public, in which timber, in its various forms, is extensively used, are to be found in the free States—we say, let all these things be remembered, and the truth will at once flash across the mind that the forests of the North are a source of far greater income than those of the South. The difference is simply this: At the North everything is turned to advantage. When a tree is cut down, the main body is sold or used for lumber, railing, or paling, the stump for matches or shoepegs, the knees for ship-building and the branches for fuel. At the South everything is either neglected or mismanaged.

Whole forests are felled by the ruthless hand of slavery, the trees are cut into logs, rolled into heaps, covered with the limbs and brush, and then burned on the identical soil that gave them birth. The land itself next falls a prey to the fell destroyer, and that which was once a beautiful, fertile, and luxuriant woodland, is soon despoiled of all its treasures, and converted into an eye-offending desert.

Were we to go beneath the soil and collect all the mineral and lapida-rious wealth of the free States, we should find it so much greater than the corresponding wealth of the slave States, that no ordinary combination of figures would suffice to express the difference. To say nothing of the gold and quicksilver of California, the iron and coal of Pennsylvania, the copper of Michigan, the lead of Illinois, or the salt of New York, *the marble and free-stone quarries of New England are, incredible as it may seem to those unacquainted with the facts, far more important sources of revenue than all the subterranean deposits of the slave States.* From the most reliable statistics within our reach, we are led to the inference that the total value of all the precious metals, rocks, minerals and medicinal waters, annually extracted from the bowels of the free States, is not less than eighty-five million of dollars ; the whole value of the same substances annually brought up from beneath the surface of the slave States does not exceed twelve millions. In this respect to what is our poverty ascribable ? To the same cause that has impoverished and dis-honored us in all other respects—the thriftless and degrading system of human slavery.

Nature has been kind to us in all things. The strata and substrata of the South are profusely enriched with gold and silver, and precious stones, and from the natural orifices and aqueducts in Virginia and North Carolina, flow the purest healing waters in the world. But of what avail is all this latent wealth ? Of what avail will it ever be, so long as slavery is permitted to play the dog in the manger ? To these queries there can be but one reply. Slavery must be throttled ; the South, so great and so glorious by nature, must be reclaimed from her infamy and degradation ; our cities, fields and forests, must be kept intact from the unsparing monster ; the various and ample resources of our vast domain, subterraneous as well as superficial, must be developed, and made to contribute to our pleasures and to the necessities of the world.

A very significant chapter, and one particularly pertinent to many of the preceding pages, might be written on the Decline of Agriculture in the Slave States ; but as the press of other subjects admonishes us to be concise upon this point, we shall present only a few of the more striking instances. In the first place, let us compare the crops of wheat and rye in Kentucky, in 1850, with the corresponding crops in the same State in 1840—after which, we will apply a similar rule of comparison to two or three other slaveholding States.

KENTUCKY.

	Wheat, bus.	Rye, bus.
Crop of 1840	4,803,152	1,321,373
" 1850	2,142,822	415,073
	Decrease 2,660,330 bus.	Decrease 906,300 bus.

TENNESSEE.

	Wheat, bus.	Tobacco, lbs.
Crop of 1840	4,569,692	29,550,432
" 1850	1,619,386	20,148,932
	Decrease 2,950,306 bus.	Decrease 9,401,500 lbs.

VIRGINIA.

	Rye, bus.	Tobacco, lbs.
Crop of 1840	1,482,799	75,347,106
" 1850	458,930	56,803,227
	Decrease 1,023,869 bus.	Decrease 18,543,879 lbs.

ALABAMA.

	Wheat, bus.	Rye, bus.
Crop of 1840	838,052	51,000
" 1850	294,044	17,261
	Decrease 544,008 bus.	Decrease 33,739 bus

The story of these figures is too intelligible to require words of explanation ; we shall, therefore, drop this part of our subject, and proceed to compile a couple of tables that will exhibit on a single page the wealth, revenue and expenditure, of the several States of the confederacy. Let it be distinctly understood, however, that, in the compilation of these tables, three million two hundred and four thousand three hundred and thirteen negroes are valued as personal property, and credited to the Southern States as if they were so many horses and asses, or bridles and blankets—and that no monetary valuation whatever is placed on any creature, of any age, color, sex or condition, that bears the upright form of man in the free States.

TABLE 10.

WEALTH, REVENUE, AND EXPENDITURE OF THE FREE AND OF THE SLAVE STATES — 1850.

WEALTH, REVENUE, AND EXPENDITURE OF THE FREE STATES—1850.				WEALTH, REVENUE, AND EXPENDITURE OF THE SLAVE STATES—1850.			
States.	Real and Personal Property.	Revenue.	Expenditure.	States.	Real and Personal Property.	Revenue.	Expenditure.
Cal....	$22,161,872	$366,825	$925,625	Ala....	$228,204,332	$658,976	$518,559
Conn....	155,707,980	150,189	137,326	Ark....	39,841,025	68,412	74,076
Illinois.	156,265,006	736,080	192,940	Del....	18,855,863	.....	.....
Indiana	202,650,264	1,288,064	1,061,605	Florida.	23,198,734	60,619	55,284
Iowa...	23,714,688	139,681	131,631	Georgia	335,425,714	1,142,405	597,882
Maine..	122,777,571	744,879	624,101	Ky.....	301,628,456	779,293	674,697
Mass...	573,342,286	598,170	674,622	La.....	233,998,764	1,146,568	1,098,911
Mich ..	59,787,255	548,326	431,918	Md.....	219,217,364	1,279,958	1,360,458
N. H. .	103,652,835	141,686	149,890	Miss....	228,951,130	221,200	223,637
N. J....	153,151,619	139,166	180,614	Mo.....	137,247,707	326,579	207,656
N. Y...	1,080,309,216	2,695,310	2,520,932	N. C....	226,800,472	219,000	228,173
Ohio...	504,726,120	3,016,408	2,736,060	S. C....	288,257,694	532,152	463,021
Penn...	729,144,998	7,716,552	6,876,480	Tenn...	207,454,704	502,126	623,625
R. I....	80,508,794	124,944	115,885	Texas..	55,362,840	140,688	156,622
Vt.	92,205,049	185,880	188,058	Va.....	391,646,438	1,265,744	1,272,382
Wis. ...	42,056,595	135,155	136,096				
	$4,102,172,108	$18,725,211	$17,076,733		$2,936,090,737	$8,343,715	$7,549,933

Entire Wealth of the Free States,................................. $4,102,172,108
Entire Wealth of the Slave States, including Slaves, ... 2,936,090,737

Balance in favor of the Free States,........................... $1,166,081,371

What a towering monument to the beauty and glory of Free Labor! What irrefragable evidence of the unequalled efficacy and grandeur of free institutions! These figures are, indeed, too full of meaning to be passed by without comment. The two tables from which they are borrowed are at least a volume within themselves; and, after all the pains we have taken to compile them, we shall, perhaps, feel somewhat disappointed if the reader fails to avail himself of the important information they impart.

Human life, in all ages, has been made up of a series of adventures and experiments, and even at this stage of the world's existence, we are, perhaps, almost as destitute of a perfect rule of action, secular or religious, as were the erratic contemporaries of Noah. It is true, however, that we have made some progress in the right direction; and as it seems to be the tendency of the world to correct itself, we may suppose that future generations will be enabled, by intuition, to discriminate between the true and the false, the good and the bad, and that with the development of this faculty of the mind, error and discord will begin to wane, and finally cease to exist. Of all the experiments that have been tried by the people in America, slavery has proved the most fatal; and the sooner it is abolished the better it will be for us, for posterity, and for the world. One of the evils resulting from it, and that not the least, is apparent in the figures above. Indeed, the *unprofitableness* of slavery is a monstrous evil, when considered in all its bearings; it makes us poor; poverty makes us ignorant; ignorance makes us wretched ; wretchedness makes us wicked, and wickedness leads to—the devil!

> "Ignorance is the curse of God,
> Knowledge the wing wherewith we fly to heaven."

Facts truly astounding are disclosed in the two last tables, and we could heartily wish that every intelligent American would commit them to memory. The total value of all the real and personal property of the free States, with an area of only 612,597 *square miles*, is one billion one hundred and sixty-six million eighty-one thousand three hundred and seventy-one dollars greater than the total value of all the real and personal property, including the price of 3,204,313 negroes, of the slave States, which have an area of 851,508 *square miles!* But extraordinary as this difference is in favor of the North, it is much less than the true amount. *On the authority of Southrons themselves, it is demonstrable beyond the possibility of refutation that the intrinsic value of all the property in the free States is more than three times greater than the intrinsic value of all the property in the slave States.*

James Madison, a Southern man, fourth President of the United States, a most correct thinker, and one of the greatest statesmen the country has produced, "thought it wrong to admit the idea that there could be property in men," and we indorse, to the fullest extent, this opinion of the profound editor of the *Federalist.* We shall not recognize property in men; the slaves of the South are not worth a groat in any civilized community; no man of genuine decency and refinement would hold them as property on any terms; in the eyes of all enlightened nations and individuals, they are men, not merchandise. Southern pro-slavery politicians, some of whom have not hesitated to buy and sell their own sons and daughters, boast that the slaves of the South are worth sixteen hundred million of dollars, and we have seen the amount estimated as high as two thousand million. Mr. De Bow, the Southern superintendent of the seventh census, informs us that the value of all the property in the slave States, real and personal, including slaves, was, in 1850, only $2,936,090,737; while, according to the same authority, the value of all the real and personal property in the free States, genuine property, property that is everywhere recognized as property, was, at the same time, $4,102,172,108. Now all we have to do in order to ascertain the real value of all the property of the South, independent of ɩegroes, whose value, if valuable at all, is of a local and precarious character, is to subtract from the sum total of Mr. De Bow's return of the entire wealth of the slave States the estimated value of the slaves themselves; and then, by deducting the difference from the intrinsic value of all the property in the free States, we shall have the exact amount of the overplus of wealth in the glorious land of free soil, free labor, free speech, free presses, and free schools. And now to the task.

Entire Wealth of the Slave States, including Slaves,............... $2,936,090,737
Estimated Value of the Slaves, ... 1,600,000,000
    True Wealth of the Slave States, ... :......... $1,336,090,737

True Wealth of the Free States, ... $4,102,172,108
True Wealth of the Slave States, ... 1,336,090,737
    Balance in favor of the Free States, ... $2,766,081,371

There, friends of the South and of the North, you have the conclusion of the whole matter. Liberty and slavery are before you; choose which you will have; as for us, in the memorable language of the immortal Henry, we say, "give us liberty, or give us death!" In the great struggle for wealth that has been going on between the two rival systems of free and slave labor, the balance above exhibits the net profits of the former. The struggle on the one side has been calm, laudable, and eminently successful; on the other, it has been attended by tumult, unutterable cruelties and disgraceful failure. We have given the slave oligarchy every conceivable opportunity to vindicate their domestic policy, but for them to do it is a moral impossibility.

Less than three-quarters of a century ago—say in 1789, for that was about the average time of the abolition of slavery in the Northern States—the South, with advantages in soil, climate, rivers, harbors, minerals, forests, and, indeed, almost every other natural resource, began an even race with the North in all the important pursuits of 'ife; and now, in the brief space of scarce three score years and ten, we find her completely distanced, enervated, dejected and dishonored. Slave-owners and slave-drivers are the sole authors of her disgrace; as they have sown, so let them reap.

As we have seen above, a careful and correct inventory of all the real and personal *property* in the two grand divisions of the country, discloses the astounding fact, that in 1850, the free States were worth precisely *two thousand seven hundred and sixty-six million eighty-one thousand three hundred and seventy-one dollars* more than all the slave States! Twenty-seven hundred million of dollars! Think of it! What a vast and desirable sum, and how much better off the South would be with it than without it! Such is the enormous amount out of which slavery has defrauded us during the space of sixty-one years—from 1789 to 1850

—being an average of about forty-five million three hundred and fifty thousand dollars per annum. During the last twenty-five or thirty years, however, our annual losses have been far greater than they were former-ly. There has been a gradual increase every year, and now the ratio of increase is almost incredible. No patriotic Southerner can become con-versant with the facts without experiencing a feeling of alarm and indig-nation. Until the North abolished slavery, she had no advantage of us whatever; the South was more than her equal in every respect. But no sooner had she got rid of that hampering and pernicious institution than she began to absorb·our wealth, and now it is confidently believed that the merchants and slaveholding pleasure-seekers of the South an-nually pour one hundred and twenty million of dollars into her coffers! Taking into account, then, the probable amount of money that has been drawn from the South and invested in the North within the last eight years, and adding it to the grand balance above—the net profits of the North up to 1850—it may be safely assumed that, in the present year of grace, 1859, *the free States are worth at least thirty-five hundred million of dollars more than the slave States!* Let him who dares, gainsay these remarks and calculations; no truthful tongue will deny them; no hon-orable pen can controvert them.

One more word now as to the valuation of negroes. Were our nature so degraded, or our conscience so elastic as to permit us to set a price upon men, as we would set a price upon cattle and corn, we should be content to abide by the appraisement of the slaves at the South, and would then enter into a calculation to ascertain the value of foreigners to the North. Not long since, it was declared in the South that "one free laborer is equal to five slaves," and as there are two million five hundred thousand Europeans in the free States, all of whom are free la-borers, we might bring Southern authority to back us in estimating their value at *sixty-two hundred million of dollars*—a handsome sum where-withal to offset the account of *sixteen hundred million of dollars*, brought forward as to the value of Southern slaves! It is obvious, therefore, that if we were disposed to follow the barbarian example of the traffickers in human flesh, we could prove the North vastly richer than the South in bone and sinew—to say nothing of mind and morals, which shall receive our attention hereafter. The North has just as much right to appraise the Irish immigrant, as the South has to set a price on the African slave. But as it would be wrong to do either, we shall do neither. It is not our business to think of man as a merchantable com-modity; and we will not, even by implication, admit "the wild and guilty fantasy," that the condition of chattelhood may rightfully attach to sentient and immortal beings.

For the purpose of showing what Virginia, once the richest, most populous, and most powerful of the States, has become under the blight of slavery, we shall now introduce an extract from one of the speeches delivered by Governor Wise, during a late gubernatorial campaign in that degraded commonwealth. Addressing a Virginia audience, in language as graphic as it is truthful, he says:

"Commerce has long ago spread her sails, and sailed away from you. You have not, as yet, dug more than coal enough to warm yourselves at your own hearths; you have set no tilt-hammer of Vulcan to strike blows worthy of gods in your own iron-foundries; you have not yet spun more than coarse cotton enough, in the way of manufacture, to clothe your own slaves. You have no commerce, no mining, no manufactures. You have relied alone on the single power of agriculture, and *such agriculture!* Your sedge-patches outshine the sun. Your inattention to your only source of wealth, has seared the very bosom of mother earth. Instead of having to feed cattle on a thousand hills, you have had to chase the stump-tailed steer through the sedge-patches to procure a tough beef-steak. The present condition of things has existed too long in Virginia. The landlord has skinned the tenant, and the tenant has skinned the land, until all have grown poor together."

With tears in its eyes, and truth on its lips, for the first time after an interval of twenty years, the *Richmond Enquirer* helps to paint the melancholy picture. In 1852, that journal thus bewailed the condition of Virginia:

"We have cause to feel deeply for our situation. Philadelphia herself contains a population far greater than the whole free population of Eastern Virginia. The little State of Massachusetts has an aggregate wealth exceeding that of Virginia by more than $126,000,000."

Just a score of years before these words were penned, the same paper, then edited by the elder Ritchie, made a most earnest appeal to the intelligence and patriotism of Virginia, to adopt an effectual measure for the speedy overthrow of the pernicious system of human bondage. Here is an extract from an article which appeared in its editorial column under date of January 7th, 1832:

"Something must be done, and it is the part of no honest man to deny it—of no free press to affect to conceal it. When this dark population is growing upon us; when every new census is but gathering its appalling numbers upon us; when, within a period equal to that in which this Federal Constitution has been in existence, these numbers will increase to more than two millions within Virginia; when our sister States are closing their doors upon our blacks for sale, and when our whites are moving westwardly in greater numbers than we like to hear of, when this, the fairest land on all this continent, for soil, and climate, and situation, combined, might become a sort of garden spot, if it were worked by the hands of white men alone, can we, ought we, to sit quietly down, fold our arms, and say to each other, 'Well, well; this thing will not come to the worst in our days; we will leave it to our children, and our grandchildren, and great-grandchildren, to take care of themselves, and to brave the storm!' Is this to act like wise men? Means sure but gradual, systematic but discreet, ought to be adopted, for reducing the mass of evil which is pressing upon the South, and will still more press upon her, the longer it is put off. We say now, in the utmost sincerity of our hearts, that our wisest men cannot give too much of their attention to this subject, nor can they give it too soon."

Better abolition doctrine than this is seldom heard. Why did not the *Enquirer* continue to preach it? What potent influence hushed its clarion voice, just as it began to be lifted in behalf of a liberal policy and an enlightened humanity ?   Had Mr. Ritchie continued to press the truth home to the hearts of the people, as he should have done, Virginia, instead of being worth only $392,000,000 in 1850—negroes and all— would have been worth at least $800,000,000 in genuine property; and if the State had emancipated her slaves at the time of the adoption of the Constitution, the last census would no doubt have reported her wealth, and correctly, at a sum exceeding a thousand millions of dollars.

Listen now to the statement of a momentous fact.   The value of all the property, real and personal, including slaves, in seven slave States, Virginia, North Carolina, Tennessee, Missouri, Arkansas, Florida and Texas, is less than the real and personal estate, which is unquestionable property, in the single State of New York.   Nay, worse ; if eight entire slave States, Arkansas, Delaware, Florida, Maryland, Missouri, Mississippi, Tennessee and Texas, and the District of Columbia—with all their hordes of human merchandise—were put up at auction, New York could buy them all, and then have one hundred and thirty-three millions of dollars left in her pocket !   Such is the amazing contrast between freedom and slavery, even in a pecuniary point of view.   When we come to compare the North with the South in regard to literature, general intelligence, inventive genius, moral and religious enterprises, the discoveries in medicine, and the progress in the arts and sciences, we shall, in every instance, find the contrast equally great on the side of Liberty.

It gives us no pleasure to say hard things of the Old Dominion, the mother of Washington, Jefferson, Henry, and other illustrious patriots, who, as we shall prove hereafter, were genuine abolitionists ; but the policy which she has pursued has been so utterly inexcusable, so unjust to the non-slaveholding whites, so cruel to the negroes, and so disregardful of the rights of humanity at large, that it becomes the duty of every one who makes allusion to her history, to expose her follies, her crimes, and her poverty, and to publish every fact, of whatever nature, that would be instrumental in determining others to eschew her bad example.   She has willfully departed from the faith of the founders of this Republic.   She has not only turned a deaf ear to the counsel of wise men from other States in the Union, but she has, in like manner, ignored the teachings of the great warriors and statesmen who have sprung from her own soil.   In a subsequent chapter, we expect to show that all, or nearly all, the distinguished Virginians, whose bodies have been consigned to the grave, but whose names have been given to history, and whose memoirs have a place in the hearts of their countrymen, were the friends and advocates of universal freedom—that they were inflexibly opposed to the extension of slavery into the Territories, devised measures for its restriction, and, with hopeful anxiety, looked forward to the time when it should be eradicated from the States themselves. With them, the rescue of our country from British domination, and the establishment of the General Government upon a firm basis, were considerations of paramount importance; they supposed, and no doubt earnestly desired, that the States, in their sovereign capacities, would soon abolish a system of wrong and despotism which was so palpably in conflict with the principles enunciated in the Declaration of Independence. Indeed, it would seem that, among the framers of that immortal instrument and its equally immortal sequel, the Constitution of the United States, there was a tacit understanding to this effect; and the Northern States, true to their implied faith, abolished it within a short period after our national independence had been secured. Not so with the South. She has pertinaciously refused to perform her duty. She has apostatized from the faith of her greatest men, and even at this very moment repudiates the sacred principle that " all men are endowed by their Creator with certain unalienable rights," among which " are life, liberty, and the pursuit of happiness." It is evident, therefore, that the free States are the only members of this confederacy that have established republican forms of government based upon the theories of Washington, Jefferson, Madison, Henry, and other eminent statesmen of Virginia.

The great revolutionary movement which was set on foot in Charlotte, Mecklenburg county, North Carolina, on the 20th day of May, 1775, has not yet been terminated, nor will it be, until every slave in the United States is freed from the tyranny of his master. Every victim of the vile institution, whether white or black, must be reinvested with the sacred rights and privileges of which he has been deprived by an inhuman oligarchy. What our noble sires of the revolution left unfinished it is our duty to complete. They did all that true valor and patriotism could accomplish. Not one iota did they swerve from their plighted faith; the self-sacrificing spirit which they evinced will command the applause of every succeeding age. Not in vindication of their own personal rights merely, but of the rights of humanity; not for their own generation and age simply, but for all ages to the end of time, they gave their toil, their treasure and their blood, nor deemed them all too great a price to pay for the establishment of so comprehensive and beneficent a principle. Let their posterity emulate their courage, their disinterestedness, and their zeal, and especially remember that it is the duty of every existing generation so to provide for its individual interests, as to confer superior advantages on that which is to follow. To this principle the North has adhered with the strictest fidelity. How has it been with the South? Has she imitated the praiseworthy example of our illustrious ancestors? No! She has treated it with the utmost contempt; she has been extremely selfish—so selfish, indeed, that she has robbed pos terity of its natural, inalienable rights. From the period of the formation of the government down to the present moment, her policy has been downright suicidal, and, as a matter of course, wholly indefensible. She has hugged a viper to her breast; her whole system has been paralyzed, her conscience is seared, and, still holding in her embrace the cause of her shame and suffering, she is becoming callous to every principle of justice and magnanimity. Except among the non-slaveholders, who, beside being kept in the grossest ignorance, are under the restraint of all manner of iniquitous laws, patriotism has almost ceased to exist within her borders. And here we desire to be distinctly under-stood, for we shall have occasion to refer to this matter again. We repeat, therefore, the substance of our averment, that, at this day, there is scarcely a grain of pure patriotism in the South, except among the non-slaveholders. Subsequent pages shall testify to the truth of this assertion. Here and there, it is true, a slaveholder, disgusted with the institution, becomes ashamed of himself, emancipates his negroes, and enters upon the walks of honorable life; but these cases are exceedingly rare, and do not, in any manner, disprove the general correctness of our remark. All persons who do voluntarily manumit their slaves, as mentioned above, are undeniably actuated by principles of pure patriotism, justice and humanity; and so believing, we delight to do them honor.

Once more to the Old Dominion. At her door we lay the bulk of the evils of slavery. The first African sold in America was sold on James River, in that State, on the 20th of August, 1620; and although the institution was fastened upon her and the other colonies by the mother country, she was the first to perceive its blighting and degrading influences, her wise men were the first to denounce it, and, after the British power was overthrown at Yorktown, she should have been the first to abolish it. Fifty-seven years ago she was the Empire State; now, with half a dozen other slaveholding States thrown into the scale with her, she is far inferior to New York, which, at the time Cornwallis surrendered his sword to Washington, was less than half her equal. Had she obeyed the counsels of the good, the great and the wise men of our nation—especially of her own incomparable sons, the extensible element of slavery would have been promptly arrested, and the virgin soil of nine Southern States, Kentucky, Tennessee, Louisiana, Mississippi, Alabama, Missouri, Arkansas, Florida, and Texas, would have been saved from its horrid pollutions. Confined to the original States in which it existed, the system would soon have been disposed of by legislative enactments, and long before the present day, by a gradual process that could have shocked no interest and alarmed no prejudice, we should have rid ourselves not only of African slavery, which is an abomination and a curse, but also of the negroes themselves, who, in our judgment, whether viewed in relation to their actual characteristics and condition, or through the strong antipathies of the whites, are, to say the least, an undesirable population.

This, then, is the ground of our expostulation with Virginia: that, in stubborn disregard of the advice and friendly warnings of Washington, Jefferson, Madison, Henry, and a host of other distinguished patriots who sprang from her soil—patriots whose voices shall be heard before we finish our task—and in utter violation of every principle of justice and humanity, *she still persists* in fostering an institution or system which is so manifestly detrimental to her vital interests. Every Virginian, whether living or dead, whose name is an honor to his country, has placed on record his abhorrence of slavery, and in doing so, has borne testimony to the blight and degradation that everywhere follow in its course. One of the best abolition speeches we have ever read was delivered in the Virginia House of Delegates, January 20th, 1832, by Charles James Faulkner, who still lives, and who has, we understand, generously emancipated several of his slaves, and sent them to Liberia. Here follows an extract from his speech; let Southern politicians read it attentively, and imbibe a moiety of the spirit of patriotism which it breathes:

"Sir, I am gratified to perceive that no gentleman has yet risen in this Hall, the avowed advocate of slavery. *The day has gone by when such a voice could be listened to with patience, or even with forbearance.* I even regret, sir, that we should find those amongst us who enter the lists of discussion as its *apologists*, except alone upon the ground of uncontrollable necessity. And yet, who could have listened to the very eloquent remarks of the gentleman from Brunswick, without being forced to conclude that he at least considered slavery, however *not to be defended upon principle*, yet as being divested of much of its enormity, as you approach it in practice.

"Sir, if there be one who concurs with that gentleman in the harmless character of this institution, let me request him to compare the condition of the slaveholding portion of this commonwealth—*barren, desolate and seared as it were by the avenging hand of Heaven*—with the descriptions which we have of this country from those who first broke its virgin soil. To what is this change ascribable? *Alone to the withering and blasting effects of slavery.* If this does not satisfy him, let me request him to extend his travels to the *Northern States of this Union*, and beg him to contrast the happiness and contentment which prevail throughout that country, the busy and cheerful sound of industry, the rapid and swelling growth of their population, their means and institutions of education, their skill and proficiency in the useful arts, their enterprise and public spirit, the monuments of their commercial and manufacturing industry; and, above all, their devoted attachment to the government from which they derive their protection, *with the derision, discontent, indolence and poverty of the Southern country*, To what, Sir, is all this ascribable? *To that vice in the organization of society, by which one-half of its inhabitants are arrayed in interest and feeling against the other half*—to that unfortunate state of society in which freemen regard labor as disgraceful, and slaves shrink from it as a burden tyrannically imposed upon them—to that condition of things in which half a million of your population can feel no sympathy with the society in the prosperity of which they are forbidden to participate, and no attachment to a government at whose hands they receive nothing but injustice.

"If this should not be sufficient, and the curious and incredulous inquirer should suggest that the contrast which has been adverted to, and which is so manifest, might be traced to a difference of climate, **or** other causes distinct from slavery itself, permit me to refer him to the two States of Kentucky and Ohio. No difference of soil, no diversity of climate, no diversity in the original settlement of those two States, can account for the remarkable disproportion in their natural advancement. Separated by a river alone, *they seem to have been purposely and providen-*

tially designed to exhibit in their future histories the difference which necessarily results from a country free from, and a country afflicted with, the curse of slavery.

" Vain and idle is every effort to strangle this inquiry. As well might you attempt to chain the ocean, or stay the avenging thunderbolts of Heaven, as to drive the people from any inquiry which may result in their better condition. This is too deep, too engrossing a subject of consideration. It addresses itself too strongly to our interests, to our passions, and to our feelings. I shall advocate no scheme that does not respect the right of property, *so far as it is entitled to be respected*, with a just regard to the safety and resources of the State. I would approach the subject as one of great magnitude and delicacy, as one whose varied and momentous consequences demand the calmest and most deliberate investigation. But still, sir, I would approach it—aye, delicate as it may be, encompassed as it may be with difficulties and hazards, I would still approach it. The people demand it. Their security requires it. In the language of the wise and prophetic Jefferson, ' You must approach it—you must bear it—you must adopt some plan of emancipation, or worse will follow.' "

Mr. Curtis, in a speech in the Virginia Legislature in 1832, said :

" There is a malaria in the atmosphere of these regions, which the new comer shuns, as being deleterious to his views and habits. See the wide-spreading ruin which the avarice of our ancestral government has produced in the South, as witnessed in a sparse population of freemen, deserted habitations, and fields without culture ! Strange to tell, even the wolf, driven back long since by the approach of man, now returns, after the lapse of a hundred years, to howl over the desolations of slavery."

Mr. Moore, also a member of the Legislature of Virginia, in speaking of the evils of slavery, said :

" The first I shall mention is the irresistible tendency which it has to undermine and destroy everything like virtue and morality in the community. If we look back through the long course of time which has elapsed since the creation to the present moment, we shall scarcely be able to point out a people whose situation was not, in many respects, preferable to our own, and that of the other States, in which negro slavery exists.

" In that part of the State below tide-water, the whole face of the country wears an appearance of almost utter desolation, distressing to the beholder. The very spot on which our ancestors landed, a little more than two hundred years ago, appears to be on the eve of again becoming the haunt of wild beasts."

Mr. Rives, of Campbell county, said :

" On the multiplied and desolating evils of slavery, he was not disposed to say much. The curse and deteriorating consequence were within the observation and experience of the members of the House and the people of Virginia, and it did not seem to him that there could be two opinions about it."

Mr. Powell said :

" I can scarcely persuade myself that there is a solitary gentleman in this House who will not readily admit that slavery is an evil, and that its removal, if practicable, is a consummation most devoutly to be wished. I have not heard, nor do I expect to hear, a voice raised in this Hall to the contrary."

In the language of the *New York Times,* " we might multiply extracts almost indefinitely from Virginia authorities—testifying to the blight and degradation that have overtaken the Old Dominion, in every department of her affairs. Her commerce gone, her agriculture decaying, her land falling in value, her mining and manufactures nothing, her schools dying out,—she presents, according to the testimony of her own sons,

the saddest of all pictures—that of a sinking and dying State." Every
year leaves her in a worse condition than it found her; and as it is with
Virginia, so it is with the entire South. In the terse language of Gov.
Wise, "all have grown poor together." The black god of slavery,
which the South has worshipped for two hundred and thirty-nine
years, is but a devil in disguise; and if we would save ourselves from
being ingulfed in utter ruin we must repudiate this foul god, for a
purer deity, and abandon his altars for a holier shrine. No time is to
be lost; his fanatical adorers, the despotic adversaries of human liberty,
are concocting schemes for the enslavement of all the laboring classes,
irrespective of race or color. The issue is before us; we cannot evade
it; we must meet it with firmness, and with unflinching valor.

We have been credibly informed by a gentleman from Powhattan
county in Virginia, that in the year 1836 or '37, or about that time, the
Hon. Abbott Lawrence, of Boston, backed by his brother Amos and
other millionaires of New England, went down to Richmond with the
sole view of reconnoitering the manufacturing facilities of that place—
fully determined, if pleased with the water-power, to erect a large number of cotton-mills and machine-shops. He had been in the capital of
Virginia only a day or two before he discovered, much to his gratifica-
tion, that nature had shaped everything to his liking; and as he was a
business man who transacted business in a business-like manner, he lost
no time in making preliminary arrangements for the consummation of
his noble purpose. His mission was one of peace and promise; others
were to share the benefits of his concerted and laudable scheme; thousands of poor boys and girls in Virginia, instead of growing up in extreme poverty and ignorance, or of having to emigrate to the free States
of the West, were to have avenues of profitable employment opened to
them at home; thus they would be enabled to earn an honest and reputable living, to establish and sustain free schools, free libraries, free lec-
tures, and free presses, to become useful and exemplary members of society, and to die fit candidates for heaven. The magnanimous New
Englander was in ecstasies with the prospect that opened before him.
Individually, so far as mere money was concerned, he was perfectly independent; his industry and economy in early life had secured to him
the ownership and control of an ample fortune. With the aid of eleven
other men, each equal to himself, he could have bought the whole city of
Richmond—negroes and all—though it is not to be presumed that he
would have disgraced his name by becoming a trader in human flesh.
But he was not selfish; unlike the arrogant and illiberal slaveholder, he
did not regard himself as the centre around whom everybody else should
revolve. On the contrary, he was a genuine philanthropist. While,
with a shrewdness that will command the admiration of every practical
business man, he engaged in nothing that did not swell the dimensions

of his own purse, he was yet always solicitous to invest his capital in a manner calculated to promote the interests of those around him. Nor was he satisfied with simply furnishing the means whereby his less fortunate neighbors were to become prosperous, intelligent and contented. With his generous heart and sagacious mind, he delighted to aid them in making a judicious application of his wealth to their own use. Moreover, as a member of society, he felt that the community had some reasonable claims upon him, and he made it obligatory on himself constantly to devise plans and exert his personal efforts for the public good. Such was the character of the distinguished manufacturer who honored Richmond with his presence twenty years since; such was the character of the men whom he represented, and such were the grand designs which they sought to accomplish.

To the enterprising and moneyed descendant of the Pilgrim Fathers it was a matter of no little astonishment, that the immense water-power of Richmond had been so long neglected. He expressed his surprise to a number of Virginians, and was at a loss to know why they had not, long prior to the period of his visit amongst them, availed themselves of the powerful element that is eternally gushing and foaming over the falls of James River. Innocent man! He was utterly unconscious of the fact that he was " interfering with the beloved institutions of the South," and little was he prepared to withstand the terrible denunciations that were immediately showered on his head through the columns of the Richmond papers. Few words will suffice to tell the sequel. Those negro-driving sheets, whose hireling policy, for the last five and twenty years, has been to support the worthless black slave and his tyrannical master at the expense of the free white laborer, *wrote down the enterprise,* and the noble son of New England, abused, insulted and disgusted, quietly returned to Massachusetts, and there employed his capital in building up the cities of Lowell and Lawrence, either of which, in all those elements of material and social prosperity that make up the greatness of States, is already far in advance of the most important of all the seedy and squalid slave-towns in the Old Dominion. Such is an inkling of the infamous means that have been resorted to, from time to time, for the purpose of upholding and perpetuating in America the accursed system of human slavery.

How any rational man in this or any other country, with the astounding contrasts between Freedom and Slavery ever looming in his view. can offer an apology for the existing statism of the South, is to us a most inexplicable mystery. Indeed, we cannot conceive it possible that the conscience of any man, who is really sane, would permit him to become the victim of such an egregious and diabolical absurdity. Therefore, at this period of our history, with the light of the past, the reality of the present, and the prospect of the future, all so prominent and se palpable, we infer that every person who sets up an unequivocal defence of the institution of slavery, must, of necessity, be either a fool, a knave, or a madman.

It is much to be regretted that pro-slavery men look at but one side of the question. Of all the fanatics in the country, they have, of late, become the most unreasonable and ridiculous. Let them deliberately view the subject of slavery in all its aspects and bearings, and if they are possessed of honest hearts and convincible minds, they will readily perceive the grossness of their past errors, renounce their allegiance to a cause so unjust and disgraceful, and at once enroll themselves among the hosts of Freedom and the friends of universal Liberty. There are thirty-one States in the Union; let them drop California, or any other new free State, and then institute fifteen comparisons, first comparing New York with Virginia, Pennsylvania with Carolina, Massachusetts with Georgia, and so on, until they have exhausted the catalogue. Then, for once, let them be bold enough to listen to the admonitions of their own souls, and if they do not soon start to their feet *demanding* the abolition of slavery, it will only be because they have reasons for suppressing their inmost sentiments. Whether we compare the old free States with the old slave States, or the new free States with the new slave States, the difference, unmistakable and astounding, is substantially the same. All the free States are alike, and all the slave States are alike. In the former, wealth, intelligence, power, progress, and prosperity, are the prominent characteristics; in the latter, poverty, ignorance, imbecility, inertia, and extravagance, are the distinguishing features. To be convinced, it is only necessary for us to open our eyes and look at facts—to examine the *statistics* of the country, to free ourselves from obstinacy and prejudice, and to unbar our minds to the convictions of truth. Let figures be the umpire. Close attention to the preceding and subsequent tables is all we ask; so soon as they shall be duly considered and understood, the primary object of this work will have been accomplished.

Not content with eating out the vitals of the South, slavery, in keeping with the character which it has acquired for insatiety and rapine, is beginning to make rapid encroachments on new territory; and as a basis for a few remarks on the blasting influence which it is shedding over the broad and fertile domains of the West, which, in accordance with the views and resolutions offered by the immortal Jefferson, should have been irrevocably dedicated to freedom, we beg leave to call the attention of the reader to a plain, faithful presentation of the philosophy of free and slave labor. Says the *North American and United States Gazette :*

"We have but to compare the States, possessing equal natural advantages, in which the two kinds of labor are employed, in crder to decide with entire confi dence as to which kind is the more profitable. At the origin of the government, Virginia, with a much larger extent of territory than New York, contained a population of seven hundred and fifty thousand, and sent ten representatives to Congress; while New York contained a population of three hundred and forty thousand, and sent six representatives to Congress. Behold how the figures are reversed. The population of New York is three and a half millions, represented by thirty-three members in Congress; while the population of Virginia is but little more than one and a half millions, represented by thirteen members in Congress. It is the vital sap of free labor that makes the one tree so thrifty and vigorous, so capable of bearing with all ease the fruit of such a population. And it is slave labor which strikes a decadence through the other, drying up many of its branches with a fearful sterility, and rendering the rest but scantily fruitful; really incapable of sustaining more. Look at Ohio, teeming with inhabitants, its soil loaded with every kind of agricultural wealth, its people engaged in every kind of freedom's diversified employments, abounding with numberless happy homes, and with all the trophies of civilization, and it exhibits the magic effect of free labor, waking a wilderness into life and beauty; while Kentucky, with equal or superior natural advantages, nature's very garden in this Western world, which commenced its career at a much earlier date, and was in a measure populous when Ohio was but a slumbering forest, but which in all the elements of progress, is now left far, very far, behind its young rival, shows how slave labor hinders the development of wealth among a people, and brings a blight on their prosperity. The one is a grand and beautiful poem in honor of free labor. The other is an humble confession to the world of the inferiority of slave labor."

Were we simply a freesoiler, or anything else less than a thorough and uncompromising abolitionist, we should certainly tax our ability to the utmost to get up a cogent argument against the extension of slavery over any part of our domain where it does not now exist; but as our principles are hostile to the institution even where it does exist, and, therefore, by implication and in fact, more hostile still to its introduction into new territory, we forbear the preparation of any special remarks on this particular subject.

With regard to the unnational and demoralizing system of slavery, we believe the majority of Northern people are too scrupulous. They seem to think that it is enough for them to be mere freesoilers, to keep in check the diffusive element of slavery, and to prevent it from crossing over the bounds within which it is now regulated by municipal law. Remiss in their *national* duties, as we contend, they make no positive attack upon the institution in the Southern States. Only a short while since, one of their ablest journals—the *North American and United States Gazette*, published in Philadelphia—made use of the following language:

"With slavery in the States, we make no pretence of having anything politically to do. For better or for worse, the system belongs solely to the people of those States; and is separated by an impassable gulf of State sovereignty from any legal intervention of ours. We cannot vote it down any more than we can vote down the institution of caste in Hindostan, or abolish polygamy in the Sultan's dominions. Thus, precluded from all political action in reference to it, prevented from touching one stone of the edifice, not the slightest responsibility attaches to us as citizens for its continued existence. But on the question of extending slavery over the free Territories of the United States, it is our right, it is our imperative duty to think, to feel, to speak and to vote. We cannot interfere to cover the shadows of slavery with the sunshine of freedom, but we can interfere to prevent the sunshine of freedom from being eclipsed by the shadows of slavery. We can interpose to stay the progress of that institution, which aims to drive free labor from its own holdings. Kansas should be divided up into countless homes for the ownership of men who have a right to the fruit of their own labors. Free labor would make it bud and blossom like the rose; would cover it with beauty, and draw from it boundless wealth; would throng it with population; would make States, nations, empires out of it, prosperous, powerful, intelligent and free, illustrating on a wide theatre the beneficent ends of Providence in the formation of our government, to advance and elevate the millions of our race, and, like the heart in the body, from its central position, sending out on every side, far and near, the vital influences of freedom and civilization. May that region, therefore, be secured to free labor."

Now we fully and heartily indorse every line of the latter part of this extract; but, with all due deference to our sage contemporary, we do most emphatically dissent from the sentiments embodied in the first part. Pray, permit us to ask—have the people of the North no interest in the United States as a *nation*, and do they not see that slavery is a great injury and disgrace to the *whole country?* Did they not, in "the days that tried men's souls," strike as hard blows to secure the independence of Georgia as they did in defending the liberties of Massachusetts, and is it not notoriously true that the Toryism of South Carolina prolonged the war two years at least? Is it not, moreover, equally true that the oligarchs of South Carolina have been unmitigated pests and bores to the General Government ever since it was organized, and that the free and conscientious people of the North are virtually excluded from her soil, in consequence of slavery? It is a well-known and incontestable fact, that the Northern States furnished about two-thirds of all the American troops engaged in the Revolutionary War; and, though they were neither more nor less brave or patriotic than their fellow-soldiers of the South, yet, inasmuch as the independence of our country was mainly secured by virtue of their numerical strength, we think they ought to consider it not only their right but their *duty* to make a firm and deci- sive effort to save the States which they fought to free, from falling under the yoke of a worse tyranny than that which overshadowed them under the reign of King George the Third. Freemen of the North! we earnestly entreat you to think of these things. Hitherto, as mere free- soilers, you have approached but half-way to the line of your duty ; now, for your own sakes and for ours, and for the purpose of perpetuating this great Republic, which your fathers and our fathers founded in sep- tennial streams of blood, we ask you, in all seriousness, to organize your- selves as *one man* under the banners of Liberty, and to aid us in *exter- minating* slavery, which is the only thing that militates against our complete aggrandizement as a nation.

In this extraordinary crisis of affairs, no man can be a true patriot without first becoming an abolitionist. And here, perhaps, we may be pardoned for the digression necessary to show the exact definition of the terms *abolish, abolition, abolitionist.* We have looked in vain for an explanation of the signification of these words in any Southern pub- lication ; for no dictionary has ever yet been published in the South, nor is there the least probability that one ever will be published within her borders, until slavery is *abolished;* but, thanks to Heaven, a portion of this continent is what our Revolutionary Fathers, and the Fathers of the Constitution, fought and labored and prayed to make it—a land of freedom, of power, of progress, of prosperity, of intelligence, of religion, of literature, of commerce, of science, of arts, of agriculture, of manufactures, of ingenuity, of enterprise, of wealth, of renown, of goodness, and of grandeur. From that glorious part of our confederacy —from the North, whence, on account of slavery in the South, we are under the humiliating necessity of procuring almost everything that is useful or ornamental, from primers to Bibles, from wafers to printing presses, from ladles to locomotives, and from portfolios to portraits and pianos—comes to us a huge volume bearing the honored name of Webster—Noah Webster, who, after thirty-five years of unremitting toil, completed a work which is, we believe, throughout Great Britain and the United States, justly regarded as the standard vocabulary of the English language—and in it the terms *abolish, abolition,* and *abolitionists,* are defined as follows :

"Abolish, *v. t.* To make void ; to annul ; to abrogate ; applied chiefly and appropriately to established laws, contracts, rites, customs and institutions ; as to *abolish* laws by a repeal, actual or virtual. To destroy or put an end to ; as to *abolish* idols."

"Abolition, *n.* The act of abolishing ; or the state of being abolished; an annulling ; abrogation ; utter destruction ; as the *abolition* of laws, decrees, ordinances, rites, customs, etc. The putting an end to slavery ; emancipation."

"Abolitionist, *n.* A person who favors abolition, or the immediate emancipation of slaves."

There, gentlemen of the South, you have the definitions of the transitive verb *abolish,* and its two derivative nouns, *abolition* and *abolitionist ;* can you, with the keenest possible penetration of vision, detect in either of these words even a tittle of the opprobrium which the oligarchs, in their wily and inhuman efforts to enslave all working classes irrespective of race or color, have endeavored to attach to them ? We know you cannot ; abolition is but another name for patriotism, and its other special synonyms are generosity, magnanimity, reason, prudence, wisdom, religion, progress, justice and humanity.

Non-slaveholders of the South ! farmers, mechanics and workingmen, we take this occasion to assure you that the slaveholding politicians whom you have elected to offices of honor and profit, have hoodwinked you, trifled with you, and used you as mere tools for the consummation of their wicked designs. They have purposely kept you in ignorance, and have, by molding your passions and prejudices to suit themselves, induced you to act in direct opposition to your dearest rights and interests. By a system of the grossest subterfuge and misrepresentation, and in order to avert, for a season, the vengeance that will most assuredly overtake them ere long, they have taught you to hate the lovers of liberty, who are your best and only true friends. Now, as one of your own number, we appeal to you to join us in our earnest and timely efforts to rescue the generous soil of the South from the usurped and desolating control of these political vampires. Once and forever, at least so far as this country is concerned, the infernal question of slavery must be disposed of; a speedy and absolute abolishment of the whole system is the true policy of the South—and this is the policy which we propose to pursue. Will you aid us, will you assist us, will you be freemen, or will you be slaves? These are questions of vital importance; weigh them well in your minds; come to a prudent and firm decision, and hold yourselves in readiness to act in accordance therewith. You must either be for us or against us—anti-slavery or pro-slavery; it is impossible for you to occupy a neutral ground; it is as certain as fate itself, that if you do not voluntarily oppose the usurpations and outrages of the slavocrats, they will force you into involuntary compliance with their infamous measures. Consider well the aggressive, fraudulent and despotic power which they have exercised in the affairs of Kansas; and remember that, if, by adhering to erroneous principles of neutrality or non-resistance, you allow them to force the curse of slavery on that or any other vast and fertile field, the broad area of all the surrounding States and Territories—the whole nation, in fact—will soon fall a prey to their diabolical intrigues and machinations. Thus, if you are not vigilant, will they take advantage of your neutrality, and make you and others the victims of their inhuman despotism. Do not reserve the strength of your arms until you shall have been rendered powerless to strike; the present is the proper time for action; under all the circumstances, apathy or indifference is a crime. First ascertain, as nearly as you can, the precise nature and extent of your duty, and then, without a moment's delay, perform it in good faith. To facilitate you in determining what considerations of right, justice and humanity require at your hands, is one of the primary objects of this work; and we shall certainly fail in our desire if we do not accomplish our task in a manner acceptable to God and advantageous to man.

But we are carrying this chapter beyond all ordinary bounds; and yet, there are many important particulars in which we have drawn no comparison between the free and slave States. The more weighty remarks which we intended to offer in relation to the new States of the West and Southwest, free and slave, shall appear in the succeeding chapter. With regard to agriculture, and all the multifarious interests of husbandry, we deem it quite unnecessary to say more. Cotton has been shorn of its magic power, and is no longer King; *dried grass*, commonly called hay, is, it seems, the rightful heir to the throne. Commerce, Manufactures, Literature, and other important subjects, shall be considered as we progress.

CHAPTER II.

Our age, marked by res'less activity in almost all departments of knowledge, and by struggles and aspirations before unknown, is stamped by no characteristic more deeply than by a desire to establish or extend freedom in the political societies of mankind. . . . . There are many persons who pretend to admire liberty, but withhold it from the people on the plea that they are not prepared for it. Unquestionably, all races are not prepared for the same amount of liberty. But two things are certain, that all nations, and especially those belonging to our own civilized family, prove that they are prepared for the beginning of liberty, by desiring it and insisting upon it and that you cannot otherwise prepare nations for enjoying liberty than by beginning to establish it, as you best prepare nations for a high christianity by beginning to preach it. —LIEBER.

PRELIMINARY to our elucidation of what we conceive to be the most discreet, fair and feasible plan for the abolition of slavery, we propose to offer a few additional reasons why it should be abolished. Among the thousand and one arguments that present themselves in support of our position—which, before we part with the reader, we shall endeavor to define so clearly, that it shall be regarded as ultra only by those who imperfectly understand it—is the influence which slavery invariably exercises in depressing the value of real estate; and as this is a matter in which the non-slaveholders of the South, of the West, and of the Southwest, are most deeply interested, we shall discuss it in a sort of preamble of some length.

The slaveholding oligarchy say we cannot abolish slavery without infringing on the right of property. Again we tell them we do not recognize property in men; but even if we did, and if we were to inventory the negroes at quadruple the value of their last assessment, still, impelled by a sense of duty to others, and as a matter of simple justice, to ourselves, we, the non-slaveholders of the South, would be fully warranted in emancipating all the slaves at once, and that, too, without any compensation whatever to those who claim to be their absolute masters and owners. We will explain. In 1850, the average value per acre, of land in the Northern States was $28 07; in the Northwestern $11 39; in the Southern $5 34; and in the Southwestern $6 26. Now, in consequence of numerous natural advantages, among which may be enumerated the greater mildness of climate, richness of soil, deposits of precious metals, abundance, and spaciousness of harbors, and superexcellence of water-power, we contend that, had it not been for slavery, the average value of land in all the Southern and

Southwestern States, would have been *at least* equal to the average value of the same in the Northern States. We conclude, therefore, and we think the conclusion is founded on principles of equity, that you, the slaveholders, are indebted to us, the non-slaveholders, in the sum of $22 73, which is the difference between $28 07 and $5 34, on every acre of Southern soil in our possession. This claim we bring against you, because slavery, which has inured exclusively to your own benefit, if, indeed, it has been beneficial at all, has shed a blighting influence over our lands, thereby keeping them out of market, and damaging every acre to the amount specified. Sirs! are you ready to settle the account? Let us see how much it is. There are in the fifteen slave States, 346,048 slaveholders, and 544,926,720 acres of land. Now the object is to ascertain how many acres are owned by slaveholders, and how many by non-slaveholders. Suppose we estimate five hundred acres as the average landed property of each slaveholder; will that be fair? We think it will, taking into consideration the fact that 174,503 of the whole number of slaveholders hold less than five slaves each— 68,820 holding only one each. According to this hypothesis, the slaveholders own 173,024,000 acres, and the non-slaveholders the balance, with the exception of about 40,000,000 of acres which belong to the General Government. The case may be stated thus:

$$\text{Estimates} \begin{cases} \text{Acres owned by slaveholders} \dots \dots \dots 173,024,000 \\ \text{Acres owned by the government} \dots \dots 40,000,000 = 213,024,000 \\ \text{Acres owned by non-slaveholders} \dots \dots \dots \dots 331,902,720 \end{cases}$$

Area of the Slave States 544,926,720 acres.

Now, chevaliers of the lash, and conservators of slavery, the total value of three hundred and thirty-one million nine hundred and two thousand seven hundred and twenty acres, at twenty-two dollars and seventy-three cents per acre, is *seven billion five hundred and forty-four million one hundred and forty-eight thousand eight hundred and twenty-five dollars;* and this is our account against you on a single score. Considering how your pernicious institution has retarded the development of our commercial and manufacturing interests, how it has stifled the aspirations of inventive genius; and, above all, how it has barred from us the heaven-born sweets of literature and religion— concernments too sacred to be estimated in a pecuniary point of view— might we not, with perfect justice and propriety, duplicate the amount, and still be accounted modest in our demands? Fully advised, however, of your indigent circumstances, we feel it would be utterly useless to call on you for the whole amount that is due us; we shall, therefore, in your behalf, make another draft on the fund of non-slaveholding generosity, and let the account, meagre as it is, stand as above. Though we have given you all the offices, and you have given us none of the benefits of legislation; though we have fought the battles of the South, while you were either lolling in your piazzas, or in active fellowship with the enemy, and endeavoring to filch from us our birthright of freedom; though you have absorbed the wealth of our communities in sending your own children to Northern seminaries and colleges, or in employing Yankee teachers to officiate exclusively in your own families, and have refused to us the limited privilege of common schools; though you have scorned to patronize our mechanics and industrial enterprises, and have passed to the North for every article of apparel, utility, and adornment; and though you have maltreated, outraged and defrauded us in every relation of life, civil, social, and political, yet we are willing to forgive and forget you, if you will but do us justice on a single count. Of you, the introducers, aiders and abettors of slavery, we demand indemnification for the damage our lands have sustained on account thereof; the amount of that damage is $7,544,148,825; and now, sirs, we are ready to receive the money, and if it is perfectly convenient to you, we would be glad to have you pay it in specie! It will not avail you, sirs, to parley or prevaricate. We must have a settlement. Our claim is just and overdue. We have already indulged you too long. Your reckless extravagance has almost ruined us. We are determined that you shall no longer play the profligate, and fare sumptuously every day at our expense. How do you propose to settle? Do you offer us your negroes in part payment? We do not want your negroes. We would not have all of them, nor any number of them, even as a gift. We hold ourselves above the disreputable and iniquitous practices of buying, selling, and owning slaves. What we demand is damages in money, or other absolute property, as an equivalent for the pecuniary losses we have suffered at your hands. You value your negroes at sixteen hundred millions of dollars, and propose to sell them to us for that sum; we should consider ourselves badly cheated, and disgraced for all time, here and hereafter, if we were to take them off your hands at sixteen farthings! We tell you emphatically, we are firmly resolved never to degrade ourselves by becoming the mercenary purchasers or proprietors of human beings. Except for the purpose of liberating them, we would not give a handkerchief or a tooth-pick for all the slaves in the world. But, in order to show how ridiculously absurd are the howls and groans which you invariably set up for compensation, whenever we speak of the abolition of slavery, we will suppose your negroes are worth all you ask for them, and that we are bound to secure to you every cent of the sum before they can become free—in which case, our accounts would stand thus:

Non-slaveholders' account against Slaveholders........$7,544,148,825
Slaveholders' account against Non-slaveholders..... .. 1,600,000,000

Balance due Non-slaveholders.......... ·····.$5,944,148,825

Now, Sirs, we ask you in all seriousness, Is it not apparent that you nave filched from us nearly five times the amount of the assessed value of your slaves? Why, then, do you still clamor for more? Is it your purpose to make the game perpetual? Think you that we will ever continue to bow at the wave of your wand, that we will bring humanity into everlasting disgrace by licking the hand that smites us, and that with us there is no point beyond which forbearance ceases to be a virtue? Sirs, if these be your thoughts, you are laboring under a most fatal delusion. You can goad us no further; you shall oppress us no longer; heretofore, earnestly but submissively, we have asked you to redress the more atrocious outrages which you have perpetrated against us; but what has been the invariable fate of our petitions? With scarcely a perusal, with a degree of contempt that added insult to injury, you have laid them on the table, and from thence they have been swept into the furnace of oblivion. Henceforth, Sirs, we are demandants, not suppliants. We demand our rights, nothing more, nothing less. It is for you to decide whether we are to have justice peaceably or by violence, for whatever consequences may follow, we are determined to have it one way or the other.

Slavery has polluted and impoverished your lands; freedom will restore them to their virgin purity, and add from twenty to thirty dollars to the value of every acre. Correctly speaking, emancipation will cost you nothing; the moment you abolish slavery, that very moment will the putative value of the slave become actual value in the soil. Though there are ten millions of people in the South, and though you the slaveholders are only three hundred and forty-seven thousand in number, you have within a fraction of one-third of all the territory belonging to the fifteen slave States. You have a landed estate of 173,024,000 acres, the present average market value of which is only $5 34 per acre; emancipate your slaves on Wednesday morning, and on the Thursday following the value of your lands, and ours too, will have increased to an average of at least $28 07 per acre. Let us see, therefore, even in this one particular, whether the abolition of slavery will not be a real pecuniary advantage to you. The present total market value of all your landed property, at $5 34 per acre, is only $923,248,160. With the beauty and sunlight of freedom beaming on the same estate, it would be worth, at $28 07 per acre, $4,856,873,680! The former sum, deducted from the latter, leaves a balance of $3,933,535,520, and to the full extent of this amount will *your* lands be increased in value whenever you abolish slavery; that is, provided you abolish it before it completely "dries up all the organs of increase." Here is a more manifest and distinct statement of the case:

Estimated value of slaveholders' lands after slavery shall have been abolished......................................	$4,856,783,680
Present value of slaveholders' lands.....................	923,248,160
Probable aggregate enhancement of value..............	$3,933,535,520

Now, Sirs, this last sum is considerably more than twice as great as the estimated value of all your negroes; and those of you, if any there be, who are yet heirs to sane minds and generous hearts, must, it seems to us, admit that the bright prospect which freedom presents for a wonderful increase in the value of real estate, ours as well as yours, to say nothing of the thousand other kindred considerations, ought to be quite sufficient to induce all the Southern States, in their sovereign capacities, to abolish slavery at the earliest practicable period. You yourselves, instead of losing anything by the emancipation of your negroes—even though we suppose them to be worth every dime of $1,600,000,000, would, in this one particular, the increased value of land, realize a *net profit* of over *twenty-three hundred million of dollars.* Here are the exact figures ·

Net increment of value which it is estimated will accrue to slaveholders' lands in consequence of the abolition of slavery......................................	$3,933,535,520
Putative value of the slaves............................	1,600,000,000
Slaveholders' estimated net landed profits of emancipation	$2,333,535,520

What is the import of these figures? They are full of meaning. They proclaim themselves the financial intercessors for freedom, and, with that open-hearted liberality which is so characteristic of the sacred cause in whose behalf they plead, they propose to pay you upward of three thousand nine hundred million of dollars for the very " property" which you, in all the extravagance of your unchastened avarice, could not find a heart to price at more than one thousand six hundred million. In other words, your own lands, groaning and languishing under the monstrous burden of slavery, announce their willingness to pay you all you ask for the negroes, and offer you, besides, a bonus of more than twenty-three hundred million of dollars, if you will but convert those lands into free soil! *Our* lands, also, cry aloud to be spared from the further pollutions and desolations of slavery; and now, sirs, we want to know explicitly whether, or not, it is your intention to heed these lamentations of the ground? We, the non-slaveholders of the South, have many very important interests at stake—interests which, heretofore, you have steadily despised and trampled under foot, but which, henceforth, we shall foster and defend in utter defiance of all the unhallowed influences which it is possible for you, or any other class of slaveholders or slavebreeders to bring against us. Not the least among these interests is our landed property, which, to command a decent price, only needs to be disencumbered of slavery.

In his present condition, we believe, man exercises one of the noblest virtues with which heaven has endowed him, when without taking any undue advantage of his fellow-men, and with a firm, unwavering purpose to confine his expenditures to the legitimate pursuits and pleasures of life, he covets money and strives to accumulate it. Entertaining this view, and having no disposition to make an improper use of money, we are free to confess that we have a greater penchant for twenty-eight dollars than for five; for ninety than for fifteen; for a thousand than for one hundred. South of Mason and Dixon's line we, the non-slaveholders, have 331,902,720 acres of land, the present average market value of which, as previously stated, is only $5 34 per acre; by abolishing slavery we expect to enhance the value to an average of at least $28 07 per acre, and thus realize an average net increase of wealth of more than *seventy-five hundred million of dollars*. The hope of realizing smaller sums has frequently induced men to perpetrate acts of injustice; we can see no reason why the certainty of becoming immensely rich in real estate, or other property, should make us falter in the performance of a *sacred duty*.

As illustrative of our theme, a bit of personal history may not be out of place in this connection. Only a few months have elapsed since we sold to an elder brother an interest we held in an old homestead which was willed to us many years ago by our deceased father. The tract of land, containing two hundred acres, or thereabouts, is situated two and a half miles west of Mocksville, the capital of Davie county, North Carolina, and is very nearly equally divided by Bear Creek, a small tributary of the South Yadkin. More than one-third of this tract—on which we have ploughed, and hoed, and harrowed, many a long summer without ever suffering from the effects of *coup de soleil*—is under cultivation; the remaining portion is a well-timbered forest, in which, without being very particular, we counted, while hunting through it not long since, sixty-three different kinds of indigenous trees—to say nothing of either coppice, shrubs or plants—among which the hickory, oak, ash, beech, birch, and black walnut, were most abundant. No turpentine or rosin, is produced in our part of the State; but there are, on the place of which we speak, several species of the genus Pinus, by the light of whose flammable knots, as radiated on the contents of some half-dozen old books which, by hook or by crook, had found their way into the neighborhood, we have been enabled to turn the long winter evenings to some advantage, and have thus *partially* escaped from the prison-grounds of those loathsome dungeons of illiteracy in which it has been the constant policy of the oligarchy to keep the masses, the non-slaveholding whites and the negroes, forever confined. The fertility of the soil may be inferred from the quality and variety of its natural productions; the meadow and the bottom, comprising, perhaps, an era of forty acres, are hardly surpassed by the best lands in the valley of the Yadkin. A thorough examination of the orchard will disclose the fact that considerable attention has been paid to the selection of fruits ; the buildings are tolerable ; the water is good. Altogether, to be frank, and nothing more, it is, for its size, one of the most desirable farms in the country, and will, at any time, command the maximum price of land in Western Carolina. Our brother, anxious to become the sole proprietor, readily agreed to give us the highest market price, which we shall publish by and bye. While reading the Baltimore *Sun*, the morning after we had made the sale, our attention was allured to a paragraph headed " Sales of Real Estate," from which, among other significant items, we learned that a tract of land containing exactly two hundred acres, and occupying a portion of one of the rural districts in the southeastern part of Pennsylvania, near the Maryland line, had been sold the week before, at *one hundred and five dollars and fifty cents* per acre. Judging from the succinct account given in the *Sun*, we are of the opinion that, with regard to fertility of soil, the Pennsylvania tract always has been, is now, and perhaps always will be, rather inferior to the one under special consideration. One is of the same size as the other ; both are used for agricultural purposes ; in all probability the only *essential* difference between them is this : one is blessed with the pure air of freedom, the other is cursed with the malaria of slavery. For our interest in the old homestead we received a nominal sum, amounting to an average of precisely *five dollars and sixty cents* per acre. No one but our brother, who was keen for the purchase, would have given us quite so much.

And now, pray let us ask, what does this narrative teach ? We shall use few words in explanation ; there is an extensive void, but it can be better filled with reflection. The aggregate value of the one tract is $21,100 ; that of the other is only $1,120 ; the difference is $19,980. We contend, therefore, in view of all the circumstances detailed, that the advocates and retainers of slavery, have, to all intents and purposes, defrauded our family out of this last-mentioned sum. In like manner, and on the same basis of deduction, we contend that almost every non-slaveholder, who either is or has been the owner of real estate in the South, would in a court of strict justice, be entitled to damages—the amount in all cases to be determined with reference to the quality of the land in question. We say this, because in violation of every principle of expediency, justice, and humanity, and in direct opposition to our solemn protests, slavery was foisted upon us, and has been thus far perpetuated by and through the wily intrigues of the oligarchy, and by them alone ; and furthermore, because the very best agricultural lands in the Northern States being worth from one hundred to one hundred and seventy-five dollars per acre, there is no possible reason, except slavery, why the more fertile and congenial soil of the South should not be worth at least as much. If, on this principle, we could ascertain, in the matter of real estate, the total indebtedness of the slaveholders to the non-slaveholders, we should doubtless find the sum quite equivalent to the amount estimated on a preceding page—$7,544,148,825.

We have recently conversed with two gentlemen who, to save themselves from the poverty and disgrace of slavery, left North Carolina six or seven years ago, and who are now residing in the territory of Minnesota, where they have accumulated handsome fortunes. One of them had travelled extensively in Kentucky, Missouri, Ohio, Indiana, and other adjoining States; and, according to his account, and we know him to be a man of veracity, it is almost impossible for persons at a distance, to form a proper conception of the magnitude of the difference between the current value of lands in the Free and the Slave States of the West. On one occasion, embarking at Wheeling, he sailed down the Ohio; Virginia and Kentucky on the one side, Ohio and Indiana on the other. He stopped at several places along the river, first on the right bank, then on the left, and so on, until he arrived at Evansville; continuing his trip, he sailed down to Cairo, thence up the Mississippi to the mouth of the Des Moines; having tarried at different points along the route, sometimes in Missouri, sometimes in Illinois. Wherever he landed on free soil, he found it from one to two hundred per cent. more valuable than the slave soil on the opposite bank. If, for instance, the maximum price of land was eight dollars in Kentucky, the minimum price was sixteen in Ohio; if it was seven dollars in Missouri, it was fourteen in Illinois. Furthermore, he assured us, that, so far as he could learn, two years ago, when he travelled through the States of which we speak, the range of prices of agricultural lands, in Kentucky, was from three to eight dollars per acre; in Ohio, from sixteen to forty; in Missouri, from two to seven; in Illinois, from fourteen to thirty; in Arkansas, from one to four; in Iowa, from six to fifteen.

In all the old slave States, as is well known, there are vast bodies of land that can be bought for the merest trifle. We know an enterprising capitalist in Philadelphia, who owns in his individual name, in the State of Virginia, *one hundred and thirty thousand acres*, for which he paid only *thirty-seven and a half cents* per acre! Some years ago, in certain parts of North Carolina, several large tracts were purchased at the rate of *twenty-five cents* per acre?

Hiram Berdan, the distinguished inventor, who has frequently seen freedom and slavery side by side, and who is, therefore, well qualified to form an opinion of their relative influence upon society, says:

" Many comparisons might be drawn between the free and the slave States, either of which should be sufficient to satisfy any man that slavery is not only ruinous to free labor and enterprise, but injurious to morals, and blighting to the soil where it exists. The comparison between the States of Michigan and Arkansas, which were admitted into the Union at the same time, will fairly illustrate the difference and value of free and slave labor, as well as the difference of moral and intellectual progress in a free and in a slave State.

" In 1836, those young Stars were admitted into the constellation of the Union. Michigan, with one-half the extent of territory of Arkansas, challenged her sister State for a twenty years' race, and named as her rider, 'Neither slavery, nor involuntary servitude, unless for the punishment of crime, shall ever be tolerated in this State.' Arkansas accepted the challenge, and named as her rider, 'The General Assembly shall have no power to pass laws for the emancipation of slaves without the consent of the owners.' Thus mounted, these two States, the one free and the other slave, started together twenty years ago, and now, having arrived at the end of the proposed race, let us review and mark the progress of each. Michigan comes out in 1856 with three times the population of slave Arkansas, with five times the assessed value of farms, farming implements and machinery, and with eight times the number of public schools."

In the foregoing part of our work, we have drawn comparisons between the old free States and the old slave States, and between the new free States and the new slave States; had we sufficient time and space, we might with the most significant results, change this method of comparison, by contrasting the new free States with the old slave States. Can the slavery-extensionists compare Ohio with Virginia, Illinois with Georgia, or Indiana with South Carolina, without experiencing the agony of inexpressible shame? If they can, then indeed has slavery debased them to a lower deep than we care to contemplate.

We shall now introduce two tables of valuable and interesting statistics, to which philosophic and discriminating readers will doubtless have frequent occasions to refer. Table 11 will show the area of the several States, in square miles and in acres, and the number of inhabitants to the square mile in each State; also the grand total, or the average, of every statistical column; table 12 will exhibit the total number of inhabitants residing in each State, according to the census of 1850, the number of whites, the number of free colored, and the number of slaves. The recapitulations of these tables will be followed by a complete list of the number of slaveholders in the United States, showing the exact number in each Southern State, and in the District of Columbia. Most warmly do we commend all these statistics to the *studious* attention of the reader. Their language is more eloquent than any possible combination of Roman vowels and consonants. We have spared no pains in arranging them so as to express at a single glance the great truths of which they are composed; and we doubt not that the plan we have adopted will meet with general approbation. Numerically considered, it will be perceived that the slaveholders are, in reality, a very insignificant class. Of them, however we shall have more to say hereafter.

TABLE 11.

AREA OF THE FREE AND OF THE SLAVE STATES.

States.	Square Miles.	Acres.	Inhabitants to sq. mile.	States.	Square Miles.	Acres.	Inhabitants to sq. mile.
California	155,980	99,827,200	.59	Alabama	50,722	32,027,490	15.21
Conn.....	4,674	2,991,360	79.33	Arkansas	52,198	33,406,720	4.03
Illinois...	55,405	35,359,200	15.37	Delaware	2,120	1,356,800	43.18
Indiana..	33,809	21,637,760	29.24	Florida..	59,268	37,931,520	1.48
Iowa.....	50,914	32,584,960	3.78	Georgia..	58,000	37,120,000	15.62
Maine....	31,766	20,330,240	18.36	Kentucky	37,680	24,115,200	26.07
Mass.....	7,800	4,992,000	127.50	Louisiana	41,255	26,403,200	12.55
Michigan.	56,243	35,995,520	7.07	Maryland	11,124	7,119,360	52.41
N. Hamp.	9,280	5,939,200	34.26	Miss.....	47,156	30,179,840	12.86
N. Jersey	8,320	5,224,800	58.84	Missouri.	67,380	43,123,200	10.12
New York	47,000	30,080,000	65.90	N. C.....	50,704	32,450,560	17.14
Ohio.....	39,964	26,576,960	49.55	S. C.....	29,385	18,805,400	22.75
Penn.....	46,000	29,440,000	50.26	Tenn. ...	45,600	29,184,000	21.99
Rhode Is.	1,306	835,840	112.97	Texas...	237,504	152,002,560	.89
Vermont.	10,212	6,535,680	30.76	Virginia.	61,352	39,165,280	23.17
Wisconsin	53,924	34,511,360	5.66				
	612,597	392,062,080	21.91		851,448	544,926,720	11.29

TABLE 12.

POPULATION OF THE FREE AND OF THE SLAVE STATES—1850.

States.	Whites.	Free Colored.	Total.	States.	Whites.	Free Colored.	Slaves.	Total.
California	91,635	962	92,597	Alabama	426,514	2,265	342,844	771,623
Conn.....	363,099	7,693	370,792	Arkansas	162,189	608	47,100	209,897
Illinois...	846,034	5,436	851,470	Delaware	71,169	18,073	2,290	91,532
Indiana..	977,154	11,262	988,416	Florida .	47,203	932	39,310	87,445
Iowa.....	191,881	333	192,214	Georgia.	521,572	2,931	381,622	906,185
Maine ...	581,813	1,356	583,169	Kentucky	761,413	10,011	210,981	982,405
Mass.....	985,450	9,064	994,514	Louisiana	255,491	17,462	244,809	517,762
Michigan.	395,071	2,583	397,654	Maryland	417,943	74,723	90,368	583,034
N. Hamp.	317,456	520	317,976	Miss.....	295,718	930	309,878	606,326
N. Jersey	465,509	23,810	489,555	Missouri.	592,004	2,618	87,422	682,044
New York	3,048,325	49,069	3,097,394	N. C. ...	553,028	27,463	288,548	869,039
Ohio.....	1,955,050	25,279	1,980,329	S. C. ...	274,563	8,960	384,984	668,507
Penn.....	2,258,160	53,626	2,311,786	Tenn. ...	756,836	6,422	239,459	1,002,717
Rhode Is.	143,875	3,670	147,545	Texas...	154,034	397	58,161	212,592
Vermont..	313,402	718	314,120	Virginia.	894,800	54,333	472,528	1,421,661
Wisconsin	304,756	535	305,391					
	13,233,670	196,116	13,434,922		6,184,477	228,138	3,200,364	9,612,979

RECAPITULATION—AREA.

	Square Miles.	Acres.
Area of the Slave States	851,448	544,926,720
Area of the Free States........................	612,597	392,062,082
Balances in favor of Slave States, ...	238,851	152,864,638

RECAPITULATION—POPULATION—1850.

	Whites.	Total.
Population of the Free States	13,233,670	13,434,922
Population of the Slave States	6,184,477	9,612,976
Balances in favor of the Free States, ...	7,049,193	3,821,946

FREE COLORED AND SLAVE—1850.

Free Negroes in the Slave States..	228,138
Free Negroes in the Free States...	196,116
Excess of Free Negroes in the Slave States............................	32,022

Slaves in the Slave States	3,200,364
Free Negroes in the Slave States......................................	228,138
Aggregate Negro Population of the Slave States in 1850.......... .	3,428,502

THE TERRITORIES AND THE DISTRICT OF COLUMBIA.

	Area in Square Miles.	Population.
Indian Territory.............................	71,127	
Kansas "	114,798	
Minnesota "	166,025	6,077
Nebraska "	335,882	
N. Mexico "	207,007	61,547
Oregon "	185,030	13,294
Utah "	269,170	11,380
Washington "	123,022	
Columbia, Dist. of.............................	60	*51,687
Aggregate of Area and Population 1,472,121		143,985

NUMBER OF SLAVEHOLDERS IN THE UNITED STATES—1850.

Alabama	29,295
Arkansas..............................	5,999
Columbia, District of..	1,477
Delaware..	809
Florida...	3,520
Georgia	38,456
Kentucky	38,385
Louisiana...	20,670
Carried forward,..................	138,611

* Of the 51,687 inhabitants in the District of Columbia, in 1850, 10,057 were Free **Colored,** and 3,687 were slaves.

	Brought forward	138,611
Maryland		16,040
Mississippi		23,116
Missouri		19,185
North Carolina		28,303
South Carolina		25,596
Tennessee		33,864
Texas		7,747
Virginia		55,063

Total Number of Slaveholders in the United States.................... 347,525

CLASSIFICATION OF SLAVEHOLDERS—1850.

Holders of	1 slave		68,820
Holders of	1 and under	5	105,683
Holders of	5 and under	10	80,765
Holders of	10 and under	20	54,595
Holders of	20 and under	50	29,733
Holders of	50 and under	100	6,196
Holders of	100 and under	200	1,479
Holders of	200 and under	300	187
Holders of	300 and under	500	56
Holders of	500 and under 1,000		9
Holders of	1,000 and over		2

Aggregate Number of Slaveholders in the United States................. 347,525

It thus appears that there are in the United States, three hundred and forty-seven thousand five hundred and twenty-five slaveholders. But this appearance is deceptive. The actual number is certainly less than two hundred thousand. Professor De Bow, the Superintendent of the Census, informs us that "the number includes slave-hirers," and furthermore, that "where the party owns slaves in different counties, or in different States, he will be entered more than once." Now every Southerner, who has any practical knowledge of affairs, must know, and does know, that every New Year's day, like almost every other day, is desecrated in the South, by publicly hiring out slaves to large numbers of non-slaveholders. The slave-owners, who are the exclusive manufacturers of public sentiment, have popularized the dictum that white servants are unfashionable; and there are, we are sorry to say, nearly one hundred and sixty thousand non-slaveholding sycophants, who have subscribed to this false philosophy, and who are giving constant encouragement to the infamous practices of slaveholding and slave-breeding, by hiring at least one slave every year.

With the statistics at our command, it is impossible for us to ascertain the exact numbers of slaveholders and non-slaveholding slave-hirers in the slave States; but we have data which will enable us to approach very near to the facts. The town from which we hail, Salisbury, the capital of Rowan county, North Carolina, contains about twenty-three hundred inhabitants, including three hundred and seventy-two slaves,

4

fifty-one slaveholders, and forty-three non-slaveholding slave-hirers. Taking it for granted that this town furnishes a fair relative proportion of all the slaveholding, and non-slaveholding slave-hirers in the slave States, the whole number of the former, including those who have been "entered more than once," is one hundred and eighty-eight thousand five hundred and fifty-one; of the latter, one hundred and fifty-eight thousand nine hundred and seventy-four; and, now, estimating that there are in Maryland, Virginia, and other grain-growing States, an aggregate of two thousand slave-owners, who have cotton plantations *stocked* with negroes in the far South, and who have been "entered more than once," we find, as the result of our calculations, that the total number of actual slaveholders in the Union, is precisely one hundred and eighty-six thousand five hundred and fifty-one—as follows:

Number of actual slaveholders in the United States.............. 186,551
Number "entered more than once ".......................... 2,600
Number of non-slaveholding slave-hirers...................... 158,974

Aggregate number, according to De Bow............ 347,525

The greater number of non-slaveholding slave-hirers, are a kind of third-rate aristocrats—persons who formely owned slaves, but whom slavery, as is its custom, has dragged down to poverty, leaving them, in their false and shiftless pride, to eke out a miserable existence over the hapless chattels personal of other men.

Thus far in giving expression to our sincere and settled opinions, we have endeavored to show, in the first place, that slavery is a great moral, social, civil, and political evil—a dire enemy to true wealth and national greatness, and an atrocious crime against both God and man; and, in the second place, that it is a paramount duty which we owe to heaven, to the earth, to America, to humanity, to our posterity, to our consciences, and to our pockets, to adopt effectual and judicious measures for its immediate suppression. The questions now arise, How can the evil be averted? What are the most prudent and practicable means that can be devised for the abolition of slavery? In the solution of these problems it becomes necessary to deal with a multiplicity of stubborn realities. And yet, we can see no reason why North Carolina, in her sovereign capacity, may not with equal ease and success, do what forty-five other States of the world have done within the last forty-five years. Nor do we believe any good reason exists why Virginia should not perform as great a deed in ·1869 as did New York in 1799. Massachusetts abolished slavery in 1780; would it not be a masterly stroke of policy in Tennessee, and every other slave State, to abolish it in or before 1870?

To the non-slaveholding whites of the South, as a deeply-wronged and vitally distinct political party, we must look for that change of law, or reorganization of society, which, at an early day, we hope, is to result in the substitution of liberty for slavery; and, under all the circumstances, it now becomes their duty to mark out an independent course for themselves, and to utterly contemn and ignore the many base instruments of power, animate and inanimate, which have been so freely and so effectually used for their enslavement. Steering entirely clear of the oligarchy, now is the time for the non-slaveholders to assert their rights and liberties; never before was there such an appropriate period to strike for Freedom in the South.

Had it not been for the better sense, the purer patriotism, and the more practical justice of the non-slaveholders, the Middle States and New England would still be groaning and grovelling under the ponderous burden of slavery; New York would never have risen above the dishonorable level of Virginia; Pennsylvania, trampled beneath the iron-heel of the black code, would have remained the unprogressive parallel of Georgia; Massachusetts would have continued till the present time, and Heaven only knows how much longer, the contemptible coequal of South Carolina.

Succeeded by the happiest moral effects and the grandest physical results, we have seen slavery crushed beneath the wisdom of the non-slaveholding statesmen of the North; followed by corresponding influences and achievements, many of us who have not yet passed the meridian of life, are destined to see it equally crushed beneath the wisdom of the non-slaveholding statesmen of the South. With righteous indignation, we enter our protest against the base yet baseless admission that Louisiana and Texas are incapable of producing as great statesmen as Rhode Island and Connecticut. What has been done for New Jersey by the statesmen of New Jersey, can be done for Kentucky by the statesmen of Kentucky; the wisdom of the former State has abolished slavery ; as sure as the earth revolves on its axis, the wisdom of the latter will not do less.

That our plan for the abolition of slavery is the best that can be devised, we have not the vanity to contend ; but that it is a good one, and will do to act upon until a better shall have been suggested, we do firmly and conscientiously believe. Though but little skilled in the delicate art of surgery, we have pretty thoroughly probed slavery, the frightful tumor on the body politic, and have, we think, ascertained the precise remedies requisite for a speedy and perfect cure. Possibly the less ardent friends of freedom may object to our prescription, on the ground that some of its ingredients are too griping, and that it will cost the patient a deal of most excruciating pain. But let them remember that the patient is exceedingly refractory, that the case is a desperate one, and that drastic remedies are indispensably necessary. When they shall have discovered milder yet equally efficacious ones, it will be time enough to discontinue the use of ours—then no one will be readier than we to discard the infallible strong recipe for the infallible mild. Not at the persecution of a few thousand slaveholders, but at the restitution of natural rights and prerogatives to several million of non-slaveholders, do we aim.

Inscribed on the banner, which we herewith unfurl to the world, with the full and fixed determination to stand by it or die by it, unless one of more virtuous efficacy shall be presented, are the mottoes which, in substance, embody the principles, as we conceive, that should govern us in our patriotic warfare against the most subtle and insidious foe that ever menaced the inalienable rights and liberties and dearest interests of America:

1st. Thorough Organization and Independent Political Action on the part of the Non-Slaveholding Whites of the South.

2nd. Ineligibility of Pro-slavery Slaveholders—Never another vote to any one who advocates the Retention and Perpetuation of Human Slavery.

3rd. No Coöperation with Pro-slavery Politicians—No Fellowship with them in Religion—No Affiliation with them in Society.

4th. No Patronage to Pro-slavery Merchants—No Guestship in Slave-waiting Hotels—No Fees to Pro-slavery Lawyers—No Employment of Pro-slavery Physicians—No audience to Pro-slavery Parsons.

5th. No more Hiring of Slaves by Non-Slaveholders.

6th. Abrupt Discontinuance of Subscription to Pro-slavery Newspapers.

7th. The Greatest Possible Encouragement to Free White Labor.

This, then, is the outline of our scheme for the abolition of slavery in the Southern States. Let it be acted upon with due promptitude, and, as certain as truth is mightier than error, fifteen years will not elapse before every foot of territory, from the mouth of the Delaware to the emboguing of the Rio Grande, will glitter with the jewels of freedom. Some time during this year, next, or the year following, let there be a general convention of non-slaveholders from every slave State in the Union, to deliberate on the momentous issues now pending. First, let them adopt measures for holding in restraint the mischievous excesses of the oligarchy; secondly, in order to cast off the thralldom which the despotic slave-power has fastened upon them, and, as the first step necessary to be taken to regain the inalienable rights and liberties with which they were invested by nature, but of which they have been divested by the Vandalic dealers in human flesh, let them devise ways and means for the complete annihilation of slavery; thirdly, let them put forth an equitable and comprehensive platform, fully defining their position, and inviting the active sympathy and coöperation of the millions of down-trodden non-slaveholders throughout the Southern and Southwestern States. Let all these things be done, not too hastily, but with calmness deliberation, prudence and circumspection; if need be, let the delegates to the convention continue in session one or two weeks; only let their labors be wisely and thoroughly performed; let them, on Wednesday morning, present to the poor whites of the South, a well-digested scheme for the reclamation of their ancient rights and prerogatives, and, on the Thursday following, slavery in the United States will be worth absolutely less than nothing; for then, besides being so despicable and precarious that nobody will want it, it will be a lasting reproach to those in whose hands it is lodged.

Were it not that other phases of the subject admonish us to be economical of space, we could suggest more than a dozen different plans, either of which, if scrupulously carried out, would lead to a wholesome, speedy, and perfect termination of slavery. Under all the circumstances, however, it might be difficult for us—perhaps it would not be the easiest thing in the world for anybody else—to suggest a better plan than the one above. Let it, or one embodying its principal features, be adopted forthwith, and the last wail of slavery will soon be heard, growing fainter and fainter, till it dies utterly away, to be succeeded by the jubilant shouts of emancipated millions.

At the very moment we write, as has been the case ever since the United States have had a distinct national existence, and as will always continue to be the case, unless right triumphs over wrong, all the civil, political, and other offices, within the gift of the South, are filled with negro-nursed incumbents from the ranks of that artful band of misanthropes—three hundred and forty-seven thousand in number—who, for the most part, obtain their living by breeding, buying and selling slaves. The magistrates in the villages, the constables in the districts, the commissioners of the towns, the mayors of the cities, the sheriffs of the counties, the judges of the various courts, the members of the legislatures, the governors of the States, the representatives and senators in Congress—are all slaveholders. Nor does the catalogue of their usurpations end here. By means of much barefaced arrogance and corruption, they have obtained control of the General Government, and all the consuls, ambassadors, envoys extraordinary, and ministers plenipotentiary, who are chosen from the South, and commissioned to foreign countries, are selected with especial reference to the purity of their proslavery antecedents. If credentials have ever been issued to a single non-slaveholder of the South, we are ignorant of both the fact and the hearsay ; indeed, it would be very strange if this much abused class of persons were permitted to hold important offices abroad, when they are not allowed to hold unimportant ones at home.

And, then, there is the Presidency of the United States, which office has been held *forty-eight* years by slaveholders from the South, and only *twenty* years by non-slaveholders from the North. Nor is this the full record of oligarchica. obtrusion.   On an average, the offices of Secretary of State, Secretary of the Treasury, Secretary of the Interior, Secretary of the Navy, Secretary of War, Postmaster-General and Attorney-General, have been under the control of slave-drivers nearly two-thirds of the time. The Chief Justices and the Associate Justices of the Supreme Court of the United States, the Presidents pro tem. of the Senate, and the Speakers of the House of Representatives, have, in a large majority of instances, been slave-breeders from the Southern side of the Potomac. Five slave-holding Presidents have been reëlected to the chief magistracy of the Republic, while no non-slaveholder has ever held the office more than a single term. Thus we see plainly that even the non-slaveholders of the North, to whose freedom, energy, enterprise, intelligence, wealth, population, power, progress, and prosperity, our country is almost exclusively indebted for its high position among the nations of the·earth, have been arrogantly denied a due participation in the honors of federal office. When "the sum of all villainies" shall have ceased to exist, then the rights of the non-slaveholders of the North, of the South, of the East, and of the West, will be duly recognized and respected; not before.

For the last sixty-eight years, slaveholders have been the sole and constant representatives of the South, and what have they accomplished? It requires but little time and few words, to tell the story of their indiscreet and unhallowed performances. In fact, with what we have already said, gestures alone would suffice to answer the inquiry. We can make neither a more truthful nor emphatic reply than to point to our thinly inhabited States, to our fields despoiled of their virgin soil, to the despicable price of lands, to our unvisited cities and towns, to our vacant harbors and idle water-power, to the dreary absence ot shipping and manufactories, to our unpensioned soldiers of the Revolution, to the millions of living monuments of ignorance, to the squalid poverty of the whites, and to the utter wretchedness of the blacks.

Either directly or indirectly, are pro-slavery politicians, who have ostentatiously set up pretensions to statesmanship, responsible for every dishonorable weakness and inequality that exists between the North and the South. Let them shirk the responsibility if they can; but it is morally impossible for them to do so. We know how ready they have always been to cite the numerical strength of the North, as a valid excuse for their inability to procure appropriations from the General Government, for purposes of internal improvement, for the establishment of lines of ocean steamers to South American and European ports, and for the accomplishment of other objects. Before that apology ever escapes from their lips again, let them remember that the numerical weakness of the South is wholly attributable to their own imbecile statism. Had the Southern States, in accordance with the principles enunciated in the Declaration of Independence, abolished slavery at the same time the Northern States abolished it, there would have been, long since, and most assuredly at this moment, a larger, wealthier, wiser, and more powerful population, south of Mason and Dixon's line, than there now is north of it. This fact being so well established that no reasonable man denies it, it is evident that the oligarchy will have to devise another subterfuge for even temporary relief.

Until slavery and slaveholders cease to be the only favored objects of legislation in the South, the North will continue to maintain the ascendency in every important particular. With those mischievous objects out of the way, it would not require the non-slaveholders of the South more than a quarter of a century to bring her up, in all respects, to a glorious equality with the North ; nor would it take them much longer to surpass the latter, which is the most vigorous and honorable rival that they have in the world. Three-quarters of a century hence, if slavery is abolished within the next ten years, as it ought to be, the South will, we believe, be as much greater than the North, as the North is now greater than the South. Three-quarters of a century hence, if the South retains slavery, which God forbid ! she will be to the North much the same that Poland is to Russia, that Cuba is to Spain, or that Ireland is to England.

What we want and must have, as the only sure means of attaining to a position worthy of Sovereign States in this eminently progressive and utilitarian age, is an energetic, intelligent, enterprising, virtuous, and unshackled population ; an untrammelled press, and the Freedom of Speech. For ourselves, as white people, and for the negroes and other persons of whatever color or condition, we demand all the rights, interests and prerogatives, that are guaranteed to corresponding classes of mankind in the North, in England, in France, in Germany, or in any other civilized and enlightened country. Any proposition that may be offered conceding less than this demand, will be promptly and disdainfully rejected.

Speaking of the non-slaveholders of the South, George M. Weston, a zealous co-laborer in the cause of Freedom, says :

" The non-slaveholding whites of the South, being not less than seven-tenths of the whole number of whites, would seem to be entitled to some inquiry into their actual condition ; and especially, as they have no real political weight or consideration in the country, and little opportunity to speak for themselves. I have been for twenty years a reader of Southern newspapers, and a reader and hearer of Congressional debates ; but, in all that time, I do not recollect ever to have seen or heard these non-slaveholding whites referred to by Southern ' gentlemen,' as constituting any part of what they call ' *the South.*' When the rights of the South, or its wrongs, or its policy, or its interests, or its institutions, are spoken of, reference is always intended to the three hundred and forty-seven thousand slaveholders. Nobody gets into Congress from the South but by their direction ; nobody speaks at Washington for any Southern interest except theirs. Yet there is, at the South, quite another interest than theirs ; embracing from two to three times as many white people ; and, as we shall presently see, entitled to the deepest sympathy and commiseration, in view of the material, intellectual, and moral privations to which it has been subjected, the degradation to which it has already been reduced, and the still more fearful degradation with which it is threatened by the inevitable operation of existing causes and influences.''

The following extract, from a paper on "Domestic Manufactures in the South and West," published by M. Tarver, of Missouri, may be appropriately introduced in this connection:

"The non-slaveholders possess, generally, but very small means, and the land which they possess is almost universally poor, and so sterile that a scanty subsistence is all that can be derived from its cultivation; and the more fertile soil, being in the possession of the slaveholders, must ever remain out of the power of those who have none. This state of things is a great drawback, and bears heavily upon and depresses the moral energies of the poorer classes. The acquisition of a respectable position in the scale of wealth appears so difficult, that they decline the hopeless pursuit, and many of them settle down into habits of idleness, and become the almost passive subjects of all its consequences. And I lament to say that I have observed, of late years, that an evident deterioration is taking place in this part of the population, the younger portion of it being less educated, less industrious, and in every point of view less respectable than their ancestors.''

Equally worthy of attention is the testimony of Gov. Hammond, of South Carolina, who says:

"According to the best calculation, which, in the absence of statistic facts, can be made, it is believed, that of the three hundred thousand white inhabitants of South Carolina, there are not less than fifty thousand whose industry, such as it is, and compensated as it is, is not, in the present condition of things, and does not promise to be hereafter, adequate to procure them, honestly, such a support as every white person is, and feels himself entitled to. And this, next to emigration, is, perhaps, the heaviest of the weights that press upon the springs of our prosperity. Most of those now follow agricultural pursuits, in feeble, yet injurious competition with slave labor. Some, perhaps, not more from inclination than from the want of due encouragement, can scarcely be said to work at all. They obtain a precarious subsistence, by occasional jobs, by hunting, by fishing, sometimes by plundering fields or folds, and too often by what is, in its effects, far worse—trading with slaves, and seducing them to plunder for their benefit.''

Conjoined with the sundry plain, straightforward facts which have issued from our own pen, these extracts show conclusively that immediate and independent political action on the part of the non-slaveholding whites of the South, is, with them, a matter, not only of positive duty, but also of the utmost importance. As yet, it is in their power to rescue the South from the gulf of shame and guilt, into which slavery has plunged her; but if they do not soon arouse themselves from their apathy, this power will be wrenched from them, and then, unable to resist the strong arm of the oppressor, they will be completely degraded to a social and political level with the negroes, whose condition of servitude will, in the meantime, become far more abject and forlorn than it is now.

In addition to the reasons which we have already assigned why no slavocrat should, in the future, be elected to any office whatever, there are others that deserve to be carefully considered. Among these, to speak plainly, may be mentioned the ill-breeding and the ruffianism of slaveholding officials. Tedious, indeed, would be the task to enumerate all the homicides, duels, assaults and batteries, and other crimes, of which they are the authors in the course of a single year. To the general reader their career at the seat of government is well known; there, on frequent occasions, choking with rage at seeing their wretched sophistries scattered to the winds by the sound, logical reasoning of the champions of Freedom, they have overstepped the bounds of common decency, vacated the chair of honorable controversy, and, in the most brutal and cowardly manner, assailed their unarmed opponents with bludgeons, bowie knives and pistols. Compared with some of their barbarisms at home, however, their frenzied onslaughts at the national Capital have been but the simplest breaches of civil deportment; and it is only for the purpose of avoiding personalities that we now refrain from divulging a few instances of the unparalleled atrocities which they have perpetrated in legislative halls south of the Potomac. Nor is it alone in the national and State legislatures that they substitute brute force for genteel behavior and acuteness of intellect. Neither court-houses nor public streets, hotels nor private dwellings, rum-holes nor law-offices, are held sacred from their murderous conflicts. About certain silly abstractions that no practical business man ever allows to occupy his time or attention, they are eternally wrangling; and thus it is that rencounters, duels, homicides, and other demonstrations of personal violence, have become so popular in all slaveholding communities. A few years of entire freedom from the cares and perplexities of public life would, we have no doubt, greatly improve both their manners and their morals; and we suggest that it is a Christian duty, which devolves on the non-slaveholders of the South, to disrobe them of the mantle of office, which they have so long worn with disgrace to themselves, injustice to their constituents, and ruin to their country.

But what shall we say of such men as Botts, Stuart, and Macfarland of Virginia; of Raynor, Morehead, Stanley, Graves, and Graham of North Carolina; of Davis and Hoffman of Maryland; of Blair and Brown of Missouri; of the Marshalls of Kentucky; and of Etheridge of Tennessee? All these gentlemen, and many others of the same school, entertain, we believe, sentiments similar to those that were entertained by the immortal Fathers of the Republic—that slavery is a great moral, social, civil, and political evil, to be got rid of at the earliest practicable period—and if they do, in order to secure our votes, it is only necessary for them to "have the courage of their opinions," to renounce slavery, and to come out frankly, fairly and squarely in favor of freedom. To neither of these patriotic sons of the South, nor to any one of the class to which they belong, would we give any offence whatever. In our strictures on the criminality of pro-slavery demagogues we have had heretofore, and shall have hereafter, no sort of reference to any respect-

4*

able slaveholder—by which we mean, any slaveholder who admits the injustice and inhumanity of slavery, and who is not averse to the discussion of measures for its speedy and total extinction. Such slaveholders are virtually on our side—that is, on the side of the non-slaveholding whites, with whom they may very properly be classified. On this point, once for all, we desire to be distinctly understood; for it would be manifestly unjust not to discriminate between the anti-slavery proprietor who owns slaves by the law of entailment, and the pro-slavery proprietor who engages in the traffic and becomes an aider an abettor of the system from sheer turpitude of heart; hence the propriety of this special disclaimer.

If we have a correct understanding of the positions which they assumed, some of the gentlemen whose names are written above, gave, during the last presidential campaign, ample evidence of their unswerving devotion to the interests of the great majority of the people, the non-slaveholding whites; and it is our unbiased opinion that a more positive truth is nowhere recorded in Holy Writ, than Kenneth Raynor uttered, when he said, in substance, that the greatest good that could happen to this country would be the complete overthrow of Black Democracy, *alias* the pro-slavery party, which has for its head and front the Ritchies and Wises of Virginia, and for its caudal termination the Keitts and Quattlebums of South Carolina.

Peculiarly illustrative of the material of which sham democracy is composed was the vote polled at the Five Points precinct, in the city of New York, on the 4th of November, 1856, when James Buchanan was chosen President by a *minority* of the people. We will produce the figures:

Five Points Precinct, New York City, 1856.

Votes cast for James Buchanan....................................... 574
"   "   John C. Fremont.................................. 16
"   "   Millard Fillmore 9

It will be recollected that Col. Fremont's majority over Buchanan, in the State of New York, was between seventy-eight and seventy-nine thousand, and that he ran ahead of the Fillmore ticket to the number of nearly one hundred and fifty one thousand. We have not the shadow of a doubt that he is perfectly satisfied with Mr. Buchanan's triumph at the Five Points, which, with the exception of the slave-pens in Southern cities, is, perhaps, the most vile and heart-sickening locality in the United States.

One of the most noticeable and commendable features of the last general election is this: almost every State, whose inhabitants have enjoyed the advantages of free soil, free labor, free speech, free presses, and free schools, and who have, in consequence, become great in numbers, in virtue, in wealth, and in wisdom, voted for Fremont, the Republican candidate, who was pledged to use his influence for the extension of like advantages to other parts of the country.   On the other hand, with a single honorable exception, all the States which "have got to hating everything with the prefix Free, from free negroes down and up through the whole catalogue—free farms, free labor, free society, free will, free thinking, free children, and free schools," and which have exposed their citizens to all the perils of numerical weakness, absolute ignorance, and hopeless poverty, voted for Buchanan, the Democratic candidate, who, in reply to the overtures of his pro-slavery partisans, had signified his willingness to pursue a policy that would perpetuate and disseminate, without limit, the multitudinous evils of human bondage.

That less than *three* per cent. of those who voted for Col. Fremont, that only about *five* per cent. of those who gave their suffrages to Mr. Fillmore, and that more than *eighteen* per cent. of those who supported Mr. Buchanan, were persons over one-and-twenty years of age who could not read and write, are estimates which we have no doubt are not far from the truth, and which, in the absence of reliable statistics, we venture to give, hoping, by their publicity, to draw closer attention to the fact, that the illiterate foreigners of the North, and the unlettered natives of the South, were cordially united in their suicidal adherence to the pro-slavery party.   With few exceptions, all the intelligent non-slaveholders of the South, in concert with the more respectable slaveholders, voted for Mr. Fillmore ; certain rigidly patriotic persons of the former class, whose hearts were so entirely with the gallant Fremont that they refused to vote at all—simply because they did not dare to express their preference for him—form the exceptions to which we allude.

Though the Whig, Democratic, and Know-Nothing newspapers, in all the States, free and slave, denounced Col. Fremont as an intolerant Catholic, it is now generally conceded that he was nowhere supported by the peculiar friends of Pope Pius IX.   The votes polled at the Five Points precinct, which is almost exclusively inhabited by low Irish Catholics, show how powerfully the Jesuitical influence was brought to bear against him.   At that delectable locality, as we have already shown, the timid Sage of Wheatland received five hundred and seventy-four votes —whereas the dauntless Finder of Empire received only sixteen.

True to their instincts for Freedom, the Germans, generally, voted the right ticket, and they will do it again, and continue to do it.   With the intelligent Protestant element of the Fatherland on our side, we can well afford to dispense with the ignorant Catholic element of the Emerald Isle.   In the influences which they exert on society, there is so little difference between Slavery, Popery, and Negro-driving Democracy, that we are not at all surprised to see them going hand in hand in their diabolical work of inhumanity and desolation.

There is, indeed, no lack of evidence to show that the Democratic party of to-day is simply and unreservedly a sectional slavery party.   On the 15th of December, 1856, but a few weeks subsequent to the appearance of a scandalous message from an infamous governor of South Carolina, recommending the reopening of the African slave trade, Emerson Etheridge of Tennessee—honor to his name!—submitted, in the House of Representatives, the following timely resolution:

'Resolved—That this House regard all suggestions or propositions of every kind, by whomsoever made, for a revival of the slave trade, as shocking to the moral sentiments of the enlightened portion of mankind, and that any act on the part of Congress, legislating for, conniving at, or legalizing that horrid and inhuman traffic, would justly subject the United States to the reproach and execration of all civilized and Christian people throughout the world.'

Who voted *for* this resolution? and who voted *against* it? Let the yeas and nays answer; they are on record, and he who takes the trouble to examine them will find that the resolution encountered no opposition worth mentioning, except from members of the Democratic party. Scrutinize the yeas and nays on any other motion or resolution affecting the question of slavery, and the fact that a majority of the members of this party have uniformly voted for the retention and extension of the "sum of all villainies," will at once be apparent.

For many years the slave-driving Democrats of the South have labored most strenuously, both by day and by night—we regret to say how unsuccessfully—to point out abolition proclivities in the Whig and Know-Nothing parties, the latter of which is now buried, and deservedly, so deep in the depths of the dead, that it is quite preposterous to suppose it will ever see the light of resurrection.

For its truckling concessions to the slave power, the Whig party merited defeat, and defeated it was, and that, too, in the most decisive and overwhelming manner. But there is yet in this party much vitality, and if its friends will reorganize, detach themselves from the burden of slavery, and hoist the fair flag of freedom, the time may come, at a day by no means remote, when their hearts will exult in triumph over the ruins of miscalled Democracy.

It is not too late, however, for the Democratic party to secure to itself a pure renown and an almost certain perpetuation of its power. Let it at once discard the worship of slavery, and do earnest battle for the principles of freedom, and it will live victoriously to a period far in the future. On the other hand, if it does not soon repudiate the fatal heresies which it has incorporated into its creed, its doom will be inevitable. Until the black flag entirely disappears from its array, we warn the non-slaveholders of the South to repulse and keep it at a distance, as they would the emblazoned skull and cross-bones that flout them from the flag of the pirate.

With regard to the sophistical reasoning which teaches that abolitionists, before abolishing slavery, should compensate the slaveholders for all or any number of the negroes in their possession, we shall endeavor not to be wearisome ; but wishing to brace our arguments, in every important particular, with unequivocal testimony from men whom we are accustomed to regard as models of political sagacity and integrity—from Southern men as far as possible—we herewith present an extract from a speech delivered in the Virginia House of Delegates, January 20, 1832, by Charles James Faulkner, whose sentiments, as then and there expressed, can hardly fail to find a response in the heart of every intelligent, upright man :

" But, sir, it is said that society having conferred this property on the slaveholder, it cannot *now* take it from him without an adequate compensation, by which is meant full value. I may be singular in the opinion, but I defy the legal research of the House to point me to a principle recognized by the law, even in the ordinary course of its adjudications, where the community pays for property which is removed or destroyed because it is a nuisance, and found injurious to that society. There is, I humbly apprehend, no such principle. There is no obligation upon society to continue your right one moment after it becomes injurious to the best interests of society; nor to compensate you for the loss of that, the deprivation of which is demanded by the safety of the State, and in which general benefit you participate as a member of the community. Sir, there is to my mind a manifest distinction between condemning private property to be applied to some beneficial public purpose, and condemning or removing private property which is ascertained to be a positive wrong to society. It is a distinction which pervades the whole genius of the law ; and is founded upon the idea, that any man who holds property injurious to the peace of that society of which he is a member. thereby violates the condition upon the observance of which his right to the property is alone guaranteed. For property of the first class condemned there ought to be compensation; but for the property of the latter class, none can be demanded upon principle, none accorded as a matter of right.

" It is conceded that, at this precise moment of our legislation, slaves are injurious to the interests and threaten the subversion and ruin of this Commonwealth. Their present number, their increasing number, all admonish us of this. In different terms, and in more measured language, the same fact has been conceded by all who have yet addressed this House. ' *Something must be done*,' emphatically exclaimed the gentleman from Dinwiddie ; and I thought I could perceive a response to that declaration, in the countenance of a large majority of this body. And why must something be done? Because if not, says the gentleman from Campbell, the throats of all the *white* people of Virginia will be cut. No, says the gentleman from Dinwiddie—' The whites cannot be conquered—the throats of the *blacks* will be cut.' It is a trifling difference, to be sure, sir, and matters not to the argument. For the fact is conceded, that one race or the other must be exterminated.

" Sir, such being the actual condition of this Commonwealth, I ask if we would not be justified *now*, supposing all considerations of policy and humanity concurred, without even a moment's delay, in staving off this appalling and overwhelming calamity? Sir, if this immense negro population were now in arms, gathering into black and formidable masses of attack, would that man be listened to, who spoke about property, who prayed you not to direct your artillery to such or such a point, for you would destroy some of *his* property? Sir, to the eye of the Statesman, as to the eye of Omniscience, dangers pressing, and dangers that must *necessarily* press, are alike present. With a single glance he embraces Virginia now, with the elements of destruction reposing quietly upon her bosom, and Virginia is lighted from one extremity to the other with the torch of servile insurrection and massacre. It is not sufficient for him that the match is not yet applied. It is enough that the magazine is open, and the match will shortly be applied.

" Sir, it is true in national as it is in private contracts, that loss and injury to one party may constitute as fair a consideration as gain to the other. Does the slaveholder, while he is enjoying his slaves, reflect upon the deep injury and incalculable loss which the possession of that property inflicts upon the true interests of the country? Slavery, it is admitted, is an evil—it is an institution which presses heavily against the best interests of the State. It banishes free white labor, it exterminates the mechanic, the artisan, the manufacturer. It deprives them of occupation. It deprives them of bread. It converts the energy of a community into indolence, its power into imbecility, its efficiency into weakness. Sir, being thus injurious, have we not a right to demand its extermination? shall society suffer, that the slaveholder may continue to gather his *crop* of human flesh? What is his mere pecuniary claim compared with the great interests of the common weal? Must the country languish, droop, die, that the slaveholder may flourish? Shall all the interests be subservient to one—all rights subordinate to those of the slaveholder? Has not the mechanic, have not the middle classes their rights— rights incompatible with the existence of slavery?

"Sir, so great and overshadowing are the evils of slavery—so sensibly are they felt by those who have traced the causes of our national decline—so perceptible is the poisonous operation of its principles in the varied and diversified interests in this Commonwealth, that all, whose minds are not warped by prejudice or interest, must admit that the disease has now assumed that mortal tendency, as to justify the application of any remedy which, under the great law of State necessity, we might consider advisable."

At once let the good and true men of this country, the patriot sons of the patriot fathers, determine that the sun which rises to celebrate the centennial anniversary of our national independence, shall not set on the head of any slave within the limits of this Republic. Will not the non-slaveholders of the North, of the South, of the East, and of the West, heartily, unanimously sanction this proposition? Will it not be cheerfully indorsed by many of the slaveholders themselves? Will any respectable man enter a protest against it? On the 4th of July, 1876— sooner, if we can—let us make good, at least so far as we are concerned, the Declaration of Independence, which was proclaimed in Philadelphia on the 4th of July, 1776—that "all men are endowed by their Creator with certain inalienable rights; that among these, are life, liberty, and the pursuit of happiness; that to secure these rights, governments are instituted among men, deriving their just powers from the consent of the governed; that whenever any form of government becomes destructive of these ends, it is the right of the people to alter or to abolish it, and to institute a new government, laying its foundation on such principles, and organizing its powers in such form, as to them shall seem most likely to effect their safety and happiness." In purging our land of the iniquity of negro slavery, we shall only be carrying on the great work that was so successfully commenced by our noble sires of the Revolution; some future generation may possibly complete the work by annulling the last and least form of oppression.

To turn the slaves away from their present homes—away from all the property and means of support which their labor has mainly produced, would be unpardonably cruel—exceedingly unjust. Still more cruel and unjust would it be, however, to the non-slaveholding whites no less than to the negroes, to grant further toleration to the existence of slavery. In any event, come what will, transpire what may, the system must be abolished. The evils, if any, which are to result from abolition, cannot, by any manner of means, be half as great as the evils which are certain to overtake us in case of its continuance. The perpetuation of slavery is the climax of iniquity

Two hundred and thirty-nine years have the negroes in America been held in inhuman bondage. During the whole of this long period they have toiled unceasingly, from the grey of dawn till the dusk of eve, for their cruel task-masters, who have rewarded them with scanty allowances of the most inferior qualities of victuals and clothes, with heartless separations of the tenderest ties of kindred, with epithets, with scoldings, with execrations, and with the lash—and, not unfrequently, with the fatal bludgeon or the more deadly weapon. From the labor of their hands, and from the fruit of their loins, the human-mongers of the South have become wealthy, insolent, corrupt and tyrannical. In reason and in conscience, it must be admitted, the slaves might claim for themselves a liberal allowance of the proceeds of their labor. If they were to demand an equal share of all the property, real and personal, which has been accumulated or produced through their efforts, Heaven, we believe, would recognize them as honest claimants.

Elsewhere we have shown, by just and liberal estimates, that, on the single score of damages to lands, the slaveholders are, at this moment, indebted to the non-slaveholding whites in the extraordinary sum of $7,544,148,825. Considered in connection with the righteous claim of wages for services which the negroes might bring against their masters, these figures are the heralds of the significant fact that, if strict justice could be meted out to all parties in the South, the slaveholders would not only be stripped of every dollar, but they would become in law as they are in reality, the hopeless debtors of the myriads of unfortunate slaves, white and black, who are now cringing, and fawning, and festering around them.

For the services of the blacks from the 20th of August, 1620, up to the 4th of July, 1869—an interval of precisely two hundred and forty-eight years ten months and fourteen days—their masters, if unwilling, ought, in our judgment, to be compelled to grant them their freedom, and to pay each and every one of them at least sixty dollars cash in hand. The aggregate sum thus raised would amount to about two hundred and fifty million of dollars, which is less than the total market value of two entire crops of cotton—one-half of which sum would be amply sufficient to land every negro in this country on the coast of Liberia, whither, if we had the power, we would ship them all within the next six months. As a means of protection against the exigencies which might arise from a sudden transition from their present homes in America to their future homes in Africa, and for the purpose of enabling them there to take the iniatory step in the walks of civilized life, the remainder of the sum—say about one hundred and twenty-five million of dollars—might, very properly, be equally distributed amongst them after their arrival in the land of their fathers.

Dr. James Hall, the Secretary of the Maryland Colonization Society, informs us that the average cost of sending negroes to Liberia does not exceed thirty dollars each ; and it is his opinion that arrangements might be made on an extensive plan for conveying them thither at an average expense of not more than twenty-five dollars each.

The American colonization movement, as now systematized and conducted, is, in our opinion, simply an American humane farce. At present the slaves are increasing in this country at the rate of nearly one hundred thousand per annum ; within the last twelve years, as will appear below, the American Colonization Society has sent to Liberia less than five thousand negroes.

Emigrants sent to Liberia by the American Colonization Society, during the twelve years ending January 1st, 1859.

In 1847	39	
In 1848	213	
In 1849	474	
In 1850	590	
In 1851	279	
In 1852	568	Emigrants
In 1853	583	to
In 1854	783	Liberia.
In 1855	207	
In 1856	544	
In 1857	370	
In 1858	163	
Total	4,813	

The average of this total is a fraction over four hundred and one, which may be said to be the number of negroes annually colonized by the society ; while the yearly increase of slaves, as previously stated, is little less than one hundred thousand ? Fiddlesticks for such colonization ! Once for all, within a reasonably short period, let us, by an equitable system of legislation, and by such other measures as may be right and proper, compel the slaveholders to do something like justice to their negroes by giving each and every one of them his freedom, and sixty dollars in current money ; then let us charter all the ocean steamers, packets and clipper ships that can be had on liberal terms, and keep them constantly plying between the ports of America and Africa, until all the slaves who are here held in bondage shall enjoy freedom in the land of their fathers. Under a well-devised and properly conducted system of operations, but a few years would be required to redeem the United States from the monstrous curse of negro slavery.

Some few years ago, when certain ethnographical oligarchs proved to their own satisfaction that the negro was an inferior "type of mankind," they chuckled wonderfully, and avowed, in substance, that it was right for the stronger race to kidnap and enslave the weaker—that because Nature had been pleased to do a trifle more for the Caucasian race than for the African, the former, by virtue of its superiority, was perfectly justifiable in holding the latter in absolute and perpetual bondage! No system of logic could be more antagonistic to the spirit of true democracy. It is probable that the world does not contain two persons who are exactly alike in all respects; yet " *all* men are endowed by their Creator with certain *inalienable* rights, among which are life, *liberty*, and the pursuit of happiness." All mankind may or may not be the descendants of Adam and Eve. In our own humble way of thinking, we are frank to confess, we do not believe in the unity of the races. This is a matter, however, which has little or nothing to do with the great question at issue. Aside from any theory concerning the original parentage of the different races of men, facts, material and immaterial, palpable and impalpable—facts of the eyes and facts of the conscience—crowd around us on every hand, heaping proof upon proof, that slavery is a shame, a crime, and a curse—a great moral, social, civil, and political evil—an oppressive burden to the blacks, and an incalculable injury to the whites—a stumbling-block to the nation, an impediment to progress, a damper on all the nobler instincts, principles, aspirations and enterprises of man, and a dire enemy to every true interest.

Waiving all other counts, we have, we think, shown, to the satisfaction of every impartial reader, that, as elsewhere stated, on the single score of damages to lands, the slaveholders are, at this moment, indebted to us, the non-slaveholding whites, in the enormous sum of nearly seventy-six hundred million of dollars. What shall be done with this amount? It is just; shall payment be demanded? No; all the slaveholders in the country could not pay it; nor shall we ever ask them for even a moiety of the amount—no, not even for a dime, nor yet for a cent; we are willing to forfeit every farthing for the sake of freedom; for ourselves we ask no indemnification for the past: we only demand justice for the future.

But sirs, slaveholders, chevaliers and lords of the lash, we are unwilling to allow you to cheat the negroes out of all the rights and claims to which, as human beings, they are most sacredly entitled. Not alone for ourself as an individual, but for others also—particularly for five or six million of Southern non-slaveholding whites, whom your iniquitous statism has debarred from almost all the mental and material comforts of life—do we speak, when we say, you must, sooner or later, emancipate your slaves, and pay each and every one of them at least sixty dollars cash in hand. By doing this, you will be restoring to them their natural rights, and remunerating them at the rate of less than twenty-six cents per annum for the long and cheerless period of their servitude, from the 20th of August, 1620, when, on James River, in Virginia, they became the unhappy slaves of heartless tyrants. Moreover, by doing this you will be performing but a simple act of justice to the non-slaveholding whites, upon whom the system of slavery has weighed scarcely less heavily than upon the negroes themselves. You will also be applying a saving balm to your own outraged hearts and consciences, and your children—yourselves in fact—freed from the accursed stain of slavery, will become respectable, useful, and honorable members of society.

And now, sirs, we have thus laid down our ultimatum. What are you going to do about it? Something dreadful, of course! Perhaps you will dissolve the Union *again*. Do it, if you dare! Our motto, and we would have you to understand it, is *The Abolition of Slavery, and the Perpetuation of the American Union.* If, by any means, you do succeed in your treasonable attempts, to take the South out of the Union to-day, we will bring her back to-morrow—if she goes away with you, she will return without you.

Do not mistake the meaning of the last clause of the last sentence; we could elucidate it so thoroughly that no intelligent person could fail to comprehend it; but, for reasons which may hereafter appear, we forego the task.

Henceforth there are other interests to be consulted in the South, aside from the interests of negroes and slaveholders. A profound sense of duty incites us to make the greatest possible efforts for the abolition of slavery; an equally profound sense of duty calls for a continuation of those efforts until the very last foe to freedom shall have been utterly vanquished. To the summons of the righteous monitor within, we shall endeavor to prove faithful; no opportunity for inflicting a mortal wound in the side of slavery shall be permitted to pass us unimproved.

Thus, terror-engenderers of the South, have we fully and frankly defined our position; we have no modifications to propose, no compromises to offer, nothing to retract. Frown, sirs, fret, foam, prepare your weapons, threat, strike, shoot, stab, bring on civil war, dissolve the Union, nay annihilate the solar system if you will—do all this, more, less, better, worse, anything—do what you will, sirs, you can neither foil nor intimidate us; our purpose is as firmly fixed as the eternal pillars of Heaven; we have determined to abolish slavery, and, so help us God, abolish it we will! Take this to bed with you to-night, sirs, and think about it, dream over it, and let us know how you feel to-morrow morning.

CHAPTER III.

SOUTHERN TESTIMONY AGAINST SLAVERY.

"Slavery is detested—we feel its fatal effects—we deplore it with all the earnestness of humanity."—PATRICK HENRY.

IF it please the reader, let him forget all that we have written on the subject of slavery; if it accord with his inclination, let him ignore all that we may write hereafter. We seek not to give special currency to our own peculiar opinions; our greatest ambition, in these pages, is to popularize the sayings and admonitions of wiser and better men. Miracles, we believe, are no longer wrought in this bedeviled world; but if, by any conceivable or possible supernatural event, the great Founders of the Republic, Washington, Jefferson, Henry, and others, could be reinvested with corporeal life, and returned to the South, there is scarcely a slaveholder between the Potomac and the mouth of the Mississippi, that would not burn to pounce upon them with bludgeons, bowie-knives and pistols! Yes, without adding another word, Washington would be *mobbed* for what he has already said. Were Jefferson now employed as a professor in a Southern college, he would be dismissed and driven from the State, perhaps murdered before he reached the border. If Patrick Henry were a bookseller in Alabama, though it might be demonstrated beyond the shadow of a doubt that he had never bought, sold, received, or presented, any kind of literature except Bibles and Testaments, he would first be subjected to the ignominy of a coat of tar and feathers, and then limited to the option of unceremonious expatriation or death. How seemingly impossible are these statements, and yet how true! Where do we stand? What is our faith? Are we a flock without a shepherd? a people without a prophet? a nation without a government?

Has the past, with all its glittering monuments of genius and patriot ism, furnished no beacon by which we may direct our footsteps in the future? If we but prove true to ourselves, and worthy of our ancestry, we have nothing to fear; our Revolutionary sires have devised and bequeathed to us an almost perfect national polity. Let us cherish, and defend, and build upon, the fundamental principles of that polity, and we shall most assuredly reap the golden fruits of unparalleled power, virtue and prosperity. Heaven forbid that a desperate faction of pro-slavery mountebanks should succeed in their infamous efforts to quench the

91

spirit of liberty, which our forefathers infused into those two sacred charts of our political faith, the Declaration of Independence, and the Constitution of the United States. Oligarchal politicians are alone responsible for the continuance of African slavery in the South. For purposes of self-aggrandizement, they have kept learning and civilization from the people; they have willfully misinterpreted the national compacts and have outraged their own consciences by declaring to their illiterate constituents, that the Founders of the Republic were not abolitionists. When the dark clouds of slavery, error and ignorance shall have passed away,—and we believe the time is near at hand when they are to be dissipated,—the freemen of the South, like those of other sections, will learn the glorious truth, that inflexible opposition to Human Bondage has formed one of the distinguishing characteristics of every really good or great man that our country has produced.

Non-slaveholders of the South! up to the present period, neither as a body, nor as individuals, have you ever had an independent existence; but, if true to yourselves and to the memory of your fathers, you, in equal copartnership with the non-slaveholders of the North, will soon become the honored rulers and proprietors of the most powerful, prosperous, virtuous, free, and peaceful nation, on which the sun has ever shone. Already has the time arrived for you to decide upon what basis you will erect your political superstructure. Upon whom will you depend for an equitable and judicious form of constitutional government? Whom will you designate as models for your future statesmen? Your choice lies between the dead and the living—between the Washingtons, the Jeffersons and the Madisons of the past, and the Quattlebums, the Iversons and the Slidells of the present. We have chosen; choose ye, remembering that freedom or slavery is to be the issue of your option.

As the result of much reading and research, and at the expenditure of no inconsiderable amount of time, labor and money, we now proceed to make known the anti-slavery sentiments of those noble abolitionists, the Fathers of the Republic, whose liberal measures of public policy have been so criminally perverted by the treacherous advocates of slavery.

Let us listen, in the first place, to the voice of him who was "first in war, first in peace, and first in the hearts of his countrymen," to

THE VOICE OF WASHINGTON.

In a letter to John F. Mercer, dated September 9th, 1786, General Washington says:

" I never mean, unless some particular circumstances should compel me to it, to possess another slave by purchase, it being among my *first wishes* to see some plan adopted by which slavery, in this country, may be abolished by law."

In a letter to Robert Morris, dated April 12, 1786, he says:

"I hope it will not be conceived from these observations that it is my wish to hold the unhappy people who are the subject of this letter in Slavery. I can only say, that there is not a man living, who wishes more sincerely than I do, to see a plan adopted for the abolition of it; but there is only one proper and effectual mode by which it can be accomplished, and that is by legislative authority; and this, as far as my suffrage will go, shall never be wanting."

He says, in a letter

" To the MARQUIS DE LAFAYETTE: *April 5th,* 1783.

"The scheme, my dear Marquis, which you propose as a precedent, to encourage the emancipation of the black people in this country from the state of bondage in which they are held, is a striking evidence of the benevolence of your heart. I shall be happy to join you in so laudable a work; but will defer going into a detail of the business till I have the pleasure of seeing you."

In another letter to Lafayette, he says:

" The benevolence of your heart, my dear Marquis, is so conspicuous on all occasions, that I never wonder at any fresh proofs of it; but your late purchase of an estate in the Colony of Cayenne, with the view of emancipating the slaves on it, is a generous and noble proof of your humanity. Would to God a like spirit might diffuse itself generally into the minds of the people of this country."

In a letter to Sir John Sinclair, he further said:

"There are in Pennsylvania laws for the gradual abolition of slavery, which neither Virginia nor Maryland have at present, but which nothing is more certain than they must have, and at a period not remote."

In a letter to Charles Pinckney, Governor of South Carolina, on the 17th of March, 1792, he says:

"I must say that I lament the decision of your Legislature upon the question of importing slaves after March, 1793. I was in hopes that motives of policy, as well as other good reasons, supported by the direful effects of Slavery, which at this moment are presented, would have operated to produce a total prohibition of the importation of slaves, whenever the question came to be agitated in any State that might be interested in the measure."

From his last will and testament we make the following extract:

" Upon the decease of my wife, it is my will and desire that all the slaves which I hold in my own right shall receive their freedom. To emancipate them during her life would, though earnestly wished by me, be attended with such insuperable difficulties, on account of their intermixture by marriage with the dower negroes, as to excite the most painful sensation, if not disagreeable consequences, from the latter, while both descriptions are in the occupancy of the same proprietor, it not being in my power, under the tenure by which the dower negroes are held, to manumit them."

It is said that, "when Mrs. Washington learned, from the will of her deceased husband, that the only obstacle to the immediate perfection of this provision was her right of dower, she at once gave it up, and the slaves were made free." A man might possibly concentrate within himself more real virtue and influence than ever Washington possessed, and yet he would not be too good for such a wife.

From the Father of his Country, we now turn to the author of the Declaration of Independence. We will listen to

THE VOICE OF JEFFERSON.

On the 39th and 40th pages of his "Notes on Virginia," Jefferson says:

" There must doubtless be an unhappy influence on the manners of our people, produced by the existence of slavery among us. The whole commerce between master and slave is a perpetual exercise of the most boisterous passions--the most unremitting despotism on the one part, and degrading submissions on the other. Our children see this, and learn to imitate it; for man is an imitative animal. This quality is the germ of all education in him. From his cradle to his grave, he is learning to do what he sees others do. If a parent could find no motive, either in his philanthropy or his self-love, for restraining the intemperance of passion towards his slave, it should always be a sufficient one that his child is present. But generally it is not sufficient. The parent storms, the child looks on, catches the lineaments of wrath, puts on the same airs in the circle of smaller slaves, gives a loose rein to the worst of passions, and, thus nursed, educated, and daily exercised in tyranny, cannot but be stamped by it with odious peculiarities. The man must be a prodigy who can retain his manners and morals undepraved by such circumstances. And with what execration should the statesman be loaded, who, permitting one half the citizens thus to trample on the rights of the other, transforms those into despots and these into enemies, destroys the morals of the one part, and the *amor patriæ* of the other; for if a slave can have a country in this world, it must be any other in preference to that in which he is born to live and labor for another; in which he must look up the faculties of his nature, contribute, as far as depends on his individual endeavors, to the evanishment of the human race, or entail his own miserable condition on the endless generations proceeding from him. With the morals of the people, their industry is also destroyed; for, in a warm climate, no man will labor for himself who can make another labor for him. This is so true, that of the proprietors of slaves a very small proportion, indeed, are ever seen to labor. And can the liberties of a nation be thought secure, when we have removed their only firm basis—a conviction in the minds of the people that these liberties are the gift of God? that they are not to be violated but by his wrath? Indeed, I tremble for my country when I reflect that God is just; that his justice cannot sleep forever; that considering numbers, nature, and natural means only, a revolution of the wheel of fortune, an exchange of situation is among possible events; that it may become probable by supernatural interference! The Almighty has no attribute which can take side with us in such a contest."

While Virginia was yet a Colony, in 1774, she held a Convention to appoint delegates to attend the first general Congress, which was to assemble, and did assemble, in Philadelphia, in September of the same year. Before that convention, Mr. Jefferson made an exposition of the rights of British America, in which he said:

" The abolition of domestic slavery is the greatest object of desire in these Colonies, where it was unhappily introduced in their infant State. But previous to the enfranchisement of the slaves, it is necessary to exclude further importations from Africa. Yet our repeated attempts to effect this by prohibitions, and by imposing duties which might amount to prohibition, have been hitherto defeated by his majesty's negative; thus preferring the immediate advantage of a few African corsairs to the lasting interests of the American States, and the rights of human nature, deeply wounded by this infamous practice."

In the original draft of the Declaration of Independence, of which it is well known he was the author, we find this charge against the King of Great Britain:

"He has waged cruel war against human nature itself, violating its most sacred rights of life and liberty, in the persons of a distant people who never offended him, captivating and carrying them into slavery in another hemisphere, or to incur miserable death in their transportation thither. This piratical warfare, the opprobrium of infidel powers, is the warfare of the Christian King of Great Britain. Determined to keep a market where men should be bought and sold, he has at length prostituted his negative for suppressing any legislative attempt to prohibit and restrain this execrable commerce."

Hear him further; he says:

"We hold these truths to be self-evident, that all men are created equal; that they are endowed by their Creator with certain unalienable rights; that among these are life, liberty, and the pursuit of happiness: that to secure these rights, governments are instituted among men, deriving their just powers from the consent of the governed."

Under date of August 7th, 1785, in a letter to Dr. Price, of London, he says:

"Northward of the Chesapeake you may find, here and there, an opponent of your doctrine, as you may find, here and there, a robber and murderer; but in no great number. Emancipation is put into such a train, that in a few years there will be no slaves northward of Maryland. In Maryland I do not find such a disposition to begin the redress of this enormity, as in Virginia. This is the next State to which we may turn our eyes for the interesting spectacle of justice in conflict with avarice and oppression; a conflict wherein the sacred side is gaining daily recruits from the influx into office of young men grown up, and growing up. These have sucked in the principles of liberty, as it were, with their mother's milk; and it is to them I look with anxiety to turn the fate of the question."

In another letter, written to a friend in 1814, he made use of the following language:

"Your favor of July 31st was duly received, and read with peculiar pleasure. The sentiments do honor to the head and heart of the writer. Mine on the subject of the slavery of negroes have long since been in the possession of the public, and time has only served to give them stronger root. The love of justice and the love of country plead equally the cause of these people, and it is a reproach to us that they should have pleaded it so long in vain."

Again, he says:

"What an incomprehensible machine is man! who can endure toil, famine, stripes, imprisonment, and death itself, in vindication of his own liberty; and the next moment be deaf to all those motives whose power supported him through his trial, and inflict on his fellow man a bondage, one hour of which is fraught with more misery than ages of that which he rose in rebellion to oppose."

Throughout the South, at the present day, especially among slaveholders, negroes are almost invariably spoken of as "goods and chattels," "property," "human cattle." In our first quotation from Jefferson's works, we have seen that he spoke of the blacks as *citizens*. We shall now hear him speak of them as *brethren*. He says:

"We must wait with patience the workings of an overruling Providence, and hope that that is preparing the deliverance of these our brethren. When the measure of their tears shall be full, when their groans shall have involved Heaven itself in darkness, doubtless a God of justice will awaken to their distress. Nothing is more certainly written in the Book of Fate, than that this people shall be free."

In a letter to James Heaton, on this same subject, dated May 20, 1826, only six weeks before his death, he says:

"My sentiments have been forty years before the public. Had I repeated them forty times, they would have only become the more stale and thread-bare. Although I shall not live to see them consummated, they will not die with me."

From the Father of the Declaration of Independence, we now turn to the Father of the Constitution. We will listen to

THE VOICE OF MADISON.

In the Convention that drafted the Constitution, Mr. Madison

"Thought it wrong to admit in the Constitution the idea that there could be property in men."

Advocating the abolition of the slave-trade, as we find in the 42d No. of the *Federalist*, he said:

"It were, doubtless, to be wished, that the power of prohibiting the importation of slaves, had not been postponed until the year 1808, or rather, that it had been suffered to have immediate operation. But it is not difficult to account, either for this restriction on the general government, or for the manner in which the whole clause is expressed. It ought to be considered as a great point gained in favor of humanity, that a period of twenty years may terminate forever within these States, a traffic which has so long and so loudly upbraided the barbarism of modern policy; that within that period it will receive a considerable discouragement from the Federal Government, and may be totally abolished by a concurrence of the few States which continue the unnatural traffic, in the prohibitory example which has been given by so great a majority of the Union."

In the 39th No. of the *Federalist*, he says:

"The first question that offers itself is, whether the general form and aspect of the government be strictly Republican. It is evident that no other form would be reconcilable with the genius of the people of America, and with the fundamental principles of the Revolution, or with that honorable determination which animates every votary of freedom, to rest all our political experiments on the capacity of mankind for self-government."

Again, he contends that:

"Where slavery exists, the Republican theory becomes still more fallacious."

On another occasion, he says:

"We have seen the mere distinction of color made, in the most enlightened period of time, a ground of the most oppressive dominion ever exercised by man over man."

THE VOICE OF MONROE.

In a speech in the Virginia Convention, Mr. Monroe said:

"We have found that this evil has preyed upon the very vitals of the Union, and has been prejudicial to all the States in which it has existed."

THE VOICE OF HENRY.

The eloquent Patrick Henry, in a letter dated January 18, 1773, asks·

"Is it not a little surprising that the professors of Christianity, whose chief excellence consists in softening the human heart, in cherishing and improving its finer feelings, should encourage a practice so totally repugnant to the first impressions of right and wrong? What adds to the wonder is, that this abominable practice has been introduced in the most enlightened ages. Times that seem to have pretensions to boast of high improvements in the arts and sciences, and refined morality, have brought into general use, and guarded by many laws, a species of violence and tyranny which our more rude and barbarous, but more honest ancestors detested. Is it not amazing that at a time when the rights of humanity are defined and understood with precision, in a country above all others fond of liberty—that in such an age and in such a country, we find men professing a religion the most mild, humane, gentle, and generous, adopting such a principle, as repugnant to humanity as it is inconsistent with the Bible, and destructive to liberty? Every thinking, honest man rejects it in speculation. How free in practice from conscientious motives! Would any one believe that I am master of slaves of my own purchase? I am drawn along by the general inconvenience of living here without them. I will not, I cannot justify it. However culpable my conduct, I will so far pay my devoir to virtue as to own the excellence and rectitude of her precepts, and lament my want of conformity to them. I believe a time will come when an opportunity will be offered to abolish this lamentable evil. Everything we can do is to improve it, if it happens in our day; if not, let us transmit to our descendants, together with our slaves, a pity for their unhappy lot, and an abhorrence for slavery. If we cannot reduce this wished-for reformation to practice, let us treat the unhappy victims with lenity. It is the furthest advance we can make toward justice. It is a debt we owe to the purity of our religion, to show that it is at variance with that law which warrants slavery."

Again, this great orator says

"It would rejoice my very soul, that every one of my fellow-beings was emancipated. We ought to lament and deplore the necessity of holding our fellow-men in bondage. Believe me; I shall honor the Quakers for their noble efforts to abolish slavery."

THE VOICE OF RANDOLPH.

That very eccentric genius, John Randolph, of Roanoke, in a letter to William Gibbons, in 1820, says:

"With unfeigned respect and regard, and as sincere a deprecation on the extension of slavery and its horrors, as any other man, be him whom he may, I am your friend, in the literal sense of that much abused word. I say much abused, because it is applied to the leagues of vice and avarice and ambition, instead of good will toward man from love of him who is the Prince of Peace."

While in Congress, he said:

"Sir, I envy neither the heart nor the head of that man from the North who rises here to defend slavery on principle."

It is well known that he emancipated all his negroes. The following lines from his will are well worth perusing and preserving:

"I give to my slaves their freedom, to which my conscience tells me they are justly entitled. It has a long time been a matter of the deepest regret to me that the circumstances under which I inherited them, and the obstacles thrown in the way by the laws of the land, have prevented my emancipating them in my lifetime, which it is my full intention to do in case I can accomplish it."

THOMAS M. RANDOLPH.

In an address to the Virginia Legislature, in 1820, Gov. Randolph said:

"We have been far outstripped by States to whom nature has been far less

oountiful. It is painful to consider what might have been, under other circum
stances, the amount of general wealth in Virginia."

THOMAS JEFFERSON RANDOLPH.

In 1832, Mr. Randolph, of Albemarle, in the Legislature of Virginia,
used the following most graphic and emphatic language :

" I agree with gentlemen in the necessity of arming the State for internal
defence. I will unite with them in any effort to restore confidence to the public
mind, and to conduce to the sense of the safety of our wives and our children.
Yet, sir, I must ask upon whom is to fall the burden of this defence ? Not upon
the lordly masters of their hundred slaves, who will never turn out except to retire
with their families when danger threatens. No, sir ; it is to fall upon the less
wealthy class of our citizens, chiefly upon the non-slaveholder. I have known
patrols turned out when there was not a slaveholder among them ; and this is the
practice of the country. I have slept in times of alarm quiet in bed, without having
a thought of care, while these individuals, owning none of this property themselves,
were patrolling under a compulsory process, for a pittance of seventy-five cents
for twelve hours, the very curtilage of my house, and guarding that property which
was alike dangerous to them and myself. After all, this is but an expedient. As
this population becomes more numerous, it becomes less productive. Your guard
must be increased, until finally its profits will not pay for the expense of its subjection. Slavery has the effect of lessening the free population of a country.

" The gentleman has spoken of the increase of the female slaves being a part of
the profit. It is admitted ; but no great evil can be averted, no good attained,
without some inconvenience. It may be questioned how far it is desirable to foster and encourage this branch of profit. It is a practice, and an increasing practice, in parts of Virginia, to rear slaves for market. How can an honorable mind,
a patriot, and a lover of his country, bear to see this Ancient Dominion, rendered
illustrious by the noble devotion and patriotism of her sons in the cause of liberty,
converted into one grand menagerie, where men are to be reared for the market,
like oxen for the shambles ? Is it better, is it not worse, than the slave trade—that
trade which enlisted the labor of the good and wise of every creed, and every clime,
to abolish it ? The trader receives the slave, a stranger in language, aspect, and
manners, from the merchant who has brought him from the interior. The ties of
father, mother, husband, and child, have all been rent in twain ; before he receives
him, his soul has become callous. But here, sir, individuals whom the master has
known from infancy, whom he has seen sporting in the innocent gambols of childhood, who have been accustomed to look to him for protection, he tears from the
mother's arms and sells into a strange country among strange people, subject to
cruel taskmasters.

" He has attempted to justify slavery here, because it exists in Africa, and has
stated that it exists all over the world. Upon the same principle he could justify
Mahometanism, with its plurality of wives, petty wars for plunder, robbery, and
murder, or any other of the abominations and enormities of savage tribes. Does
slavery exist in any part of civilized Europe ? No, sir, in no part of it."

PEYTON RANDOLPH.

On the 20th of October, 1774, while Congress was in session in Philadelphia, Peyton Randolph, President, the following resolution, among
others, was unanimously adopted :

" That we will neither import nor purchase any slaves imported after the first
day of December next ; after which time we will wholly discontinue the slave trade,
and will neither be concerned in it ourselves, nor will we hire our vessels, nor sell
our commodities or manufactures, to those who are concerned in it."

EDMUND RANDOLPH.

The Constitution of the United States contains the following provision :

" No person held to service or labor in another State, under the laws thereof,
escaping to another, shall, in consequence of any law or regulation therein, be dis

charged from such service or labor, but shall be delivered up on claim of the party to whom such service or labor may be due."

To the studious attention of those Vandals who contend that the above provision requires the rendition of fugitive *slaves*, we respectfully commend the following resolution, which, it will be observed, was *unanimously* adopted :

"On motion of Mr. Randolph, the word '*servitude*' was struck out, and '*service*' unanimously inserted—the former being thought to express the condition of *slaves*. and the latter the obligation of *free* persons."—*Madison Papers*, vol. iii. p. 1569.

Well done for the Randolphs!

THE VOICE OF CLAY.

Henry Clay, whom nearly everybody loved, and at the mention of whose name the American heart always throbs with emotions of grateful remembrance, said, in an address before the Kentucky Colonization Society, in 1829 :

"It is believed that nowhere in the *farming* portion of the United States would slave labor be generally employed, if the proprietor were not tempted to raise slaves by the high price of the Southern market, which keeps it up in his own."

In the United States Senate, in 1850, he used the following memorable words :

"I am extremely sorry to hear the Senator from Mississippi say that he requires, first the extension of the Missouri Compromise line to the Pacific, and also that he is not satisfied with that, but requires, if I understand him correctly, a positive provision for the admission of slavery south of that line. And now, sir, coming from a slave State, as I do, I owe it to myself, I owe it to truth, I owe it to the subject, to say that no earthly power could induce me to vote for a specific measure for the introduction of slavery where it had not before existed, either south or north of that line. Coming as I do from a slave State, it is my solemn, deliberate and well-matured determination that no power, no earthly power, shall compel me to vote for the positive introduction of slavery either south or north of that line. Sir, while you reproach, and justly, too, our British ancestors for the introduction of this institution upon the continent of America, I am, for one, unwilling that the posterity of the present inhabitants of California and of New Mexico shall reproach us for doing just what we reproach Great Britain for doing to us. If the citizens of those territories choose to establish slavery, and if they come here with constitutions establishing slavery, I am for admitting them with such provisions in their constitutions; but then it will be their own work, and not ours, and their posterity will have to reproach them, and not us, for forming constitutions allowing the institution of slavery to exist among them. These are my views, sir, and I choose to express them ; and I care not how extensively or universally they are known."

Hear him further ; he says:

"So long as God allows the vital current to flow through my veins, I will never, never, never, by word or thought, by mind or will, aid in admitting one rood of free territory to the everlasting curse of human bondage."

Blest is the memory of noble Harry of the West!

THE VOICE OF BENTON.

In his "Thirty Years' View," Thomas H. Benton says:

"My opposition to the extension of slavery dates further back than 1844— forty years further back ; and as this is a suitable time for a general declaration, and a sort of general conscience delivery, I will say that my opposition to it dates from 1804, when I was a student at law in the State of Tennessee, and studied the subject of African slavery in an American book—a Virginian book—Tucker's edition of Black-stone's Commentaries."

Again, in a speech delivered in St. Louis, on the 3d of November, 1856, he says :

"I look at white people, and not at black ones ; I look to the peace and reputation of the race to which I belong. I look to the peace of this land—the world's last hope for a free government on the earth. One of the occasions on which I saw Henry Clay rise higher than I thought I ever saw him before, was when in the debate on the admission of California, a dissolution was apprehended if slavery was not carried into this Territory, where it never was. Then Mr. Clay rising, loomed colossally in the Senate of the United States, as he rose declaring that for no earthly purpose, no earthly object, could he carry slavery into places where it did not exist before. It was a great and proud day for Mr. Clay, toward the latter days of his life, and if an artist could have been there to catch his expression as he uttered that sentiment, with its reflex on his face, and his countenance beaming with firmness of purpose, it would have been a glorious moment in which to transmit him to posterity—his countenance all alive and luminous with the ideas that beat in his bosom. That was a proud day. I could have wished that I had spoken the same words. I speak them now, telling you they were his, and adopting them as my own."

THE VOICE OF MASON.

Colonel Mason, a leading and distinguished member of the Convention that formed the Constitution, from Virginia, when the provision for prohibiting the importation of slaves was under consideration, said :

"The present question concerns not the importing States alone, but the whole Union. Slavery discourages arts and manufactures. The poor despise labor when performed by slaves. They prevent the emigration of whites, who really enrich and strengthen a country. They produce the most pernicious effect on manners. Every master of slaves is born a petty tyrant. They bring the judgment of heaven on a country. As nations cannot be rewarded or punished in the next world, they must be in this. By an inevitable chain of causes and effects, Providence punishes national sins by national calamities. He lamented that some of our Eastern brethren had, from a lust of gain, embarked in this nefarious traffic. As to the States being in possession of the right to import, this was the case with many other rights now to be properly given up. He held it essential, in every point of view, that the General Government should have power to prevent the increase of slavery."

THE VOICE OF MCDOWELL.

In 1832, Gov. McDowell used this language in the Virginia Legislature :

"Who that looks to this unhappy bondage of an unhappy people, in the midst of our society, and thinks of its incidents or issues, but weeps over it as a curse as great upon him who inflicts it as upon him who suffers it? Sir, you may place the slave where you please—you may dry up, to your uttermost, the fountains of his feelings, the springs of his thought—you may close upon his mind every avenue of knowledge, and cloud it over with artificial night—you may yoke him to your labors, as the ox, which liveth only to work and worketh only to live—you may put him under any process which, without destroying his value as a slave, will debase and crush him as a rational being—you may do this, and the idea that he was born to be free will survive it all. It is allied to his hope of immortality—it is the ethereal part of his nature which oppression cannot rend. It is a torch lit up in his soul by the hand of Deity, and never meant to be extinguished by the hand of man."

THE VOICE OF IREDELL.

In the debates of the North Carolina Convention, Mr. Iredell, afterwards a Judge of the United States Supreme Court, said :

"When the entire abolition of slavery takes place, it will be an event which must be pleasing to every generous mind, and every friend of human nature."

THE VOICE OF PINKNEY.

William Pinkney, of Maryland, in the House of Delegates in that State, in 1789, made several powerful arguments in favor of the abolition of slavery. Here follows a brief extract from one of his speeches:

"Iniquitous and most dishonorable to Maryland, is that dreary system of partial bondage which her laws have hitherto supported with a solicitude worthy of a better object, and her citizens, by their practice countenanced. Founded in a disgraceful traffic, to which the parent country lent its fostering aid, from motives of interest, but which even she would have disdained to encourage, had England been the destined mart of such inhuman merchandise, its continuance is as shameful as its origin.

"I have no hope that the stream of general liberty will forever flow unpolluted through the mire of partial bondage, or that they who have been habituated to lord it over others, will not, in time, become base enough to let others lord it over them. If they resist, it will be the struggle of pride and selfishness, not of principle."

THE VOICE OF LEIGH.

In the Legislature of Virginia, in 1832, Mr. Leigh said:

"I thought till very lately that it was known to everybody that, during the Re volution, and for many years after, the abolition of slavery was a favorite topic with many of our ablest statesmen, who entertained with respect all the schemes which wisdom or ingenuity could suggest for its accomplishment."

THE VOICE OF MARSHALL.

Thomas Marshall, of Fauquier, said, in the Virginia Legislature, in 1832:

"Wherefore, then, object to slavery? Because it is ruinous to the whites— retards improvements, roots out an industrious population, banishes the yeomanry of the country—deprives the spinner, the weaver, the smith, the shoemaker, the carpenter, of employment and support."

THE VOICE OF BOLLING.

Philip A. Bolling, of Buckingham, a member of the Legislature of Virginia, in 1832, said:

"The time will come—and it may be sooner than many are willing to believe— when this oppressed and degraded race cannot be held as they now are—when a change will be effected, abhorrent, Mr. Speaker, to you, and to the feelings of every good man.

"The wounded adder will recoil, and sting the foot that tramples upon it. The day is fast approaching, when those who oppose all action upon this subject, and, instead of aiding in devising some feasible plan for freeing their country from an acknowledged curse, cry 'impossible,' to every plan suggested, will curse their perverseness, and lament their folly."

THE VOICE OF CHANDLER.

Mr. Chandler, of Norfolk, member of the Virginia Legislature, in 1832, took occasion to say:

"It is admitted, by all who have addressed this House, that slavery is a curse, and an increasing one. That it has been destructive to the lives of our citizens, history, with unerring truth, will record. That its future increase will create com motion, cannot be doubted.'

THE VOICE OF SUMMERS.

Mr. Summers, of Kanawha, member of the Legislature of Virginia, in 1832, said:

"The evils of this system cannot be enumerated. It were unnecessary to attempt it. They glare upon us at every step. When the owner looks to his wasted estate, he knows and feels them."

THE VOICE OF PRESTON.

In the Legislature of Virginia, in 1832, Mr. Preston said:

"Sir, Mr. Jefferson, whose hand drew the preamble to the Bill of Rights, has eloquently remarked that we had invoked for ourselves the benefit of a principle which we had denied to others. He saw and felt that slaves, as men, were embraced within this principle."

THE VOICE OF BIRNEY.

James G. Birney, of Kentucky, under whom the Abolitionists first became a National Party, and for whom they voted for President in 1844, giving him 66,304 votes, says:

"I allow not to human laws, be they primary or secondary, no matter by what numbers, or with what solemnities ordained, the least semblance of right to establish slavery, to make property of my fellow, created, equally with myself, in the image of God. Individually, or as political communities, men have no more right to enact slavery, than they have to enact murder or blasphemy, or incest or adultery. To establish slavery is to dethrone right, to trample on *justice*, the only true foundation of government. Governments exist not for the destruction of liberty, but for its defence; not for the annihilation of men's rights, but their preservation. Do they incorporate in their organic law the element of injustice?—do they live by admitting it in practice? Then do they destroy their own foundation, and absolve all men from the duty of allegiance. Is any man so besotted as, for a moment, to suppose that the slaveholder has an atom of right to his slave; as that the slave has resting on him an atom of obligation to obey the laws that enslave him, that rob him of everything—of himself? No one; else why do all just men of all countries rejoice when they hear that the oppressed of any country have achieved their liberty, at whatever cost to their tyrants?"

THE VOICE OF DELAWARE

Strong anti-slavery sentiments had become popular in Delaware as early as 1785. With Maryland and Missouri, it may now be ranked as merely a semi-slave State. Mr. McLane, a member of Congress from this State, in 1825, said:

"I shall not imitate the example of other gentlemen by making professions of my love of liberty and abhorrence of slavery, not, however, because I do not entertain them. I am an enemy to slavery."

THE VOICE OF MARYLAND.

Slavery has little vitality in Maryland. Baltimore, the greatest city of the South—greatest because freest—has a population of more than two hundred thousand souls, and yet less than three thousand of these are slaves. In spite of all the unjust and oppressive statutes enacted by the oligarchy, the non-slaveholders, who with the exception of a small number of slaveholding emancipationists, may in truth be said to be the on.y class of really respectable and patriotic citizens in the South, have wisely determined that their noble State shall be freed from the sin and the shame, the crime and the curse of slavery; and in accordance with this determination, long since formed, they are giving every possible encouragement to free white labor, thereby, very properly, rendering the labor of slaves both unprofitable and disgraceful. The formation of an Abolition Society in this State, in 1789, was the result of the influence of the masterly speeches delivered in the House of Delegates, by the Hon. William Pinkney, whose undying testimony we have already placed on record. Nearly seventy years ago, this eminent lawyer and statesman declared to the people of America, that if they did not mark out the bounds of slavery, and adopt measures for its total extinction, it would finally " work a decay of the spirit of liberty in the free States." Further, he said that, " by the eternal principles of natural justice, no master in the State has a right to hold his slave in bondage a single hour." In 1787, Luther Martin, of this State, said:

" Slavery is inconsistent with the genius of republicanism, and has a tendency to destroy those principles on which it is supported, as it lessens the sense of the equal rights of mankind, and habituates us to tyranny and oppression."

THE VOICE OF VIRGINIA.

After introducing the unreserved and immortal testimony of Washington, Jefferson, Madison, Henry, and the other great men of the Old Dominion, against the institution of slavery, it may, to some, seem quite superfluous to back the cause of Freedom by arguments from other Virginia abolitionists; but this State, notwithstanding all her more modern manners and inhumanity, has been so prolific of just views and noble sentiments, that we deem it eminently fit and proper to blazon many of them to the world as the redeeming features of her history. An Abolition Society was formed in this State in 1791. In a memorial which the members of this Society presented to Congress, they pronounced slavery " not only an odious degradation, but an outrageous violation of one of the most essential rights of human nature, and utterly repugnant to the precepts of the Gospel." A Bill of Rights, unanimously agreed upon by the Virginia Convention of June 12, 1776, holds—

" That all men are, by nature, equally free and independent ;

" That Government is, or ought to be, instituted for the common benefit, protec-tion, and security, of the People, Nation, or Community ;

" That elections of members to serve as representatives of the people in assembly ought to be free ;

" That all men having sufficient evidence of permanent common interest with, and attachment to, the community, have the right of suffrage, and cannot be taxed or deprived of their property, for public uses, without their own consent or that of their representatives so elected, nor bound by any law to which they have not in like manner assented, for the public good;

" That the freedom of the Press is one of the greatest bulwarks of Liberty, and can never be restrained but by despotic Governments ;

" That no free Government or the blessing of Liberty can be preserved to any people, but by a firm adherence to justice, moderation, temperance, frugality, and virtue, and by a frequent recurrence to fundamental principles."

The " Virginia Society for the Abolition of Slavery," organized in 1791, addressed Congress in these words:

" Your memorialists, fully aware that righteousness exalteth a nation, and that slavery is not only an odious degradation, but an outrageous violation of one of the most essential rights of human nature, and utterly repugnant to the precepts of the Gospel, which breathes ' peace on earth and good will to men,' lament that a practice so inconsistent with true policy and the inalienable rights of men, should subsist in so enlightened an age, and among a people professing that all mankind are, by nature, equally entitled to freedom."

THE VOICE OF NORTH CAROLINA.

If the question, *Slavery* or *No Slavery*, could be fairly presented for the decision of the legal voters of North Carolina at the next popular election, we believe that at least two-thirds of them would deposit the *No Slavery* ticket. Perhaps one-fourth of the slaveholders themselves would vote it, for the slaveholders in this State are more moderate, decent, sensible, and honorable, than the slaveholders in either of the adjoining States, or the States further South; and we know that many of them are heartily ashamed of the disreputable occupations of slaveholding and slave-breeding in which they are engaged, for we have had the assurance from many of their own lips. As a matter of course, all the non-slaveholders, who are so greatly in the majority, would vote to suppress the degrading system, which has kept them so long in poverty and ignorance, with the exception of those who are complete automatons to the beck and call of their imperious lords and masters, the major-generals of the oligarchy.

How long shall it be before the citizens of North Carolina shall have the privilege of expressing, at the ballot-box, their true sentiments with regard to this vexed question? Why not decide it at the next general election? Sooner or later, it must and will be decided—decided correctly, too—and the sooner the better. The first Southern State that abolishes slavery will do herself an immortal honor. God grant that North Carolina may be that State, and soon! There is at least one plausible reason why this good old State should be the first to move in this important matter, and we will state it. On the 20th of May, 1775, just one year, one month and fourteen days prior to the adoption of the Jeffersonian Declaration of Independence, by the Continental Congress in Philadelphia, July 4, 1776, the Mecklenburg Declaration of Independence, the authorship of which is generally attributed to Ephraim Brevard, was proclaimed in Charlotte, Mecklenburg county, North Carolina, and fully ratified in a second Convention of the people of said county, held on the 31st of the same month. And here, by the way, we may remark, that it is supposed that Mr. Jefferson made use of this last-mentioned document as the basis of his draft of the indestructible title-deed of our liberties. There is certainly an identicalness of language between the two papers that is well calculated to strengthen this hypothesis.

This, however, is a controversy about which we are but little concerned. For present purposes, it is, perhaps, enough for us to know, that on the 20th of May, 1776, when transatlantic tyranny and oppression could no longer be endured, North Carolina set her sister colonies a most valorous and praiseworthy example, and that they followed it. To her infamous slaveholding sisters of the South, it is now meet that she should set another noble example of decency, virtue, and independence. Let her at once inaugurate a policy of common justice and humanity—enact a system of equitable laws, having due regard to the rights and interests of all classes of persons, poor whites, negroes, and nabobs, and the surrounding States will ere long applaud her measures, and adopt similar ones for the governance of themselves.

Another reason, and a cogent one, why North Carolina should aspire to become the first free State of the South is this: The first slave State that makes herself respectable by casting out the "mother of harlots," and by rendering enterprise and industry honorable, will immediately receive a large accession of most worthy citizens from other States in the Union, and thus lay a broad foundation of permanent political power and prosperity. Intelligent white farmers from the Middle and New England States will flock to our more congenial clime, eager to give thirty dollars per acre for the very lands that are now a drug in the market because nobody wants them at the rate of five dollars per acre; an immediate and powerful impetus will be given to commerce, manu- factures, and all the industrial arts; science and literature will be revived, and every part of the State will reverberate with the triumphs of manual and intellectual labor.

In a pecuniary point of view, we of North Carolina are, at this present time, worth less than either of the four adjoining States; let us abolish slavery at the beginning of the next regular decade of years, and if our example is not speedily followed, we shall, on or before the 4th of July, 1876, be enabled to purchase the whole of Virginia and South Carolina, including, perhaps, the greater part of Georgia. An exclusive lease of liberty for ten years would unquestionably make us the Empire State of the South. But we have no disposition to debar others from the enjoyment of liberty or any other inalienable right; we ask no special favor; what we demand for ourselves we are willing to concede to our neighbors. Hereby we make application for a lease of freedom for ten years; shall we have it? May God enable us to secure it, as we believe He will. We give fair notice, however, that if we get it for ten years, we shall, with the approbation of Heaven, keep it twenty— forty—a thousand—forever!

We transcribe the Mecklenburg Resolutions, which, it will be ob- served, acknowledge the "inherent and inalienable rights of man," and "declare ourselves a free and independent people, are, and of right ought to be, a sovereign and self-governing association, under the control of no power other than that of our God, and the general government of the Congress."

MECKLENBURG DECLARATION OF INDEPENDENCE,

As proclaimed in the town of Charlotte, North Carolina, May 20th, 1775, and ratified by the County of Mecklenburg, in Convention, May 31st, 1775.

"I. *Resolved*—That whosoever, directly or indirectly, abetted, or in any way, form or manner, countenanced the unchartered and dangerous invasion of our rights as claimed by Great Britain, is an enemy to this country, to America, and to the inherent and inalienable rights of man.

"II. *Resolved*—That we the citizens of Mecklenburg County, do hereby dissolve the political bands which have connected us to the mother country, and hereby absolve ourselves from all allegiance to the British Crown, and abjure all political connection, contract or association with that nation, who have wantonly trampled on our rights and liberties, and inhumanly shed the blood of American patriots at Lexington.

"III. *Resolved*—That we do hereby declare ourselves a free and independent people, are, and of right ought to be, a sovereign and self-governing association, under the control of no power other than that of our God, and the general government of the Congress; to the maintenance of which independence, we solemnly pledge to each other our mutual coöperation, our lives, our fortunes, and our most sacred honor.

"IV. *Resolved*—That as we now acknowledge the existence and control of no law or legal officer, civil or military, within this county, we do hereby ordain and adopt, as a rule of life, all, each, and every of our former laws—wherein, nevertheless, the crown of Great Britain never can be considered as holding rights, privileges, immunities or authority therein."

Had it not been for slavery, which, with all its other blighting and degrading influences, stifles and subdues every noble impulse of the heart, this consecrated spot would long since have been marked by an enduring monument, whose grand proportions should bear witness that the virtues of a noble ancestry are gratefully remembered by an emulous and appreciative posterity. Yet, even as things are, we are not without genuine consolation. The star of hope and promise is beginning to beam brightly over the long-obscured horizon of the South ; and we are firm in the belief, that freedom, wealth, and magnanimity, will soon do justice to the memory of those fearless patriots, whose fair fame has been suffered to molder amidst the multifarious abominations of slavery, poverty, ignorance and grovelling selfishness.

In the Provincial Convention held in North Carolina, in August, 1774, in which there were sixty-nine delegates, representing nearly every county in the province, it was—

"*Resolved*—That we will not import any slave or slaves, or purchase any slave or slaves imported or brought into the Province by others, from any part of the world, after the first day of November next."

In Iredell's Statutes, revised by Martin, it is stated that,

"In North Carolina, no general law at all was passed, prior to the Revolution declaring who might be slaves."

That there is no *legal* slavery in the Southern States, and that slavery nowhere can be legalized, any more than theft, arson or murder can be legalized, has been virtually admitted by some of the most profound Southern jurists themselves ; and we will here digress so far as to fur nish the testimony of one or two eminent lawyers, not of North Caroina, upon this point.

In the debate in the United States Senate, in 1850, on the Fugitive Slave Bill, Mr. Mason, of Virginia, objected to Mr. Dayton's amendment, providing for a trial by jury, because, said he—

" A trial by jury necessarily carries with it a trial of the whole right, and a trial of the right to service will be gone into, according to all the forms of the Court, in determining upon any other fact. Then, again, it is proposed, as a part of the proof to be adduced at the hearing, after the fugitive has been re-captured, that evidence shall be brought by the claimant to show that slavery is established in the State from which the fugitive has absconded. Now this very thing, in a recent case in the city of New York, was required by one of the judges of that State, which case attracted the attention of the authorities of Maryland, and against which they protested. In that case the State judge went so far as to say that the only mode of proving it was by reference to the Statute book. Such proof is required in the Senator's amendment; and if he means by this that proof shall be brought that slavery is established by existing laws, it is impossible to comply with the requisition, for no such law can be produced, I apprehend, in any of the slave States. I am not aware that there is a single State in which the institution is established by positive law.'

Judge Clarke, of Mississippi says :

" In this State the legislature have considered slaves as reasonable and accountable beings ; and it should be a stigma upon the character of the State, and a reproach to the administration of justice, if the life of a slave could be taken with impunity, or if he could be murdered in cold blood, without subjecting the offender to the highest penalty known to the criminal jurisprudence of the country. Has the slave no rights, because he is deprived of his freedom? He is still a human being, and possesses all those rights of which he is not deprived by the positive provisions of the law. The right of the master exists not by force of the law of nature or nations, but by virtue only of the positive law of the State."

The Hon. Judge Ruffin, of North Carolina, says :

" Arguments drawn from the well-established principles, which confer and restrain the authority of the parent over the child, the tutor over the pupil, the master over the apprentice, have been pressed on us. The Court does not recognize their application ; there is no likeness between the cases ; they are in opposition to each other, and there is an impassable gulf between them. The difference is that which exists between freedom and slavery, and a greater cannot be imagined. In the one, the end in view is the happiness of the youth, born to equal rights with that governor on whom the duty devolves of training the young to usefulness in a station which he is afterward to assume among freemen. To such an end, and with such a subject, moral and intellectual instruction seem the natural means, and, for the most part, they are found to suffice. Moderate force is superadded only to make the others effectual. If that fail, it is better to leave the party to his own headstrong passions, and the ultimate correction of the law, than to allow it to be immoderately inflicted by a private person. With slavery it is far otherwise. The end is the profit of the master, his security, and the public safety ; the subject, one doomed, in his own person and his posterity, to live without knowledge, and without the capacity to make anything his own and to toil that another may reap the fruits. What moral considerations shall be addressed to such a being to convince him, what it is impossible but that the most stupid must feel and know can never be true, that he is thus to labor upon a principle of natural duty, or for the sake of his own personal happiness ? Such services can only be expected from one who has no will of his own ; who surrenders his will in implicit obedience to that of another. Such obedience is the consequence only of uncontrolled authority over the body. There is nothing else which can operate to produce the effect. The power

of the master must be absolute to render the submission of the slave perfect. .
most freely confess my sense of the harshness of this proposition. I feel it as
deeply as any man can; and as a principle of moral right, every person in his
retirement must repudiate it."

An esteemed friend, a physician, who was born and bred in Rowan
country, North Carolina, and who now resides there, informs us that
Judge Gaston, who was one of the half dozen statesmen whom the
South has produced since the days of the venerable fathers of the Republic, was an avowed abolitionist, and that he published an address to the
people of North Carolina, delineating, in a masterly manner, the material, moral and social disadvantages of slavery. Where is that address?
Has it been suppressed by the oligarchy? The fact that slaveholders
have, from time to time, made strenuous efforts to expunge the sentiments of freedom which now adorn the works of nobler men than the
noble Gaston, may, perhaps, fully account for the oblivious state into
which his patriotic effort seems to have fallen.

NOTE.—Three or four months after the above was published—up to
which time this work in its first form had passed through several editions—Prof. Hedrick had the kindness to hand us the address, delivered,
many years ago, before the Literary Societies of the University of North
Carolina, by

Judge Gaston, who, with much force, says:

" Disguise the truth as we may, and throw the blame where we will, it is slavery
which, more than any other cause, keeps us back in the career of improvement.
It stifles industry and represses enterprise—it is fatal to economy and providence—
it discourages skill—impairs our strength as a community, and poisons morals at
the fountain head. How this evil is to be encountered, how subdued, is indeed a
difficult and delicate inquiry, which this is not the time to examine, nor the occasion to discuss. I felt, however, that I could not discharge my duty, without
referring to this subject, as one which ought to engage the prudence, moderation,
and firmness of those who sooner or later, must act decisively upon it."

In the course of an oration which he delivered in 1830, Benjamin
Swaim, an eminent lawyer of North Carolina, asks—

" Is it nothing to us, that seventeen hundred thousand of the people of our country are doomed illegally to the most abject and vile slavery that was ever tolerated on the face of the earth? Are Carolinians deaf to the piercing cries of
humanity? Are they insensible to the demands of justice? Let any man of spirit
and feeling for a moment cast his thoughts over the land of slavery—think of the
nakedness of some, the hungry yearnings of others, the flowing tears and heaving
sighs of parting relations, the wailings of lamentation and woe, the bloody cut of
the keen lash, and the frightful scream that rends the very skies—and all this to
gratify ambition, lust, pride, avarice, vanity, and other depraved feelings of the
human heart. Indeed the worst is not generally known. Were all the miseries,
the horrors of slavery, to burst at once into view, a peal of sevenfold thunder could
scarce strike greater alarm."

THE VOICE OF SOUTH CAROLINA.

Poor South Carolina! Folly is her nightcap; fanaticism is her day-
dream; fire-eating is her pastime. She has lost her better judgment;
the dictates of reason and philosophy have no influence upon her

actions.   Like the wife who is pitiably infatuated with a drunken, worth·
less husband, she still clings, with unabated love, to the cause of her
shame, her misery, and her degradation.

A Kentuchian has recently expressed his opinion of this State in the
following language :

"South Carolina is bringing herself irrecoverably into public contempt.   It is
impossible for any impartial lover of his country, for any just, thinking man, to
witness her senseless and quenchless malignancy against the Union without the
most immeasurable disgust and scorn.   She is one vast hot-bed of disunion.   Her
people think and talk of nothing else.   She is a festering mass of treason."

In 1854, there were assessed for taxation in South Carolina,

Acres of Land 17,289,359
Valued at...$22,836,374

Average value per acre............................... $1 32

At the same time there were in New Jersey,

Acres of Land... 5,324,800
Valued at...$153,161,619

Average value per acre............................... $28 76

We hope the slaveholders will look, first on that picture, and then on
this; from one or the other, or both, they may glean a ray or two of
wisdom, which, if duly applied, will be of incalculable advantage to
them and their posterity.   We trust, also, that the non-slaveholding
whites will view, with discriminating minds, the different lights and
shades of these two pictures; they are the parties most deeply interested;
and it is to them we look for the glorious revolution that is to result in
the permanent establishment of Freedom over the last lingering ruins of
Slavery.   They have the power to retrieve the fallen fortunes of South
Carolina, to raise her up from the loathsome sink of iniquity into which
slavery has plunged her, and to make her one of the most brilliant stars
in the great constellation of States.   While their minds are occupied
with other considerations, let them not forget the difference between
twenty-eight dollars and seventy-six cents, the value of land per acre in
New Jersey, which is a second-rate free State, and *one dollar and thirty-
two cents*, the value of land per acre in South Carolina, which is, *par
excellence*, the model slave State.   The difference between the two sums
is twenty-seven dollars and forty-four cents, which would amount to
precisely two thousand seven hundred and forty-four dollars on every
one hundred acres.   To present the subject in another form, the South
Carolina tract of land, containing two hundred acres, is worth now only
two hundred and sixty-four dollars, and is depreciating every day.   Let
slavery be abolished, and in the course of a few years, the same tract
will be worth five thousand seven hundred and fifty-two dollars, with an
upward tendency.   At this rate, the increment of value on the total
area of the State will amount to more than three times as much as the
estimated value of the slaves!

South Carolina has not always been, nor will she always continue to be, on the wrong side. From Ramsay's History of the State, we learn that, in 1774, she

"*Resolved*—That his majesty's subjects in North America (without respect to color or other accidents) are entitled to all the inherent rights and liberties of his natural born subjects within the Kingdom of Great Britain ; that it is their fundamental right, that no man should suffer in his person or property without a fair trial, and judgment given by his peers, or by the law of the land."

During the Revolution, when Baron de Kalb met General Francis Marion, the former expressed amazement that so many "South Carolinians were running to take British protection." Marion replied :

" The people of Carolina form two classes, the rich and the poor. The poor are very poor ; the rich, who have slaves to do all their work, give them no employment. Unsupported by the rich, they continue poor and low-spirited. The little they get is laid out in brandy, not in books and newspapers ; hence they know nothing of the comparative blessings of our country, or of the dangers which threaten it ; therefore they care nothing about it. The rich are generally very rich ; afraid to stir lest the British should burn their houses, and carry off their negroes."

After the war, he estimated that " poor Carolina lost, through her ignorance, $15,000,000 ; for ignorance begat toryism, and toryism begat losses." In regard to the importance of educating the people, he said :

" Look at the people of New England. Religion has taught them that God created men to be happy ; to be happy they must have virtue ; that virtue is not to be attained without knowledge ; nor knowledge without instruction : nor public instruction without free schools ; nor free schools without legislative order."

One of her early writers, under the *nom de plume* of Philodemus, in a political pamphlet published in Charleston in 1784, declares that—

" Such is the fatal influence of slavery on the human mind, that it almost wholly effaces from it even the boasted characteristic of rationality."

This same writer, speaking of the particular interests of South Carolina, says :

" It has been too common with us to search the records of other nations, to find precedents that may give sanction to our own errors, and lead us unwarily into confusion and ruin. It is our business to consult their histories, not with a view to tread right or wrong in their steps, but in order to investigate the real sources of the mischiefs that have befallen them, and to endeavor to escape the rocks which they have all unfortunately split upon. It is paying ourselves but a poor compliment, to say that we are incapable of profiting by others, and that, with all the information which is to be derived from their fatal experience, it is in vain for us to attempt to excel them. If, with all the peculiar advantages of our present situation, we are incapable of surpassing our predecessors, we must be a degenerate race indeed, and quite unworthy of those singular bounties of Heaven, which we are so unskilled or undesirous to turn to our benefit."

A recent number of Frazer's Magazine contains a well-timed and well-written article from the pen of William Henry Hurlbut of this State ; and from it we make the following extract :

" As all sagacious observers of the operation of the system of slavery have demonstrated, the profitable employment of slave-labor is inconsistent with the development of agricultural science, and demands a continual supply of new and unexhausted soil. The slaveholder, investing his capital in the purchase of the laborers themselves, and not merely in soil and machines, paying his free laborers out of the profit, must depend for his continued and progressive prosperity upon the cheapness and facility with which he can transfer his slaves to fresh and fertile lands. An enormous additional item, namely the price of slaves, being added to the cost of production, all other elements of that cost require to be proportionably smaller, or profits fail." •

In an address delivered before the South Carolina Institute, in Charleston, November 20th, 1856, Mr. B. F. Perry, of Greenville, truthfully says :

"It has been South Carolina's misfortune, in this utilitarian age, to have her greatest talents and most powerful energies directed to pursuits, which avail her nothing, in the way of wealth and prosperity. In the first settlement of a new country, agricultural industry necessarily absorbs all the time and occupation of its inhabitants. They must clear the forests and cultivate the earth, in order to make their bread. This is their first consideration. Then the mechanical arts and manufactures, and commerce, must follow in the footsteps of agriculture, to insure either individual or national prosperity. No people can be highly prosperous without them. No people ever have been. Agriculture, alone, will not make or sustain a great people. The true policy of every people is to cultivate the earth, manufacture its products, and send them abroad, in exchange for those comforts and luxuries, and necessaries, which their own country and their own industry cannot give or make. The dependence of South Carolina on Europe and the Northern States for all the necessaries, comforts and luxuries, which the mechanic arts afford, has, in fact, drained her of her wealth, and made her positively poor, when compared with her sister States of the Confederacy. It is at once mortifying and alarming, to see and reflect on our own dependence in the mechanic arts and manufactures, on strangers and foreigners. In the Northern States their highest talents and energy have been diversified, and more profitably employed in developing the resources of the country, in making new inventions in the mechanic arts, and enriching the community with science and literature, commerce and manufactures."

THE VOICE OF GEORGIA.

Of the States strictly Southern, Georgia is, perhaps, the most thrifty. This prosperous condition of the State is mainly ascribable to her hundred thousand free white laborers—more than eighty-three thousand of whom are engaged in agricultural pursuits. In few other slave States are the non-slaveholders so little under the domination of the oligarchy. At best, however, even in the most liberal slave States, the social position of the non-slaveholding whites is but one short step in advance of that of the negroes ; and as there is, on the part of the oligarchy, a constantly increasing desire and effort to usurp greater power, the more we investigate the subject the more fully are we convinced that nothing but the speedy and utter annihilation of slavery from the entire nation, can save the masses of white people in the Southern States from ultimately falling to a political level with the blacks—both occupying the most abject and galling condition of servitude of which it is possible for the human mind to conceive.

Gen. Oglethorpe, under whose management the Colony of Georgia was settled, in 1733, was bitterly opposed to the institution of slavery. In a letter to Granville Sharp, dated Oct. 13th, 1776, he says :

"My friends and I settled the Colony of Georgia, and by charter were established trustees, to make laws, etc. We determined not to suffer slavery there. But the slave merchants and their adherents occasioned us not only much trouble, but at last got the then government to favor them. We would not suffer slavery (which is against the Gospel, as well as the fundamental law of England) to be authorized under our authority; we refused, as trustees, to make a law permitting such a horrid crime. The government, finding the trustees resolved firmly not to concur with what they believed unjust, took away the charter by which no law could be passed without our consent."

On the 12th of January, 1775, in indorsing the proceedings of the first American Congress, among other resolutions, " the Representatives of the extensive District of Darien, in the Colony of Georgia," adopted the following:

" 5. To show the world that we are not influenced by any contracted or interested motives, but a general philanthropy for all mankind, of whatever climate, language or complexion, we hereby declare our disapprobation and abhorrence of the unnatural practice of slavery in America (however the uncultivated state of our country or other specious arguments may plead for it), a practice founded in injustice and cruelty, and highly dangerous to our liberties (as well as lives), debasing part of our fellow creatures below men, and corrupting the virtue and morals of the rest; and is laying the basis of that liberty we contended for (and which we pray the Almighty to continue to the latest posterity), upon a very wrong foundation. We therefore resolve, at all times, to use our utmost endeavors for the manumission of our slaves in this Colony, upon the most safe and equitable footing for the masters and themselves."

The Hon. Mr. Reid, of this State, in a speech delivered in Congress, Feb. 1, 1820, says:

" I am not the panegyrist of slavery. It is an unnatural state, a dark cloud, which obscures half the lustre of our free institutions. For my own part, though surrounded by slavery from my cradle to the present moment, yet—

" 'I hate the touch of servile hands,
I loathe the slaves who cringe around.' "

As an accompaniment to those lines, he might have uttered these:

" I would not have a slave to till my ground;
To carry me, to fan me while I sleep
And tremble when I wake, for all the wealth
That sinews bought and sold have ever earned."

Thus have we presented a comprehensive summary of the most unequivocal and irrefragable testimony of the South against the iniquitous institution of human slavery. What more can we say? What more can we do? We might fill a folio volume with similar extracts; but we must forego the task; the remainder of our space must be occupied with other arguments. In the foregoing excerpts is revealed to us, in language too plain to be misunderstood, the important fact that every truly great and good man the South has ever produced, has, with hopeful confidence, looked forward to the time when this entire Continent shall be redeemed from the crime and the curse of slavery. Our noble self-sacrificing forefathers have performed their part, and performed it well. They have laid us a foundation as enduring as the earth itself; in their dying moments they admonished us to carry out their designs in the upbuilding and completion of the superstructure. Let us obey their patriotic injunctions.

From each of the six original Southern States we have introduced the most ardent aspirations for liberty—the most positive condemnations of slavery. From each of the nine slave States which have been admitted into the Union since the organization of the General Government, we could introduce, from several of their wisest and best citizens, anti

slavery sentiments equally as strong and convincing as those that ema-
nated from the great founders of our movement—Washington, Jefferson,
Madison, Patrick Henry and the Randolphs.   As we have already
remarked, however, the limits of this chapter will not admit of the
introduction of additional testimony from either of the old or new slave
States.

The reader will not fail to observe that, in presenting these solid abolition doctrines of the South, we have been careful to make such quota-
tions as triumphantly refute, in every particular, the more specious
sophistries of the oligarchy.

The mention of the illustrious names above, reminds us of the fact,
that many of the party newspapers, whose venal columns are eternally
teeming with vituperation and slander, have long assured us that the
Whig ship was to be steered by the Washington rudder, that the Democratic bark was to sail with the Jefferson compass, and that the Know-
Nothing brig was to carry the Madison chart.   Imposed upon by these
monstrous falsehoods, we have, from time to time, been induced to
engage passage on each of these corrupt and rickety old hulks; but, in
every instance, we have been basely swamped in the sea of slavery, and
are alone indebted for our lives to the kindness of Heaven and the art
of swimming.   Washington the founder of the Whig party!   Jefferson
the founder of the Democratic party!   Voltaire the founder of Christianity!   How absurd!   God forbid that man's heart should always
continue to be the citadel of deception—that he should ever be to others
the antipode of what he is to himself.

There is now in this country but one well-organized party that pro
mises, in good faith, to put in practice the principles of Washington,
Jefferson, Madison, and the other venerable Fathers of the Republic—
the Republican party.   To this party we pledge unswerving allegiance,
so long as it shall continue to pursue the statism advocated by the great
political prototypes above-mentioned, but no longer.   We believe it is,
as it ought to be, the desire, the determination, and the destiny of this
party, to give the death-blow to slavery; should future developments
prove the party at variance with this belief—a belief, by the by, which
it has recently inspired in the breasts of little less than one and a half
million of the most intelligent and patriotic voters in America—we shall
shake off the dust of our feet against it, and join one that will, in a
summary manner, extirpate the intolerable grievance.

CHAPTER IV.

Slavery must fall, because it stands in direct hostility to all the grand movements, principles, and reforms of our age, because it stands in the way of an advancing world. One great idea stands out amidst the discoveries and improvements of modern times. It is, that man is not to exercise arbitrary, irresponsible power over man. To restrain power, to divide and balance it, to create responsibility for its just use, to secure the individual against its abuse, to substitute law for private will, to shield the weak from the strong, to give to the injured the means of redress, to set a fence round every man's property and rights, in a word, to secure liberty,—such, under various expressions, is the great object on which philosophers, patriots, philanthropists, have long fixed their thoughts and hopes.—CHANNING.

THE best evidence that can be given of the enlightened patriotism and love of liberty in the free States, is the fact that, at the Presidential election in 1856, they polled thirteen hundred thousand votes for the Republican candidate, JOHN C. FREMONT. This fact of itself seems to preclude the necessity of strengthening our cause with the individual testimony of even their greatest men. Having, however, adduced the most cogent and conclusive anti-slavery arguments from the Washingtons, the Jeffersons, the Madisons, the Randolphs, and the Clays of the South, we shall now proceed to enrich our pages with gems of Liberty from the Franklins, the Hamiltons, the Jays, the Adamses, and the Websters of the North. Too close attention cannot be paid to the words of wisdom which we have extracted from the works of these truly eminent and philosophic statesmen. We will first listen to

THE VOICE OF FRANKLIN.

Dr. Franklin was the first president of " The Pennsylvania Society for promoting the Abolition of Slavery ;" and it is now generally conceded that this was the first regularly organized American abolition Society—it having been formed as early as 1774, while we were yet subjects of the British government. In 1790, in the name and on behalf of this Society, Dr. Franklin, who was then within a few months of the close of his life, drafted a memorial "to the Senate and House of Representatives of the United States," in which he said :

"Your memorialists, particularly engaged in attending to the distresses arising from slavery, believe it to be their indispensable duty to present this subject to your notice. They have observed, with real satisfaction, that many important and salutary powers are vested in you, for 'promoting the welfare and securing the blessings of liberty to the people of the United States ;' and as they conceive that

114

these blessings ought rightfully to be administered, without distinction of color, to all descriptions of people, so they indulge themselves in the pleasing expectation that nothing which can be done for the relief of the unhappy objects of their care, will be either omitted or delayed.

From a persuasion that equal liberty was originally the portion, and is still the birthright of all men, and influenced by the strong ties of humanity and the principles of their institution, your memorialists conceive themselves bound to use all justifiable endeavors to loosen the bonds of slavery, and promote a general enjoyment of the blessings of freedom. Under these impressions, they earnestly entreat your attention to the subject of slavery ; that you will be pleased to countenance the restoration to liberty of those unhappy men, who, alone, in this land of freedom, are degraded into perpetual bondage, and who, amid the general joy of surrounding freemen, are groaning in servile subjection ; that you will devise means for removing this inconsistency of character from the American people ; that you will promote mercy and justice toward this distressed race ; and that you will step to the very verge of the power vested in you for discouraging every species of traffic in the persons of our fellow-men."

On another occasion, he says :

" Slavery is an atrocious debasement of human nature."

THE VOICE OF HAMILTON.

Alexander Hamilton, the brilliant statesman and financier, tells us that—

" The sacred rights of mankind are not to be rummaged for among old parchments or musty records. They are written as with a sunbeam, in the whole volume of human nature, by the hand of Divinity itself, and can never be erased or obscured by mortal power."

Again, in 1774, addressing himself to an American Tory, he says :

" The fundamental source of all your errors, sophisms, and false reasonings, is a total ignorance of the natural rights of mankind. Were you once to become acquainted with these, you could never entertain a thought, that all men are not, by nature, entitled to equal privileges. You would be convinced that natural liberty is the gift of the beneficent Creator to the whole human race; and that civil liberty is founded on that."

THE VOICE OF JAY.

John Jay, first Chief Justice of the United States under the Constitution of 1789, in a letter to the Hon. Elias Boudinot, dated November 17, 1819, says :

" Little can be added to what has been said and written on the subject of slavery. I concur in the opinion that it ought not to be introduced nor permitted in any of the new States, and that it ought to be gradually diminished and finally abolished in all of them.

" To me, the constitutional authority of the Congress to prohibit the migration and importation of slaves into any of the States, does not appear questionable.

" The first article of the Constitution specifies the legislative powers committed to the Congress. The 9th section of that article has these words : ' The *migration or importation* of such persons as any of the *now-existing* States shall think proper to admit, shall not be prohibited by the Congress prior to the year 1808, but a tax or duty may be imposed on such importation, not exceeding ten dollars for each person.'

" I understand the sense and meaning of this clause to be, that the power of the Congress, although competent to prohibit such migration and importation, was to be exercised with respect to the *then* existing States, and them only, until the year 1808, but the Congress were at liberty to make such prohibitions as to any *new* State, which might in the *mean* time be established. And further, that from and after *that* period, they were authorized to make such prohibitions as to *all* the States, whether *new* or *old*.

" It will, I presume, be admitted, that slaves were the persons intended. The word slaves was avoided, probably on account of the existing toleration of slavery.

and its discordancy with the principles of the Revolution, and from a consciousness of its being repugnant to the following positions in the Declaration of Independence: ' We hold these truths to be self-evident : that all men are created equal ; that they are endowed by their Creator with certain inalienable rights ; that among these are life, liberty, and the pursuit of happiness."

In a previous letter, written from Spain, whither he had been appointed as minister plenipotentiary, he says, speaking of the abolition of slavery :

" Till America comes into this measure, her prayers to Heaven will be impious. This is a strong expression, but it is just. I believe that God governs the world, and I believe it to be a maxim in His, as in our courts, that those who ask for equity ought to do it."

WILLIAM JAY.

The Hon. Wm. Jay, a noble son of Chief Justice John Jay, says :

" A crisis has arrived in which we must maintain our rights, or surrender them forever. I speak not to abolitionists alone, but to all who value the liberty our fathers achieved. Do you ask what we have to do with slavery ? Let our muzzled presses answer—let the mobs excited against us by the merchants and politicians answer—let the gag laws threatened by our governors and legislatures answer— let the conduct of the National Government answer."

THE VOICE OF ADAMS.

From the Diary of John Quincy Adams, " the old man eloquent," we make the following extract :

" It is among the evils of slavery, that it taints the very sources of moral princi- ple. It establishes false estimates of virtue and vice ; for what can be more false and more heartless than this doctrine, which makes the first and holiest rights of humanity to depend upon the color of the skin ? It perverts human reason, and induces men endowed with logical powers to maintain that slavery is sanctioned by the Christian religion ; that slaves are happy and contented in their condition ; that between master and slave there are ties of mutual attachment and affection ; that the virtues of the master are refined and exalted by the degradation of the slave, while at the same time they vent execrations upon the slave trade, curse Britain for having given them slaves, burn at the stake negroes convicted of crimes, for the terror of the example, and writhe in agonies of fear at the very mention of human rights as applicable to men of color."

THE VOICE OF WEBSTER.

In a speech which he delivered at Niblo's Garden, in the city of New York, on the 15th of March, 1837, Daniel Webster, the Great Expounder of the Constitution, said :

" On the general question of slavery, a great part of the community is already strongly excited. The subject has not only attracted attention as a question of politics, but it has struck a far deeper one ahead. It has arrested the religious feeling of the country, it has taken strong hold on the consciences of men. He is a rash man, indeed, and little conversant with human nature, and especially has he an erroneous estimate of the character of the people of this country, who supposes that a feeling of this kind is to be trifled with or despised. It will assuredly cause itself to be respected. But to endeavor to coin it into silver, or retain its free expression, to seek to compress and confine it, warm as it is, and more heated as such endeavors would inevitably render it—should this be attempted, I know nothing, even in the Constitution or Union itself, which might not be endangered by the explosion which might follow."

When discussing the Oregon Bill in 1848, he said :

" I have made up my mind, for one, that under no circumstances will I consent to the further extension of the area of slavery in the United States, or to the fur- ther increase of slave representation in the House of Representatives."

Under date of February 15th, 1850, in a letter to the Rev. Mr. Furness, he says:

"From my earliest youth I have regarded slavery as a great moral and political evil. I think it unjust, repugnant to the natural equality of mankind, founded only in superior power; a standing and permanent conquest by the stronger over the weaker. All pretence of defending it on the ground of different races, I have ever condemned. I have even said that if the black race is weaker, that is a reason against, not for, its subjection and oppression. In a religious point of view I have ever regarded it, and even spoken of it, not as subject to any express denunciation. either in the Old Testament or the New, but as opposed to the whole spirit of the Gospel and to the teachings of Jesus Christ. The religion of Jesus Christ is a religion of kindness, justice and brotherly love. But slavery is not kindly affectionate : it does not seek anothers, and not its own; it does not let the oppressed go free. It is, as I have said, but a continual act of oppression, But then, such is the influence of a habit of thinking among men, and such is the influence of what has been long established, that even minds, religious and tenderly conscientious, such as would be shocked by any single act of oppression, in any single exercise of violence and unjust power, are not always moved by the reflection that slavery is a continual and permanent violation of human rights."

While delivering a speech at Buffalo, in the State of New York, in the summer of 1851, only about twelve months prior to his decease, he made use of the following emphatic words:

"I never would consent, and never have consented, that there should be one foot of slave territory beyond what the old thirteen States had at the formation of of the Union. Never, never."

NOAH WEBSTER.

Noah Webster, the great American vocabulist, says:

"That freedom is the sacred right of every man, whatever be his color, who has not forfeited it by some violation of municipal law, is a truth established by God himself, in the very creation of human beings. No time, no circumstance, no human power or policy can change the nature of this truth, nor repeal the fundamental laws of society, by which every man's right to liberty is guarantied. The act of enslaving men is always a violation of those great primary laws of society. by which alone, the master himself holds every particle of his own freedom."

THE VOICE OF CLINTON.

De Witt Clinton, the father of the great system of internal improvements in the State of New York, speaking of despotism in Europe, and of slavery in America, asks:

"Have not prescription and precedent—patriarchal dominion—divine right of kings and masters, been alternately called in to sanction the slavery of nations? And would not all the despotisms of the ancient and modern world have vanished into air, if the natural equality of mankind had been properly understood and practised? . . . . . This declares that the same measure of justice ought to be measured out to all men, without regard to adventitious inequalities, and the intellectual and physical disparities which proceed from inexplicable causes."

THE VOICE OF WARREN.

Major General Joseph Warren, one of the truest patriots of the Revolution, and the first American officer of rank that fell in our contest with Great Britain, says:

"That personal freedom is the natural right of every man, and that property, or an exclusive right to dispose of what he has honestly acquired by his own labor, necessarily arises therefrom, are truths that common sense has placed beyond the reach of contradiction. And no man, or body of men, can, without being guilty of flagrant injustice, claim a right to dispose of the persons or acquisitions of any other man or body of men, unless it can be proved that such a right has arisen from some compact between the parties, in which it has been explicitly and freely granted."

Otis, Hancock, Ames, and others, should be heard, but for lack of space. Volumes upon volumes might be filled with extracts similar to the above, from the works of the deceased statesmen and sages of the North, who, while living, proved themselves equal to the task of exterminating from their own States the matchless curse of human slavery. Such are the men who, though no longer with us in the flesh, " still live." A living principle—an immortal interest—have they, invested in every great and good work that distinguishes the free States. The railroads, the canals, the telegraphs, the factories, the fleets of merchant vessels, the magnificent cities, the scientific modes of agriculture, the unrivalled institutions of learning, and other striking evidences of progress and improvement at the North, are, either directly or indirectly, the offspring of their gigantic intellects. When, if ever, commerce, and manufactures, and agriculture, and great enterprises, and truth, and liberty, and justice, and magnanimity, shall have become obsolete terms, then their names may possibly be forgotten, but not till then.

An army of brave and worthy successors—champions of Freedom now living, have the illustrious forefathers of the North, in the persons of Garrison, Greeley, Giddings, Goodell, Grow, and Gerrit Smith ; in Seward, Sumner, Stowe, Raymond, Parker, and Phillips ; in Beecher, Banks, Burlingame, Bryant, Hale, and Hildreth ; in Emerson, Dayton, Thompson, Tappan, King and Cheever ; in Whittier, Wilson, Wade, Wayland, Weed, and Burleigh. These are the men whom, in connection with their learned and eloquent compatriots, the Everetts, the Bancrofts, the Prescotts, the Chapins, the Longfellows, and the Danas, future historians, if faithful to their calling, will place on record as America's true statesmen, literati, preachers, philosophers, and philanthropists, of the present age.

In this connection, however, it may not be amiss to remark that the Homers, the Platos, the Bacons, the Newtons, the Shakspeares, the Miltons, the Blackstones, the Cuviers, the Humboldts, and the Macaulays of America, have not yet been produced ; nor, in our humble judgment, will they be, until slavery shall have been overthrown, and free dom established in the States of Virginia, Kentucky, and Tennessee. Upon the soil of those States, when free, or on other free soil crossed by about the same degrees of latitude, and not distant from the Appalachian chain of mountains, will, we believe, be nurtured into manhood, in the course of one or two centuries, perhaps, as great men as those mentioned above—greater, possibly, than any that have ever yet lived. Whence their ancestors may come, whether from Europe, from Asia, from Africa, from Oceanica, from North or South America, or from the islands of the sea, or whatever honorable vocation they may now be engaged in, matters nothing at all. For aught we know, their great-grandfathers are now humble artisans in Maine, or moneyed merchants in Massachusetts; illiterate poor whites in Mississippi, or slave-driving lordlings in South Carolina; frugal farmers in Michigan, or millionaires in Illinois; daring hunters in the Rocky Mountains, or metal-diggers in California; peasants in France, or princes in Germany—no matter where, or what, the scope of country above mentioned is, in our opinion, destined to be the birthplace of their illustrious offspring—the great savans of the New World, concerning whom let us console ourselves with the hope that they are not buried deeply in the matrix of the future.

CHAPTER V.

Here's Freedom to them that would read,
IIere's Freedom to them that would write,
There's none ever feared that the truth should be heard,
But they whom the truth would indict.
May Liberty meet with success,
May Prudence protect it from evil,
May tyrants and tyranny tine in their mist,
And wander their way to the devil !

BURNS.

To the true friends of freedom throughout the world, it is a pleasing thought, and one which, by being communicated to others, is well calculated to universalize the principles of liberty, that the great heroes, statesmen, and sages, of all ages and nations, ancient and modern, who have ever had occasion to speak of the institution of human slavery, have entered their most unequivocal and positive protests against it. To say that they disapproved of the system would not be sufficiently expressive of the utter detestation with which they uniformly regarded it. That they abhorred it as the vilest invention that the Evil One has ever assisted bad men to concoct, is quite evident from the very tone and construction of their language.

Having with much pleasure and profit, heard the testimony of America, through her representative men, we will now hear that of other nations, through their representative men—doubting not that we shall be more than remunerated for our time and trouble. We will first listen to

THE VOICE OF ENGLAND.

In the case of James Somerset, a negro who had been kidnapped in Africa, transported to Virginia, there sold into slavery, thence carried to England, as a waiting-boy, and there induced to institute proceedings against his master for the recovery of his freedom,

MANSFIELD says :

" The state of slavery is of such a nature that it is incapable of being introduced on any reasons moral or political, but only by positive law, which preserves its force long after the reasons, occasion, and time itself whence it was created, are erased from the memory. It is so odious that nothing can be sufficient to support it but positive law. Whatever inconveniences, therefore, may follow from the decision, I cannot say that this case is allowed or approved by the law of England and, therefore, the black must be discharged."

LOCKE says :

" Slavery is so vile, so miserable a state of man, and so directly opposite to the generous temper and courage of our nation, that it is hard to be convinced that an Englishman, much less a gentleman, should plead for it."

Again, he says :

" Though the earth, and all inferior creatures, be common to all men, yet every man has a property in his own person ; this nobody has a right to but himself."

In her speech at the opening of Parliament, on the 3d of February, 1859,

QUEEN VICTORIA said :

" I have great satisfaction in announcing to you that the Emperor of the French has abolished a system of negro emigration from the coast of Africa, against which, as unavoidably tending, however guarded, to the encouragement of the slave trade, my government has never ceased to address to his Imperial Majesty its most earnest but friendly representations. This wise act on the part of his Imperial Majesty induces me to hope that the negotiations now in progress at Paris may tend to the total abandonment of the system, and to the substitution of a duly regulated supply of free labor."

PITT says :

" It is injustice to permit slavery to remain for a single hour."

FOX says :

" With regard to a regulation of slavery, my detestation of its existence induces me to know no such thing as a regulation of robbery, and a restriction of murder. Personal freedom is a right of which he who deprives a fellow-creature is criminal in so depriving him, and he who withholds is no less criminal in withholding."

Speaking in Parliament against the slave trade,

HUDDLESTONE remarked :

" That a curse attended this trade even in the mode of defending it. By a certain fatality, none but the vilest arguments were brought forward, which corrupted the very persons who used them. Every one of these was built on the narrow ground of interest, of pecuniary profit, of sordid gain, in opposition to every motive that had reference to humanity, justice and religion, or to that great principle which comprehended them all."

SHAKSPEARE says :

" A man is master of his liberty."

Again, he says :

" It is the curse of kings to be attended
By slaves, that take their humors for a warrant
To break within the bloody house of life, -
And, on the winking of authority,
To understand a law ; to know the meaning
Of dangerous majesty, when, perchance, it frowns
More upon humor than advised respect."

Again :

" Heaven will one day free us from this slavery."

Again :

Liberty ! Freedom ! Tyranny is dead !—
Run hence, proclaim, cry it about the streets ;
Some to the common pulpits, and cry out,
Liberty, freedom, and enfranchisement."

COWPER says:

"Slaves cannot breathe in England; if their lungs
Receive our air, that moment they are free.
They touch our country and their shackles fall.
That's noble, and bespeaks a nation proud
And jealous of the blessing. Spread it then,
And let it circulate through every vein
Of all your empire, that where Britain's power
Is felt, mankind may feel her mercy too."

MILTON asks:

"Where is the beauty to see,
Like the sun-brilliant brow of a nation when free?"

Again, he exclaims:

"O execrable son, so to aspire
Above his brethren, to himself assuming
Authority usurp'd, from God not given:
He gave us only over beast, fish, fowl,
Dominion absolute; that right we hold
By his donation; but man over men
He made not lord; such title to himself
Reserving, human left from human free."

Again, he says:

"If our fathers promised for themselves, to make themselves slaves, they could make no such promise for us."

Again:

"Since, therefore, the law is chiefly right reason, if we are bound to obey a magistrate as a minister of God, by the very same reason and the very same law, we ought to resist a tyrant, and minister of the devil."

DR. JOHNSON says:

"No man is by nature the property of another. The rights of nature must be some way forfeited before they can justly be taken away."

DR. PRICE says:

"If you have a right to make another man a slave, he has a right to make you a slave."

HARRIET MARTINEAU says:

"Where a man is allowed the possession of himself, the purchaser of his labor is benefited by the vigor of his mind through the service of his limbs: where man is made the possession of another, the possessor loses at once and forever all that is most valuable in that for which he has paid the price of crime."

BLACKSTONE says:

"If neither captivity nor contract can, by the plain law of nature and reason, reduce the parent to a state of slavery, much less can they reduce the offspring."

Again, he says;

"The primary aim of society is to protect individuals in the enjoyment of those absolute rights which were vested in them by the immutable laws of nature. Hence it follows that the first and primary end of human laws is to maintain those absolute rights of individuals."

Again:

"If any human law shall allow or require us to commit crime, we are bound to transgress that human law, or else we must offend both the natural and divine."

COKE says:

"What the Parliament doth, shall be holden for naught, whenever it shall enact that which is contrary to the rights of nature."

HAMPDEN says:

"The essence of all law is justice. What is not justice is not law; and what is not law ought not to be obeyed."

HARRINGTON says:

"All men naturally are equal; for though nature with a noble variety has made different features and lineaments of men, yet as to freedom, she has made every one alike, and given them the same desires."

FORTESCUE says:

"Those rights which God and nature have established, and which are therefore called natural rights, such as life and liberty, need not the aid of human laws to be more effectually invested in every man than they are; neither do they receive any additional strength when declared by the municipal laws to be inviolable. On the contrary, no human power has any authority to abridge or destroy them, unless the owner himself shall commit some act that amounts to a forfeiture."

And again:

"The law, therefore, which supports slavery and opposes liberty, must necessarily be condemned as cruel, for every feeling of human nature advocates liberty. Slavery is introduced by human wickedness, but God advocates liberty, by the nature which he has given to man."

BROUGHAM says:

"Tell me not of rights—talk not of the property of the planter in his slaves. I deny the right; I acknowledge not the property. In vain you tell me of laws that sanction such a claim. There is a law above all the enactments of human codes, the same throughout the world, the same in all times; it is the law written by the finger of God on the hearts of men; and by that law, unchangeable and eternal, while men despise fraud, and loathe rapine, and abhor blood, they shall reject with indignation the wild and guilty phantasy that man can hold property in man."

THE VOICE OF IRELAND.

BURKE says:

"Slavery is a state so improper, so degrading, and so ruinous to the feelings and capacities of human nature, that it ought not to be suffered to exist."

CURRAN says:

"I speak in the spirit of British law, which makes liberty commensurate with and inseparable from British soil: which proclaims even to the stranger and the sojourner, the moment he steps his foot on British earth, that the ground on which he treads is holy and consecrated by the genius of Universal Emancipation. No matter in what language his doom may have been pronounced; no matter what complexion, incompatible with freedom, an Indian or African sun may have burnt upon him; no matter in what disastrous battle his liberty may have been cloven down; no matter with what solemnities he may have been devoted upon the altar of slavery, the moment he touches the sacred soil of Britain, the altar and the god sink together in the dust; his soul walks abroad in her own majesty; and he stands redeemed, regenerated and disenthralled by the irresistible genius of Universal Emancipation."

The Dublin University Magazine for December, 1856, says:

"The United States must learn, from the example of Rome, that Christianity and the pagan institution of slavery cannot coëxist together. The Republic must take her side and choose her favorite child; for if she love the one, see must hate the other."

THE VOICE OF SCOTLAND.

BEATTIE says :

"Slavery is inconsistent with the dearest and most essential rights of man's nature; it is detrimental to virtue and industry; it hardens the heart to those tender sympathies which form the most lovely part of human character; it involves the innocent in hopeless misery, in order to procure wealth and pleasure for the authors of that misery; it seeks to degrade into brutes beings whom the Lord of Heaven and Earth endowed with rational souls, and created for immortality; in short, it is utterly repugnant to every principle of reason, religion, humanity, and conscience. It is impossible for a considerate and unprejudiced mind, to think of slavery without horror."

MILLER says :

"The human mind revolts at a serious discussion of the subject of slavery. Every individual, whatever be his country or complexion, is entitled to freedom."

MACKNIGHT says :

"Men-stealers are inserted among the daring criminals against whom the law of God directed its awful curses. These were persons who kidnapped men to sell them for slaves; and this practice seems inseparable from the other iniquities and oppressions of slavery; nor can a slave dealer easily keep free from this criminality, if indeed the receiver is as bad as the thief."

THE VOICE OF FRANCE.

LAFAYETTE says :

"I would never have drawn my sword in the cause of America, if I could have conceived that thereby I was founding a land of slavery."

Again, while in the prison of Magdeburg, he says :

"I know not what disposition has been made of my plantation at Cayenne; but I hope Madame de Lafayette will take care that the negroes who cultivate it shall preserve their liberty."

O. LAFAYETTE, grandson of General Lafayette, in a letter under date of April 26th, 1851, says :

"This great question of the abolition of Negro Slavery, which has my entire sympathy, appears to me to have established its importance throughout the world. At the present time, the States of the Peninsula, if I do not deceive myself, are the only European powers who still continue to possess slaves; and America, while continuing to uphold slavery, feels daily, more and more, how heavily it weighs upon her destinies."

MONTESQUIEU asks :

"What civil law can restrain a slave from running away, since he is not a member of society?"

Again, he says :

"Slavery is contrary to the fundamental principles of all societies."

Again :

"In democracies, where they are all upon an equality, slavery is contrary to the principles of the Constitution."

Again :

"Nothing puts one nearer the condition of a brute than always to see freemen and not be free."

Again :

"Even the earth itself, which teems with profusion under the cultivating hand of the free born laborer, shrinks in barrenness from the contaminating sweat of a slave."

LOUIS X. issued the following edict:

"As all men are by nature free born, and as this Kingdom is called the Kingdom of Franks (freemen), it shall be so in reality. It is therefore decreed that enfranchisement shall be granted throughout the whole Kingdom upon just and reasonable terms."

BUFFON says:

"It is apparent that the unfortunate negroes are endowed with excellent hearts, and possess the seeds of every human virtue. I cannot write their history without lamenting their miserable condition."

ROUSSEAU says:

"The terms *slavery* and *right*, contradict and exclude each other."

BRISSOT says:

"Slavery, in all its forms, in all its degrees, is a violation of divine law, and a degradation of human nature."

THE VOICE OF GERMANY.

GROTIUS says:

"Those are men-stealers who abduct, keep, sell or buy slaves or freemen. To steal a man is the highest kind of theft."

GOETHE says:

"Such busy multitudes I fain would see
Stand upon free soil with a people free."

LUTHER says:

"Unjust violence is, by no means, the ordinance of God, and therefore can bind no one in conscience and right, to obey, whether the command comes from pope, emperor, king or master."

Carl Schurz, a distinguished German orator, patriot and statesman, now a citizen of Wisconsin—a man who was born to reflect honor on whatever state or nation in which he may reside—in a most eloquent and forcible speech which he delivered in Faneuil Hall, Boston, April 18, 1859, says:

"Look at the slave States. There is a class of men who are deprived of their natural rights. But this is not the only deplorable feature of that peculiar organization of society. Equally deplorable is it, that there is another class of men who keep the former in subjection. That there are slaves is bad; but almost worse is it, that there are masters. Are not the masters freemen? No, sir! Where is their liberty of the press? Where is their liberty of speech? Where is the man among them who dares to advocate openly principles not in strict accordance with the ruling system? They speak of a Republican form of government, they speak of Democracy, but the despotic spirit of slavery and mastership combined pervades their whole political life like a liquid poison. I am an anti-slavery man, and I have a right to my opinion in South Carolina just as well as in Massachusetts. My neighbor is a Democrat; I may be sorry for it, but I solemnly acknowledge his right to his opinion in Massachusetts as well as in South Carolina. You tell me, that for my opinion they will mob me in South Carolina. Sir, there is the difference between South Carolina and Massachusetts. There is the difference between an anti-slavery man, who is a freeman, and a slaveholder, who is himself a slave."

Frederick Kapp, an accomplished German author and orator, who, since his arrival in America—many years ago—has paid much attention to our social and political institutions, says:

"The whites who reside in the South, and are non-slaveholders, add very little weight to the scale, because they are entirely dependent upon the slaveholders, even though these latter constitute no more than perhaps the one-ninth of the whole population of the slave States. The non-slaveholders are characterized by their poverty and ignorance; and we think it a safe calculation to say that not more than one-fourth of the whole white population can read and write. It is the interest of the slaveholder to perpetuate ignorance. For this reason the free-school system of the North has no existence in the South; the greater the rawness and poverty on the part of the whites, the greater is their subordination to, and dependence on, the slave aristocracy.

"As a natural consequence growing out of these relations, it is the slaveholder only who can obtain public office, or who is elected to Congress; in fact, many of the Southern constitutions prescribe such qualifications as being requisite. The slaveholders, by these means, transmit from family to family a hereditary influence, so that they are no longer merely natural politicians, but have a political education, a general political spirit, a very decided political tradition."

To Dr. Max Langenschwarz, who, in 1833, in connection with his friend Ludwig Storch, formed an Anti-Slavery Society in Leipsic, Germany, we are indebted for the following brief but interesting annals:

"The first historical documents in regard to the abolition of slavery are to be found in Germany, whose people and governments at a very early period declared themselves against *Leibeigenschaft* (involuntary bondage), and against every right to buy or sell human beings, or to keep them as slaves. In a document of the fifth century, we find that the *Catti* united with the *Franks* in a war against the Gauls, under the express condition 'That the prisoners should be exchanged, that no prisoner should be held or brought into bondage as *Leibeigen* (a slave,) and that capital punishment should avenge such a crime against God and men.'

"The same feelings are to be found in many other documents of the old Germans. In 1372, Henry the Iron, one of the first Landgraves of Hessia, published an edict: 'Abolishing for all eternity the state of *Leibeigenschaft* (slavery), and threatening with death all those who should be discovered keeping a man, woman or child, in involuntary servitude.'

"In a bishop's edict in 1411 (*Muenster*), we find the following: 'If a man is kept in involuntary bondage and as a slave against his will, he shall ask for his immediate deliverance; and if he is kept a slave in spite of his demand, and defends himself against his master, and kills him, the killing (*Todtschlag*) shall not be considered as murder.'"

THE VOICE OF RUSSIA.

Those of our readers who keep themselves informed of the grand movements and enterprises of the age, need scarcely be reminded that the present Czar of Russia, Alexander II., who is not merely an emperor but also a man, and who, by the profound wisdom and magnanimity of his measures, bids fair to become a greater Alexander than Alexander the Great, has recently issued an elaborate ukase for the purpose of bringing about, in due time, the complete abolition of serfdom throughout his vast empire. In Moscow, at a banquet held on the 9th of January, 1858, in éclat of the emperor's ukase, and in furtherance of the plans proposed for the emancipation of the serfs, M. Bapst, the eminent Russian professor of political economy, said:

"We have met here to celebrate an event which will be an epoch in the annals of our history, and upon which future historians will dwell with pleasure. At the very commencement of this century, one of our first manufacturers said to Storch, that trade could never flourish under our system of compulsory labor or, in other words, of serfage; already, in 1849, the Free Economical Society proved by facts the inconveniences of serfage as regards agriculture. The development of national wealth has ever gone hand-in-hand with the regular organization of popular labor, which, as it gradually emancipates itself from stringent conditions, becomes more active, more progressive, and consequently more productive. In proportion as national labor gradually issues forth free from such disadvantageous conditions, the love of work increases among the people. Emulation and competition arouse the sleeping energies of the nation; they will not allow them to rust, and excite them to healthy activity and continual progress. The day of the primitive forms of the economical condition of the people has now left us forever. The wants of a great nation increase daily, and cannot be satisfied with the coarse conditions contrary to all progress of primitive economy founded on compulsory labor—a labor the limits of which are as restricted as its nature is unproductive. Our task is not to double, but to increase tenfold our productive power, our labor, our wealth, unless we wish to see taken away from us by nations more advanced than ourselves the markets which are ours by tradition and by our geographical position."

On the same occasion, M. Pauloff, one of Professor Bapst's most worthy compatriots, said:

"Heaven has allowed us to live long enough to witness the second regeneration of Russia. We may congratulate ourselves, for this movement is one of great importance. We breathe more like Christians, our hearts beat more nobly, and we may look at the light of heaven with a clearer eye. We have met to-day to express our deep and sincere sympathy for a holy and praiseworthy work, and we meet without any nervousness to mar our rejoicing. A new spirit animates us, a new era has commenced. One of our social conditions is on the eve of a change. If we consider it in a past light, we may perhaps admit that it was necessary that it should have been allowed to be as it was from the want of a better administrative organization, and of the concentration in the hands of a government of the means which have since given so great a development to the power of Russia. But what was momentarily gained to the State was lost to mankind. The advantage cost an enormous price. Order without—anarchy within—and the condition of the individual cast its shadow over society at large. The emperor has struck at the roots of this evil. The glory and prosperity of Russia cannot rest upon institutions based on injustice and falsehood. No! these blessings are henceforth to be found in the path thrown open by him whose name Russia pronounces with respect and pride. The emperor has ceded this great reform, which he might have accomplished by his own powerful will, by asking the nobles to take the initiative. Let us then hail this noble idea, inspired by the sole wish for the welfare of his people, with that enlightened heartiness which may now be expected from Russia. Let us not, however, suppose that the path traced by history is an avenue of roses without thorns. This would be sheer ignorance. When a new, a more moral and Christian state of things is about to be established, the obstacles that will have to be encountered must not be taken into consideration, except with the hope that the torrent of the new life will sweep them away. The change in the economical condition of our national existence will arouse our individual energies, the want of which is one of our greatest evils. Let us wish, then, gentlemen, from our innermost heart, a long life to him who has marshalled his faithful Russia to the conquest of truth and justice."

THE VOICE OF ITALY.

CICERO says:

"By the grand laws of nature, all men are born free, and this law is universally binding upon all men."

Again he says:

"Eternal justice is the basis of all human laws."

Again:

"Law is not something wrought out by man's ingenuity, nor is it a decree of the people, but it is something eternal, governing the world by the wisdom of its commands and prohibitions."

Again:

"Whatever is just is also the true law, nor can this true law be abrogated by any written enactments."

Again :

" If there be such a power in the decrees and commands of fools, that the nature of things is changed by their votes, why do they not decree that what is bad and pernicious shall be regarded as good and wholesome ; or why, if the law can make wrong right, can it not make bad good ?"

Again :

" Those who have made pernicious and unjust decrees, have made anything rather than laws."

Again :

" The law of all nations forbids one man to pursue his advantage at the expense of another."

LACTANTIUS says :

" Justice teaches men to know God and to love men, to love and assist one another, being all equally the children of God."

LEO X. says :

" Not only does the Christian religion, but nature herself cry out against the state of slavery."

THE VOICE OF GREECE.

SOCRATES says :

" Slavery is a system of outrage and robbery."

ARISTOTLE says :

" It is neither for the good, nor is it just, seeing all men are by nature alike, and equal, that one should be lord and master over others."

POLYBIUS says :

" None but unprincipled and beastly men in society assume the mastery over their fellows, as it is among bulls, bears, and cocks."

PLATO says :

" Slavery is a system of the most complete injustice."

From each of the above, and from other nations, additional testimony is at hand ; but, for reasons already assigned, we forbear to introduce it. Corroborative of the correctness of the position which we have assumed, even Persia has a voice, which may be easily recognized in the tones of her immortal Cyrus, who says :

" To fight, in order not to be made a slave, is noble."

Than Great Britain no nation has more heartily or honorably repented of the crime of slavery—no nation, on the perception of its error, has ever acted with more prompt magnanimity to its outraged and unhappy bondsmen. Entered to her credit, many precious jewels of liberty remain in our possession, ready to be delivered when called for ; of their value some idea may be formed, when we state that they are filigreed with such names as Wilberforce, Buxton, Granville, Grattan, Camden, Clarkson, Sharp, Sheridan, Sidney, Martin, and Macaulay.

Virginia, the Carolinas, and other Southern States, which are pro-

vided, not with republican, but with anti-republican forms of government, and which have abolished freedom, should learn, from the history
of the monarchical governments of the Old World, if not from the example of the more liberal and enlightened portions of the New, how to
abolish slavery. The lesson is before them in a variety of exceedingly
interesting forms, and, sooner or later, they must learn it, either voluntarily or by compulsion. Virginia, in particular, is a spoilt child,
having been the pet of the General Government for the last seventy
years; and like many other other spoilt children, she has become fro-
ward, peevish, perverse, sulky and irreverent—not caring to know her
duties, and failing to perform even those which she does know. Her
superiors perceive that the abolition of slavery would be a blessing to
her; she is, however, either too ignorant to understand the truth, or
else, as is the more probable, her false pride and obstinacy restrain her
from acknowledging it. What is to be done? Shall ignorance, or
prejudice, or obduracy, or willful meanness, triumph over knowledge,
and liberality, and guilelessness, and laudable enterprise? No, never!
Assured that Virginia and all the other slaveholding States are doing
wrong every day, it is our duty to make them do right, if we have the
power; and we believe we have the power now resident within their
own borders. What are the opinions, generally, of the non-slaveholding
whites? Let them speak.

CHAPTER VI.

TESTIMONY OF THE CHURCHES.

Who blushed alike to be, or have a slave—
Unchristian thought! on what pretence soe'er,
Of right inherited, or else acquired;
Of loss, or profit, or what plea you name,
To buy or sell, to barter, whip, and hold
In chains a being of celestial make—
Of kindred form, of kindred faculties,
Of kindred feelings, passions, thoughts, **desires;**
Born free, and heir of an immortal hope!
Thought villainous, absurd, detestable!
Unworthy to be harbored in a fiend!

POLLOK.

Lo! the nation is arousing,
  From its slumber, long and deep;
And the Church of God is waking,
  Never, never more to sleep,
    While a bondman,
  In his chains remains to weep.

OLIVER JOHNSON.

IN quest of arguments against slavery, we have perused the works **of** several eminent Christian writers of different denominations, and we now proceed to lay before the reader the result of a portion of our labor. As it is the special object of this chapter to operate on, to correct and cleanse the consciences of slaveholding professors of religion, we shall adduce testimony only from the five churches to which they, in their satanic piety, mostly belong—the Presbyterian, the Episcopal, the Baptist, the Methodist, and the Roman Catholic—all of which, we hope, are destined, at no distant day, to become thoroughly imbued with the spirit of Heaven-ordained Love and Freedom. With few exceptions, all the other Christian sects are, as they should be, avowedly and inflexibly opposed to the inhuman institution of slavery. The Congregational, the Quaker, the Lutheran, the Dutch and German Reformed, the Unitarian and the Universalist, especially, are all honorable, able, and eloquent defenders of the natural rights of man. We will begin by introducing a mass of

PRESBYTERIAN TESTIMONY.

The Rev. Albert Barnes, of Philadelphia, one of the most learned Presbyterian preachers and commentators of the day, says:

130

" There is a deep and growing conviction in the minds of the mass of mankind, that slavery violates the great laws of our nature ; that it is contrary to the dictates of humanity ; that it is essentially unjust, oppressive and cruel ; that it invades the rights of liberty with which the Author of our being has endowed all human beings; and that, in all the forms in which it has ever existed, it has been impossible to guard it from what its friends and advocates would call ' *abuses* of the system.' It is a violation of the first sentiments expressed in our Declaration of Independence, and on which our fathers founded the vindication of their own conduct in an appeal to arms. It is at war with all that a man claims for himself and for his own children ; and it is opposed to all the struggles of mankind, in all ages, for freedom. The claims of humanity plead against it. The struggles for freedom everywhere in our world condemn it. The instinctive feeling in every man's own bosom in regard to himself is a condemnation of it. The noblest deeds of valor, and of patriotism in our own land, and in all lands where men have struggled for freedom, are a condemnation of the system. All that is noble in man is opposed to it ; all that is base, oppressive, and cruel, pleads for it.

" The spirit of the New Testament is against slavery, and the principles of the New Testament, if fairly applied, would abolish it. In the New Testament no man is commanded to purchase and own a slave ; no man is commended as adding anything to the evidences of his Christian character, or as performing the appropriate duty of a Christian, for owning one. Nowhere in the New Testament is the institution referred to as a good one, or as a desirable one. It is commonly—indeed, it is almost universally—conceded that the proper application of the principles of the New Testament would abolish slavery everywhere, or that, the state of things which will exist when the Gospel shall be fairly applied to all the relations of life, slavery will not be found among those relations.

" Let slavery be removed from the church, and let the voice of the church, with one accord, be lifted up in favor of freedom ; let the church be wholly detached from the institution, and let there be adopted by all its ministers and members an interpretation of the Bible—as I believe there may be and ought to be—that shall be in accordance with the deep-seated principles of our nature in favor of freedom, and with our own aspirations for liberty, and with the sentiments of the world in its onward progress in regard to human rights, and not only would a very material objection against the Bible be taken away—and one which would be fatal if it were well founded—but the establishment of a very strong argument *in favor* of the Bible, as a revelation from God, would be the direct result of such a position."

Writing " To a certain elder of a certain Presbyterian Church," of which church he himself is a member,

PROF. C. D. CLEVELAND says :

" What, let me ask, can tend more to shake the belief of men in the divine inspiration of the sacred Scriptures, than to endeavor to prove to them, that these same Scriptures—the foundation rock of our faith—sanction such a man-brutalizing crime as American Slavery ? The natural conscience of man, all the world over, revolts with loathing at this monstrous crime ; and the law of nations has pronounced the slave trade to be piracy, condemning to the gallows those found guilty of it ; and a sad day will it be for Christianity, if men shall be brought to believe that their natural conscience and the laws of nations are higher, in their moral standard, than what claims to be the revealed will of God."

From a resolution denunciatory of slavery, unanimously adopted by the General Assembly of the Presbyterian Church, in 1818, we make the following extract :

" We consider the voluntary enslaving of one part of the human race by another as a gross violation of the most precious and sacred rights of human nature, as utterly inconsistent with the law of God, which requires us to love our neighbor as ourselves, and as totally irreconcilable with the spirit and principles of the Gospel of Christ, which enjoins that ' all things whatsoever ye would that men should do to you, do ye even so to them.' . . . We rejoice that the church to which we belong commenced, as early as any other in this country, the good work of endeavoring to put an end to slavery, and that in the same work many of its members have ever since been, and now are, among the most active, vigorous, and efficient laborers. . . . We earnestly exhort them to continue, and, if possible, to increase, their exertions to effect a total abolition of slavery."

A Committee of the Synod of Kentucky, in an address to the Presbyterians of that State, says

"That our negroes will be worse off, if emancipated, is, we feel, but a specious pretext for lulling our own pangs of conscience, and answering the argument of the philanthropist. None of us believes that God has so created a whole race that it is better for them to remain in perpetual bondage."

EPISCOPAL TESTIMONY.

BISHOP HORSLEY says:

"Slavery is injustice, which no consideration of policy can extenuate."

BISHOP BUTLER says:

"Despicable as the negroes may appear in our eyes, they are the creatures of God, and of the race of mankind, for whom Christ died, and it is inexcusable to keep them in ignorance of the end for which they were made, and of the means whereby they may become partakers of the general redemption."

BISHOP PORTEUS says:

"The Bible classes men-stealers or slave-traders among the murderers of fathers and mothers, and the most profane criminals on earth."

Thomas Scott, the celebrated Commentator, says:

"To number the persons of men with beasts, sheep and horses, as the stock of a farm, or with bales of goods, as the cargo of a ship, is, no doubt, a most detestable and anti-Christian practice."

John Jay, Esq., of the City of New York—a most exemplary Episcopalian—in a pamphlet entitled, "Thoughts on the Duty of the Episcopal Church, in Relation to Slavery," says:

"Alas! for the expectation that she would conform to the spirit of her ancient mother! She has not merely remained a mute and careless spectator of this great conflict of truth and justice with hypocrisy and cruelty, but her very priests and deacons may be seen ministering at the altar of slavery, offering their talents and influence at its unholy shrine, and openly repeating the awful blasphemy, that the precepts of our Saviour sanction the system of American slavery. Her Northern clergy, with rare exceptions, whatever they may feel on the subject, rebuke it neither in public nor in private, and her periodicals, far from advancing the progress of abolition, at times oppose our societies, impliedly defending slavery, as not incompatible with Christianity, and occasionally withholding information useful to the cause of freedom."

A writer in a late number of "The Anti-Slavery Churchman," published in Geneva, Wisconsin, speaking of a certain portion of the New Testament, says:

"This passage of Paul places necessary work in the hands of Gospel ministers. If they preach the whole Gospel, they must preach what this passage enjoins—and if they do this, they must preach against American slavery. Its being connected with politics does not shield them. Political connections cannot place sin under protection. They cannot throw around it guards that the public teachers of morals may not pass. Sin is a violation of God's law—and God's law must be proclaimed and enforced at all hazards. This is the business of the messenger of God, and if anything stands in its way, it is his right, rather it his solemn commission, to go forward—straightway to overpass the lines that would shut him out, and utter his warnings. Many sins there are, that in like manner, might be shielded. Fashion, and rank, and business, are doing their part to keep much sin in respectability, and excuse it from the attacks of God's ministers. But what are these, that they should seal a minister's lips—what more are the wishes of politicians?"

For further testimony from this branch of the Christian system, if desired, we refer the reader to the Rev. Dr. Tyng, the Rev. Evan M. Johnson, and the Rev. J. McNamara,—all Broad Church Episcopalians, whose magic eloquence and irresistible arguments bid fair, at an early day, to win over to the paths of progressive freedom, truth, justice and humanity, the greater number of their High and Low Church brethren.

BAPTIST TESTIMONY.

Concerning a certain text, the Rev. Wm. H. Brisbane, once a slave-holding Baptist in South Carolina, says :

" Paul was speaking of the law having been made for men-stealers. Where is the record of that law? It is in Exodus xxi. 16, and in these words: ' He that stealeth a man, and selleth him, or if he be found in his possession, he shall surely be put to death.' Here it will be perceived that it was a crime to sell the man, for which the seller must suffer death. But it was no less a crime to hold him as a slave, for this also was punishable with death. A man may be kidnapped out of slavery into freedom. There was no law against that. And why? Because kidnapping a slave and placing him in a condition of freedom, was only to restore him to his lost rights. But if a man who takes him becomes a slaveholder, or a slave seller, then he is a criminal, liable to the penalty of death, because he robs the man of liberty. Perhaps some will say this law was only applicable to the first holder of the slave, that is, the original kidnapper, but not to his successors who might have purchased or inherited him. But what is kidnapping? Suppose I propose to a neighbor to give him a certain sum of money if he will steal a white child in Carolina and deliver him to me. I pay him the money upon his delivering the child to me. Is it not my act as fully as his? Am I not also the thief? But does it alter the case whether I agree beforehand or not to pay him, for the child? He steals him, and then sells him to me. He is found by his parents in my hands. Will it avail me to say I purchased him and paid my money for him? Will it not be asked, Do you not know that a white person is not merchantable? And shall I not have to pay the damage for detaining that child in my service as a slave? Assuredly, not only in the eyes of the law, but in the judgment of the whole community, I would be regarded a criminal. So when one man steals another and offers him for sale, no one, in view of the Divine law, can buy him, for the reason that the Divine law forbids that man shall in the first place be made a merchantable article. The inquiry must be, if I buy, I buy in violation of the Divine law, and it will not do for me to plead that I bought him. I have him in possession, and that is enough, God condemns me for it as a man-stealer. My having him in possession is evidence against me, and the Mosaic law says, if he be found in my hands, I must die. Now, when Paul said the law was made for men-stealers, was it not also saying the law was made for slaveholders? I am not intending to apply this term in a harsh spirit. But I am bound, as I fear God, to speak what I am satisfied is the true meaning of the apostle."

In his " Elements of Moral Science," the Rev. Francis Wayland, D.D., one of the most erudite and distinguished Baptists now living, says:

" The moral precepts of the Bible are diametrically opposed to slavery. They are, Thou shalt love thy *neighbor* as *thyself*, and *all things whatsoever* ye would that men should do unto you, do ye even so unto them.

" The application of these precepts is universal. Our neighbor is *every one whom we may benefit.* The obligation respects *all things whatsoever.* The precept, then, manifestly, extends to *men as men,* or *men of every condition;* and if to all things whatsoever, certainly to a thing so important as the right to personal liberty.

" Again. By this precept, it is made our duty to cherish as tender and delicate a respect for the right which the meanest individual possesses over the means of happiness bestowed upon him by God, as we cherish for our own right over our own means of happiness, or as we desire any other individual to cherish for it. Now, were this precept obeyed, it is manifest that slavery could not in fact exist for a single instant. The principle of the precept is absolutely subversive of the principle of slavery. That of the one is the entire equality of right; that of the other, the entire absorption of the rights of one in the rights of the other."

"If any one doubts respecting the bearing of the Scripture precept upon this case, a few plain questions may throw additional light upon the subject. For instance:

"Do the precepts and the spirit of the Gospel allow me to derive my support from a system which extorts labor from my fellow-men, without allowing them any voice in the equivalent which they shall receive; and which can only be sustained by keeping them in a state of mental degradation, and by shutting them out. in a great degree. from the means of salvation:

"Would the master be willing that another person should subject him to slavery, for the same reasons, and on the same grounds that he holds his slaves in bondage?

"Would the Gospel allow us, if it were in our power, to reduce our fellow-citizens of our own color to slavery? If the Gospel be diametrically opposed to the *principle* of slavery, it must be opposed to the *practice* of slavery; and therefore, were the principles of the Gospel fully adopted, slavery could not exist.

"The very course which the Gospel takes on this subject, seems to have been the only one that could have been taken, in order to effect the universal abolition of slavery. The Gospel was designed, not for one race or for one time, but for all races and for all times.. It looked not at the abolition of this form of evil for that age alone, but for its universal abolition. Hence, the important object of its Author was, to gain it a lodgment in every part of the known world; so that, by its universal diffusion among all classes of society, it might quietly and peacefully modify and subdue the evil passions of men; and thus without violence, work a revolution in the whole mass of mankind.

"If the system be wrong, as we have endeavored to show, if it be at variance with our duty both to God and to man, it must be abandoned. If it be asked when, I ask again when shall a man begin to cease doing wrong? Is not the answer, *immediately?* If a man is injuring us, do we ever doubt as to the time when he ought to cease? There is, then, no doubt in respect to the time when we ought to cease inflicting injury upon others."

Abraham Booth, an eminent theological writer of the Baptist persuasion, says:

"I have not a stronger conviction of scarcely anything, than that slaveholding (except where the slave has forfeited his liberty by crimes against society), is wicked and inconsistent with Christian character. To me it is evident, that whoever would purchase an innocent black man to make him a slave, would with equal readiness purchase a white one for the same purpose, could he do it with equal impunity and no more disgrace."

At a meeting of the General Committee of the Baptists of Virginia, in 1789, the following resolution was offered by Eld. John Leland, and adopted:

"*Resolved*, That slavery is a violent deprivation of the rights of nature, and inconsistent with Republican government, and therefore we recommend it to our brethren to make use of every measure to extirpate this horrid evil from the land; and pray Almighty God that our honorable legislature may have it in their power to proclaim the great jubilee, consistent with the principles of good policy."

METHODIST TESTIMONY.

John Wesley, the celebrated founder of Methodism, says:

"Men buyers are exactly on a level with men stealers."

Again, he says:

"American slavery is the vilest that ever saw the sun; it constitutes the sum of all villainies."

The learned Dr. Adam Clarke, author of a voluminous commentary on the Scriptures, says:

"Slave-dealers, whether those who carry on the traffic in human flesh and blood, or those who steal a person in order to sell him into bondage, or those who buy such stolen men or women, no matter of what color or what country; or the nations who legalize or connive at such traffic; all these are men-stealers, and God classes them with the most flagitious of mortals."

One of the present members of the Black River (New York) Conference, a gentleman of fine ability, who is zealous in every good word and work,

PROF. HIRAM MATTISON, says:

"The attitude of the American churches in regard to slavery—that parent of every other abomination, is not only strengthening the hands of infidelity against Christianity in France and England, but in every other nominally Christian country; and especially in these United States. It is sapping the very foundations of all confidence in the Christian religion, in the minds of tens of thousands. Not distinguishing between the loathsome cancer and the rest of the body—between the counterfeit and the genuine—they condemn the whole, and are thenceforth regarded as infidels. Instead of a slaveholding religion they accept no religion. And infidelity has no more faithful allies in America, than the D.D.'s and other ministers who defend, or at least apologize for American slavery. They are making more infidels than all the infidel books, and periodicals, and lecturers in the land. Let us, then, on this account also —its tendency to infidelity—rise up and put away all slaveholding from the Church of Christ."

Again, laying before us a list of the churches which are righteously active in condemning and opposing slavery, and also of those which are wickedly passive in excusing and upholding it, he says to his brother Methodists:

"Look at our position as a Church in the light of these facts. See in what company we place ourselves. Let us range the anti-slavery and pro-slavery Northern Churches in parallel columns, that our shame may be the more apparent:

Anti-Slavery Churches.	*Slave-holding Churches.*
1. FRIENDS, or QUAKERS.	1. OLD SCHOOL PRESBYTERIAN.
2. FREE-WILL BAPTISTS.	2. PROTESTANT EPISCOPAL.
3. UNITED BRETHREN.	3. ROMAN CATHOLIC.
4. ASSOCIATE PRESBYTERIAN.	4. METHODIST EPIS. CHURCH!"
5. WESLEYAN METHODISTS.	
6. ORTHODOX CONGREGATIONAL.	
7. GENERAL BAPTISTS.	
8. REF'D PROT. DUTCH CHURCH.	
9. NEW SCHOOL PRESBYTERIAN.	
10. UNITARIAN.	
11. UNIVERSALISTS!	

One of the rules laid down in the Methodist Discipline as amended in 1784, was as follows:

"Every member of our Society who has slaves in his possession, shall, within twelve months after notice given to him by the assistant, legally execute and record an instrument, whereby he emancipates and sets free every slave in his possession."

Another rule was in these words:

"No person holding slaves shall in future be admitted into Society, or to the Lord's Supper, till he previously complies with these rules concerning slavery."

The answer to the question—"What shall be done with those who buy or sell slaves, or give them away"—is couched in the following language:

"They are immediately to be expelled, unless they buy them on purpose to free them."

In 1785, the voice of this church was heard as follows:

"We do hold in the deepest abhorrence the practice of slavery, and shall not cease to seek its destruction, by all wise and prudent means."

In 1797, the Discipline contained the following wholesome paragraph

" The preachers and other members of our Society are requested to consider the subject of Negro slavery, with deep attention, and that they impart to the General Conference, through the medium of the Yearly Conferences, or otherwise, any important thoughts on the subject, that the Conference may have full light, in order to take further steps toward eradicating this enormous evil from that part of the Church of God with which they are connected. The annual Conferences are directed to draw up addresses for the gradual emancipation of the slaves, to the legislatures of those States in which no general laws have been passed for that purpose. These addresses shall urge, in the most respectful but pointed manner, the necessity of a law for the gradual emancipation of slaves. Proper committees shall be appointed by the Annual Conferences, out of the most respectable of our friends, for conducting the business; and presiding elders, elders, deacons, and travelling preachers, shall procure as many proper signatures as possible to the addresses, and give all the assistance in their power, in every respect, to aid the committees, and to forward the blessed undertaking. Let this be continued from year to year, till the desired end be accomplished."

CATHOLIC TESTIMONY.

It has been only about twenty-two years since Pope Gregory XVI. immortalized himself by issuing the famous Bull against slavery, from which the following is an extract:

" Placed as we are on the Supreme seat of the apostles, and acting, though by no merits of our own, as the vicegerent of Jesus Christ, the Son of God, who, through his great mercy, condescended to make himself man, and to die for the redemption of the world, we regard as a duty devolving on our pastoral functions, that we endeavor to turn aside our faithful flocks entirely from the inhuman traffic in negroes, or any other human beings whatever. . . . In progress of time, as the clouds of heathen superstition became gradually dispersed, circumstances reached that point, that during several centuries there were no slaves allowed amongst the great majority of the Christian nations; but with grief we are compelled to add, that there afterwards arose, even among the faithful, a race of men, who, basely blinded by the appetite and desire of sordid lucre, did not hesitate to reduce, in remote regions of the earth, Indians, negroes, and other wretched beings, to the misery of slavery; or, finding the trade established and augmented, to assist the shameful crime of others. Nor did many of the most glorious of the Roman Pontiffs omit severely to reprove their conduct, as injurious to their soul's health, and disgraceful to the Christian name. Among these may be especially quoted the bull of Paul III., which bears the date of the 29th of May, 1537, addressed to the Cardinal Archbishop of Toledo, and another still more comprehensive, by Urban VIII., dated the 22d of April, 1636, to the collector Jurius of the Apostolic chamber in Portugal, most severely castigating by name those who presumed to subject either East or West Indians to slavery, to sell, buy, exchange, or give them away, to separate them from their wives and children, despoil them of their goods and property, to bring or transmit them to other places, or by any means to deprive them of liberty, or retain them in slavery; also most severely castigating those who should presume or dare to afford counsel, aid, favor or assistance, under any pretence, or borrowed color, to those doing the aforesaid; or should preach or teach that it is lawful, or should otherwise presume or dare to coöperate, by any possible means, with the aforesaid. . . . Wherefore, we, desiring to divert this disgrace from the whole confines of Christianity, having summoned several of our venerable brothers, their Eminences the Cardinals, of the H. R. Church, to our council, and, having maturely deliberated on the whole matter, pursuing the footsteps of our predecessors, admonished by our apostolical authority, and urgently invoke in the Lord, all Christians, of whatever condition, that none henceforth dare to subject to slavery, unjustly persecute, or despoil of their goods, Indians, negroes, or other classes of men, or be accessories to others, or furnish them aid or assistance in so doing; and on no account henceforth to exercise that inhuman traffic by which negroes are reduced to slavery, as if they were not men, but automata or chattels, and are sold in defiance of all the laws of justice and humanity, and devoted to severe and intolerable labors. We further reprobate, by our apostolical authority, all the above-described offences as utterly unworthy of the Christian name; and by the same authority we rigidly prohibit and interdict all and every individual, whether ecclesiastical or laical, from presuming to defend that commerce in negro slaves under pretence or borrowed color, or to teach or publish in any manner, publicly or privately, things contrary to the admonitions which we have given in these letters.

" And, finally, that these, our letters, may be rendered more apparent to all, and that no person may allege any ignorance thereof, we decree and order that it shall be published according to custom, and copies thereof be properly affixed to the gates of St. Peter and of the Apostolic Chancel, every and in like manner to the General Court of Mount Citatorio, and in the field of the Campus Floræ and also through the city, by one of our heralds, according to aforesaid custom.

" Given at Rome, at the Palace of Santa Maria Major, under the seal of the fisherman, on the 3d day of December, 1837, and in the ninth year of our pontificate.

" Countersigned by Cardinal A. Lambruschini."

We have already quoted the language of Pope Leo X., who says:

" Not only does the Christian religion, but nature herself, cry out against the state of slavery."

The Abbé Raynal says:

" He who supports slavery is the enemy of the human race. He divides it into two societies of legal assassins, the oppressors and the oppressed. I shall not be afraid to cite to the tribunal of reason and justice those governments which tolerate this cruelty, or which even are not ashamed to make it the basis of their power."

From the proceedings of a Massachusetts Anti-slavery Convention in 1855, we make the following extract:

" Henry Kemp, a Roman Catholic, came forward to defend the Romish Church in reply to Mr. Foster. He claimed that the Catholic Church is thoroughly anti-slavery—as thoroughly as even his friend Foster."

Thus manfully do men of pure hearts and noble minds, whether in Church or State, and without regard to sect or party, lift up their voices against the wicked and pernicious system of human slavery. Thus they speak, and thus they are obliged to speak, if they speak at all ; it is only the voice of Nature, Justice, Truth, and Love, that issues from them. The divine principle in man prompts him to speak and strike for Freedom ; the diabolical principle within him prompts him to speak and strike for slavery.

From those churches which are now—as all churches ought to be, and will be, ere the world becomes Christianized—thoroughly indoctrinated in the principles of freedom, we do not, as already intimated, deem it particularly necessary to bring forward new arguments in opposition to slavery. If, however, the reader would be pleased to hear from the churches to which we chiefly allude—and, by the by, he might hear from them with much profit to himself—we respectfully refer him to Henry Ward Beecher, George B. Cheever, Joseph P. Thompson, Theodore Parker, E. H. Chapin, and H. W. Bellows, of the North, and to M. D. Conway, John G. Fee, James S. Davis, Daniel Worth, and W. E. Lincoln, of the South. All these reverend gentlemen, ministers of different denominations, feel it their duty to preach against slavery, and, to their honor be it said, they do preach against it with unabated zeal and success. Our earnest prayer is, that Heaven may enable them, their contemporaries and successors, to preach against it with such energy and effect, as will cause it in due time, to disappear forever from the soil of our Republic.

CHAPTER VII.

BIBLE TESTIMONY.

Quench, righteous God, the thirst,
That Congo's sons hath curs'd—
 The thirst for gold !
Shall not thy thunders speak,
Where Mammon's altars reek,
Where maids and matrons shriek,
Bound, bleeding, sold ?
                          PIERPONT.

EVERY person who has read the Bible, and who has a proper under-standing of its leading moral precepts, feels in his own conscience, that it is an original and complete anti-slavery book. In a crude state of society—in a barbarous age—when men were in a manner destitute of wholesome laws, either human or divine, it is possible that a mild form of slavery may have been tolerated, and even regulated, as an insti-tution clothed with the importance of temporary recognition; but the Deity never approved it, and for the very reason that it is impossible for him to do wrong, he never will, never can approve it. The worst sys-tem of servitude of which we have any account in the Bible—and, by the way, it furnishes no account of anything so bad as slavery (the evil-one and his hot home alone excepted)—was far less rigorous and atrocious than that now established in the Southern States of this Confederacy. Even that system, however, the worst, which seems to have been prac-tised to a considerable extent by those venerable old fogies, Abraham, Isaac, and Jacob, was one of the monstrous inventions of Satan that God "winked" at; and, to the mind of the biblical scholar, nothing can be more evident than that He determined of old, that it should, in due time, be abolished. To say that the Bible sanctions slavery is equivalent to saying that the sun loves darkness; to say that one man was created to domineer over another is to call in question the justice, mercy and goodness of God.

We will now listen to a limited number of the

PRECEPTS AND SAYINGS OF THE OLD TESTAMENT.

" Proclaim liberty throughout all the land, unto all the inhabitants thereof."

" He that stealeth a man, and selleth him, or if he be found in his hand, he shall surely be put to death."

"Whoso stoppeth his ears at the cry of the poor, he also shall cry, but shall not be heard."

"He that oppresseth the poor reproacheth his Maker."

"Relieve the oppressed."

"Envy thou not the oppressor, and choose none of his ways."

"Let the oppressed go free."

"Thou shalt love thy neighbor as thyself."

"Thou shalt not respect the person of the poor, nor honor the person of the mighty; but in righteousness shalt thou judge thy neighbor."

"The wages of him that is hired shall not abide with thee all night until the morning."

"Do justice to the afflicted and needy; rid them out of the hand of the wicked."

"Execute judgment and justice; take away your exactions from my people, saith the Lord God."

"Therefore thus saith the Lord; ye have not hearkened unto me, in proclaiming liberty, every one to his brother, and every man to his neighbor: behold, I proclaim a liberty for you, saith the Lord, to the sword, to the pestilence, and to the famine; and I will make you to be removed into all the kingdoms of the earth."

"I will be a swift witness against the sorcerers, and against the adulterers, and against false swearers, and against those that oppress the hireling in his wages, the widow, and the fatherless, and that turn aside the stranger from his right, and fear not me, saith the Lord of Hosts."

"As the partridge setteth on eggs, and hatcheth them not; so he that getteth riches, and not by right, shall leave them in the midst of his days, and at his end shall be a fool."

And now let us listen to a few selected

PRECEPTS AND SAYINGS OF THE NEW TESTAMENT.

"Call no man master, neither be ye called masters."

"Where the spirit of the Lord is, there is liberty."

"If thou mayest be made free, use it rather."

"Do good to all men, as ye have opportunity."

"The laborer is worthy of his hire."

"All things whatsoever ye would that men should do to you, do ye even so to them."

"Be kindly affectionate one to another with brotherly love; in honor preferring one another."

"Stand fast therefore in the liberty wherewith Christ hath made you free, and be not entangled again with the yoke of bondage."

Some years ago a clerical sycophant of the slave power had the temerity to publish a book or pamphlet entitled " Bible defence of Slavery," which the Baltimore *Sun*, in the course of a caustic criticism, handled in the following manner :

"Bible defence of slavery! There is no such thing as a Bible defence of slavery at the present day. Slavery in the United States is a social institution, originating in the convenience and cupidity of our ancestors, existing by State laws, and recognized to a certain extent—for the recovery of slave property—by the Constitution. And nobody would pretend that, if it were inexpedient and unprofitable for any man or any State to continue to hold slaves, they would be bound to do so on the ground of a 'Bible defence' of it. Slavery is recorded in the Bible, and approved, with many degrading characteristics. War is recorded in the Bible, and approved, under what seems to us the extreme of cruelty. But are slavery and war to *endure* for ever because we find them in the Bible? or are they to *cease* at once and for ever because the Bible inculcates peace and brotherhood?"

The Haleys, Legrees and Peterkins of the South—boors of Vandalic hearts and minds—are, ever and anon, manifesting some of the most palpable and ridiculous idiosyncrasies of human nature. Ignorant of even the first lessons of a hornbook, they bandy among themselves, in traditionary order, certain garbled passages of Scripture, such, for instance, as that concerning poor old besotted Noah's intemperate curse of Ham, which, in shame and pity be it said, they regard, or pretend to regard, as investing them with full and perfect license to practise and perpetuate their most unhallowed system of iniquity. Such are the hardened, crafty creatures in human form, who, following the example of their subtle sire, when he perched himself on a pinnacle of the temple at Jerusalem, quote Scripture, without even the semblance of a blush, in the prosecution of their treasons, strategems and spoils. Such are the veritable actors, who, with "Southside Doctors of Divinity," Bible in hand, as prompters, are unceasingly performing the horrible tragedy of Human Slavery. From all such gross and irreverent distorters of Biblical truth, good Lord deliver us!

CHAPTER VIII.

It was the intention of the fathers of the Constitution that liberty should be national and slavery sectional. James Madison, himself a slaveholder, one of the framers of the Constitution, afterward Governor of Virginia, and then President of the United States, tells us why slavery was not mentioned in that instrument. He said that, when the institution of slavery had ceased to exist in this land, they did not wish the memory of it to remain on record. . . . . Shadows of the days that are past gather around me. I am standing as I have stood, as a reed shaken by the wind, as the voice of one crying in the wilderness. What argument have I not exhausted, to what sentiment have I not appealed? And I have called upon every living thing in vain; yet when I remember that all the experience of the ages is concentrated in our Constitution, I return once more to the charge, and I would that my voice could extend to every palace, and to every cabin throughout this wide Republic, that I might say to you, Arouse from your fatal delusion ; liberty and slavery cannot coexist; one or the other must die!—CASSIUS M. CLAY.

THE conflict between Freedom and Slavery is not simply a conflict between two diverse systems of labor, the one of which recognizes, while the other ignores, the manhood of the laborer; nor merely between two diverse policies, the one of which tends to enrich, and the other to impoverish society ; but it is, preëminently, a conflict between civilization with all its elevating and ameliorating influences, on the one side, and barbarism with all its rudeness and savagery, its ignorance and contempt of humanity, on the other. The very *existence* of slavery is incompatible with the highest order of social life. Fetich-worship does not more certainly indicate the degradation of the religious ideas of a people than does the chattelization of humanity mark an incomplete civilization. This element of barbarism, lingering in society wherever slavery lingers, makes itself particularly manifest in the present insane efforts of the oligarchy to reopen the foreign slave trade, not only at the expense of humanity and religion, but at the sacrifice of the national honor, and our position among the moral forces of the world.

How strikingly contrasts with this savagery of barbarism the present attitude of the great Russian Empire, as represented in the policy of the reigning emperor, Alexander the Second! With a far-seeing wisdom, which takes him out of the mob of vulgar potentates, and vindicates the kingship that belongs to a right royal nature, he has magnanimously resolved on the abolition of serfdom throughout his vast empire. The magnitude of the work proposed, considered simply in itself, and its still greater magnitude, considered in its far-reaching consequences, are beyond the grasp of any ordinary capacity, and must command for the young emperor, who has determinedly given himself to it, the sympathy and admiration of all true statesmen, philanthropists, and friends of freedom throughout the world. His enterprise is a mightier one than that which tasked the energies of his renowned ancestor, Peter the Great; and its successful accomplishment will give him a far more legitimate and lasting claim on the love and reverence of mankind. The one consolidated a great empire, the other will add millions of loyal subjects to it, by taking them out of the category of chattels, and giving them their proper status in the ranks of humanity. That this grand project will be crowned with success, the wisdom and energy with which the young emperor has set himself to the task, forbid us to doubt. And how it shames the despots of our own land, intent not only on the perpetuation of their pet barbarism, but on plunging the country into a still deeper slough of infamy and peril, by a reopening of the African slave trade, with all the bloody and sickening atrocities which it involves! Verily, the boasted enlightenment of our slavery propagandists is about on a par with that of New Zealand, and may well challenge the admiration of "South-side Doctors of Divinity," who devoutly regard the kidnapper as God's divinest messenger of salvation to the heathen world !

But a truce to these thoughts of men and measures abroad, and now to the contemporaneous Alexanders and others of our own country, beginning with

WILLIAM H. SEWARD.

In his masterly speech at Rochester, on Monday, Oct. 25, 1858, Senator Seward said :

" Free labor and slave labor—these antagonistic systems are continually coming into close contact, and collision results. Shall I tell you what this collision means ? They who think it is accidental, unnecessary, the work of interested or fanatical agitators, and therefore ephemeral, mistake the case altogether. It is an irrepressible conflict between opposing and enduring forces, and it means that the United States must and will, sooner or later, become either entirely a slaveholding nation, or entirely a free-labor nation. Either the cotton and rice fields of South Carolina and the sugar plantations of Louisiana will ultimately be tilled by free labor, and Charleston and New Orleans become marts for legitimate merchandise alone, or else the rye fields and wheat fields of Massachusetts and New York must again be surrendered by their farmers to slave culture and to the production of slaves, and Boston and New York become once more markets for trade in the bodies and souls of men."

At Buffalo, Friday, Oct. 19, 1855, he said :

" I have seen slavery in the slave States, and freedom in the free States. I have seen both slavery and freedom in this State. I know too well the evils of the former to be willing to spare any effort to prevent their return. The experience of New York tells the whole argument against slavery extension, the whole argument for universal freedom. Suppose that, fifty years ago, New York, like Virginia and Maryland, had clung to slavery, where now would have been these three composite millions of freemen, the choice and flower of Europe and America ? In that case, would superstition and false national pride have needed to organize a secret cabal, affiliated by unlawful oaths, to proscribe the exile and his children for their nativity or their conscience' sake ? Where would then have been the Erie Canal, the Genesee Valley Canal, the Oswego Canal, the Seneca and Cayuga Canal, the

Crooked Lake Canal, the Chemung Canal, the Chenango Canal, the Black River Canal, the Champlain Canal—where the imperial New York Central Railroad, the Erie Railroad, and the Ogdensburgh Railroad, with their branches penetrating not only every inhabited district in this State, but every inhabited region also in adja-cent States and in British America? Where would have been the colleges and academies, and, above all, the free common schools, yielding instruction to chil-dren of all sects and in all languages? Where the asylums and other public char-ities, and, above all, that noble emigrant charity which crowns the State with such distinguished honor? Where these ten thousand churches and cathedrals, renew-ing on every recurring Sabbath day the marvel of Pentecost, when the sojourner from every land hears the Gospel of Christ preached to him in his own tongue? Where would have been the steamers, the barges, brigs, and schooners, which crowd this harbor of Buffalo, bringing hither the productions of the Mississippi Valley and of the Gulf coast, in exchange for the fabrics of the Atlantic coast and of Europe, and of the teas and spices of Asia? Where the coasting vessels, the merchant ships, the clippers, the whale ships, and the ocean mail steamers, which are rapidly concentrating in our great seaport the commerce of the world? Where the American Navy, at once the representative and champion of the cause of uni-versal Republicanism? Where your inventors of steamboats, of electric telegraphs, and of planing machines—where your ingenious artisans—where your artists— where your mighty Press, the *Courier and Enquirer*, the *Tribune*, the *Times*, and even the *Herald* itself, defender of slavery as it is? Where your twenty cities— and where, above all, the merry, laughing agricultural industry of native-born and exotic laborers, enlivening the whole broad landscape, from the Lake coast to the Ocean's side? Go, ask Virginia—go, ask even noble Maryland, expending as she is a giant's strength in the serpent's coils, to show you her people, canals, rail-roads, universities, schools, charities, commerce, cities, and cultivated acres. Her silence is your expressive answer."

At Albany, Friday, Oct. 12, 1855, he said:

" So long as the Republican party shall be firm and faithful to the Constitution, the Union, and the Rights of Man, I shall serve it, with the reservation of that per-sonal independence which is my birthright, but at the same time with the zeal and devotion that patriotism allows and enjoins. I do not know, and personally I do not greatly care, that it shall work out its great ends this year, or the next, or in my lifetime; because I know that those ends are ultimately sure, and that time and trial are the elements which make all great reformations sure and lasting. I have not thus far lived for personal ends or temporary fame, and I shall not begin so late to live or labor for them. I have hoped that I might leave my country somewhat worthier of a lofty destiny, and the rights of human nature somewhat safer. A reasonable ambition must always be satisfied with sincere and practical endeavors. If, among those who shall come after us, there shall be any curious inquirer who shall fall upon a name so obscure as mine, he shall be obliged to confess that, however unsuccessfully I labored for generous ends, yet that I nevertheless was ever faithful, ever hopeful."

SALMON P. CHASE.

Addressing the Southern and Western Liberty Convention, at Cin-cinnati, June 11, 1845, Mr. Chase used the following unreserved, appro-priate language:

" It is our duty, and our purpose, to rescue the government from the control of the slaveholders; to harmonize its practical administration with the provisions of the Constitution, and to secure to all, without exception, and without partiality, the rights which the Constitution guarantees. We believe that slaveholding, in the United States, is the source of numberless evils, moral, social and political; that it hinders social progress; that it embitters public and private intercourse; that it degrades us as individuals, as States and as a nation; that it holds back our country from a splendid career of greatness and glory. We are, therefore, resolutely, inflexibly, at all times, and under all circumstances, hostile to its longer continu-ance in our land. We believe that its removal can be effected peacefully, con-stitutionally, without real injury to any, with the greatest benefit to all.

" We propose to effect this by repealing all legislation, and discontinuing all action, in favor of slavery at home and abroad; by prohibiting the practice of slaveholding in all places of exclusive national jurisdiction, in the District of Columbia, in American vessels upon the seas, in forts, arsenals, navy yards; by forbidding the employment of slaves upon any public work; by adopting resolutions in Congress, declaring that slaveholding, in all States created out of national territories, is unconstitutional, and recommending to the others the immediate adoption of measures for its extinction within their respective limits; and by electing and appointing to public station such men, and only such men, as openly avow our principles, and will honestly carry out our measures."

CASSIUS M. CLAY.

Of the great number of good speeches made by members of the Republican party during the Presidential campaign of 1856, it is, we believe, pretty generally admitted that the best one was made by Mr. Clay, of Kentucky, who, at the Tabernacle, in New York city, October 24th, said:

"If there are no manufactures, there is no commerce. In vain do the slaveholders go to Knoxville, to Nashville, to Memphis and to Charleston, and resolve that they will have nothing to do with these Abolition eighteen millions of Northern people; that they will build their own vessels, manufacture their own goods, ship their own products to foreign countries and break down New York, Philadelphia and Boston! Again, they resolve and reresolve, and yet there is not a single ton more shipped, and not a single article added, to the wealth of the South. But, gentlemen, they never invite such men as I am to attend their conventions. They know that I would tell them that slavery is the cause of their poverty, and that I will tell them that what they are aiming at is the dissolution of the Union—that they may be prepared to strike for that whenever the nation rises. They well know that by slave labor the very propositions which they make can never be realized; yet, when we show these things, they cry out, 'Oh, Cotton is King!' But when we look at the statistics, we find that so far from Cotton being King, Grass is King. There are nine articles of staple productions which are larger than that of cotton in this country.

"I suppose it does not follow, because slavery is endeavoring to modify the great dicta of our fathers, that cotton and free labor are incompatible. In the extreme South, at New Orleans, the laboring men—the stevedores and hackmen on the levee, where the heat is intensified by the proximity of the red brick buildings—are all white men, and they are in the full enjoyment of health. But how about cotton? I am informed by a friend of mine—himself a slaveholder, and therefore good authority—that in Northwestern Texas, among the German settlements, who, true to their national instincts, will not employ the labor of a slave, they produce more cotton to the acre, and of a better quality, and selling at prices from a cent to a cent and a half a pound higher than that produced by slave labor. This is an experiment that illustrates what I have always held, that whatever is right is expedient."

JOHN CHARLES FREMONT.

Accepting his nomination for the Presidency, in 1856, Mr. Fremont, one of the noblest sons of the South, said:

"I heartily concur in all movements which have for their object the repair of the mischiefs arising from the violation of good faith in the repeal of the Missouri Compromise. I am opposed to slavery in the abstract, and upon principles sustained and made habitual by long-settled convictions. I am inflexibly opposed to its extension on this continent beyond its present limits.

"The great body of non-slaveholding freemen, including those of the South, upon whose welfare slavery is an oppression, will discover that the power of the general government over the public lands may be beneficially exerted to advance their interests and secure their independence; knowing this, their suffrages will not be wanting to maintain that authority in the Union, which is absolutely essential to the maintenance of their own liberties, and which has more than once indicated the purpose of disposing of the public lands in such a way as would make every settler upon them a freeholder."

CHARLES SUMNER.

Speaking of the Crime against Kansas, in the United States Senate, on the 19th and 20th of May, 1856, Mr. Sumner, the scholarly and eloquent statesman—a gentleman and patriot, of whom it is not too much to say, there is not an ungenerous hair upon his head, nor an iota of discount in his composition—a prudent, fearless advocate of free labor, whom, ever since Brooks' dastardly assault upon him, on the 22d of May, 1856, we, as a Carolinian, have been eager (but have not yet had the opportunity) to grasp by the hand, and give from the South assurances of at least one hearty, unqualified condemnation of the outrage—said:

"The wickedness which I now begin to expose is immeasurably aggravated by the motive which prompted it. Not in any common lust for power did this uncommon tragedy have its origin. It is the rape of a virgin Territory, compelling it to the hateful embrace of slavery; and it may be clearly traced to a depraved longing for a new slave State, the hideous offspring of such a crime, in the hope of adding to the power of slavery in the national government. Yes, sir, when the whole world, alike Christian and Turk, is rising up to condemn this wrong, and to make it a hissing to the nations, here in our republic, force—aye, sir, force—has been openly employed in compelling Kansas to this pollution, and all for the sake of political power. There is the simple fact, which you will vainly attempt to deny, but which in itself presents an essential wickedness that makes other public crimes seem like public virtues. . . . . . In just regard for free labor in that Territory, which it is sought to blast by unwelcome association with slave labor; in Christian sympathy with the slave, whom it is proposed to task and to sell there; in stern condemnation of the crime which has been consummated on that beautiful soil; in rescue of fellow-citizens, now subjugated to a tyrannical usurpation; in dutiful respect for the early Fathers, whose aspirations are now ignobly thwarted; in the name of the Constitution, which has been outraged—of the laws, trampled down—or Justice banished—of Humanity degraded—of Peace destroyed—of Freedom crushed to earth; and, in the name of the Heavenly Father, whose service is perfect freedom, I make this last appeal."

HENRY WILSON.

Replying to Mr. Hammond, of South Carolina, in the United States Senate, March 20th, 1858, Gen. Wilson of Massachusetts, said:

" Fealty to the Administration, to the Democratic party, is now fealty to human slavery, to violence, to trickery, and to fraud. By perversions of the Constitution and the laws, by the red hand of violence, by unveiled trickeries and transparent frauds, by the indecent proscription of men of inflexible integrity, by the shameless prostitution of the honors of the government, and by the 'rank corruption, mining all within,' which 'infects unseen,' the administration is converting the American Democracy into a mere organization for the perpetuity, expansion, and domination of human slavery on the North American continent. There is not today, in all Christendom, a political organization so hostile to the rights of human nature, to the development of republican ideas, to the general progress of the human race, as the Democratic party of the United States. There is not a political organization even in Spain, Russia, or Austria, that dares, in the face of the civilized world, blazon its banners with doctrines so hostile to the rights of mankind, so abhorrent to humanity, as are avowed in these halls, and upheld by the American Democracy, under the lead of this administration. The great powers of Europe, England, France and Russia, have fixed their hungry eyes upon the coveted prizes of the Eastern World; and we are invoked to forget the lessons of Washington, to close our ears to the appeals of the people of Kansas, whose rights have been outraged, and turn our lustful eyes to the glittering prizes of dominion

7

in Mexico, Central America, Cuba, and the valleys of the distant Amazon. No party in those three European monarchies dares avow, in the face of Christendom, the sentiment we have heard proclaimed in these halls, that territorial expansion, and territorial dominion must be made, not for the advancement of the sacred and sublime principle of equal and impartial liberty to all men, but for the subjugation and personal servitude of other and inferior races. . . . . . I tell the vaunting senator from South Carolina that thousands of merchants, manufacturers and mechanics of the North are this day, and have been for months, pressed with the burden of bearing the unpaid debts owed them by the slave States. I remember that during the terrible pressure of last year, while our business men were staggering under the pressure, thirteen out of fourteen wholesale merchants in one department of business in one Southern city, imposed upon their Eastern creditors the burden of renewing their matured notes. The merchants and manufacturers of the North have lost hundreds of millions of dollars during the last thirty years in the slave States. I have personally lost, in the senator's own State, in Louisiana, Virginia, and Kentucky, thousands of dollars more than I am now able to command."

JOHN. P. HALE.

In his speech on "Kansas and the Supreme Court," delivered in the United States Senate, January 21st, 1858, Mr. Hale said:

" Peace came in 1783 ; and in 1784 Thomas Jefferson, the immortal author of the immortal Declaration of Independence, began his labors in the Continental Congress, moving that all the territory we then owned, and all the territory that we might thereafter acquire, should be forever free from what he considered the contaminating and blighting influences of human slavery. Those who are laboring with me in this great contest may take courage from the perseverance with which Jefferson adhered to his policy. In 1783–'84–'85, and '86, the measure failed, but finally, in 1787, it partially succeeded, and the ordinance was passed prohibiting slavery from all the territory which we then owned. Yet, sir, in view of all this history, written as with a sunbeam upon the very walls of the room in which this tribunal now assemble, they stand up in 1857, to declare to the world that the slave trade and slavery were so universally recognized and acknowledged, that nobody questioned the rightfulness of the traffic, and nobody supposed it capable of being questioned. Not content with overturning the whole line of judicial authority to be found in every nation of Europe, and in every State of this Union, and of their own solemn recorded decision, they go on to make the avowal ; and then go further, and undertake to tear from that chaplet which adorns the brows of the men of the Revolution the proudest and fairest of their ornaments; and that was the sincerity of the professions which they made in regard to the rights of human nature. It is true, the court in their charity undertake to throw the mantle of ignorance over these men, and say they did not understand what they meant. Sir, they did understand it, and the country understood it. There was a jealousy on the subject of liberty and slavery at that time, of which we are little prepared to judge at the present day. It is found beaming out on the pages of the writings of all these men.

" If the opinions of the Supreme Court are true, they put these men in the worst position of any men who are to be found on the pages of our history. If the opinion of the Supreme Court be true, it makes the immortal authors of the Declaration of Independence liars before God and hypocrites before the world ; for they lay down their sentiments broad, full, and explicit, and then they say that they appeal to the Supreme Ruler of the universe for the rectitude of their intentions ; but if you believe the Supreme Court, they were merely quibbling on words. They went into the courts of the Most High and pledged fidelity to their principles as the price they would pay for success ; and now it is attempted to cheat them out of the poor boon of integrity ; and it is said that they did not mean so ; and that when they said all men, they meant all white men ; and when they said that the contest they waged was for the right of mankind, the Supreme Court of the United States would have you believe they meant it was to establish slavery. Against that I protest, here, now, and everywhere ; and I tell the Supreme Court that these things are so impregnably fixed in the hearts of the people, on the page of history, in the recollections and traditions of men, that it will require mightier efforts than they have made or can make to overturn or to shake these settled convictions of the popular understanding and of the popular heart."

NATHANIEL P. BANKS.

In the course of his great speech in Wall street, New York. on the 25th of Sept., 1856, Mr. Banks said:

" For seventy-five years past the government of this country has been in the hands of southern statesmen, who have directed its policy. The North has been busy in the mechanical arts, in agriculture, and in mining, and has given less attention to the affairs of the government than it otherwise might have done—certainly less than it ought to have done. On the contrary, the South having no literature of its own, having no science of its own, having no mechanical and manufacturing industry of its own, having but little or no inventive power or genius of its own, having, in short, none of the elements of power that distinguish our civilization, has turned its attention chiefly, so far as its leading men are concerned, to the government of the country. Now, we of the North propose to divide this little matter with them. . . . . I should do wrong to our cause—the cause of the Northern States—if I failed to-day to say that there are other influences we desire to exert by the elevation to the Presidency of the man of our choice. We ask that the dead weight of human wrong shall be lifted up from the continent again, that it may rise as it was rising before these acts of wrong were done."

EDWIN D. MORGAN.

After calling to order the Convention which, in Philadelphia, in June, 1856, nominated Mr. Fremont for President, and Mr. Dayton for Vice-President, Mr. Morgan, as Chairman of the Republican National Committee—now Governor of New York—said:

" You are assembled for patriotic purposes. High expectations are cherished by the people. You are here to-day to give direction to a movement which is to decide whether the people of the United States are to be hereafter and forever chained to the present national policy of the extension of Human Slavery. Not whether the South is to rule, or the North; but whether the broad, national policy which our fathers established, cherished and maintained, is to be permitted to descend to their sons, to be the guiding star of all our people. Such is the magnitude of the question submitted. In its consideration let us avoid all extremes—plant ourselves firmly on the platform of the Constitution and the Union, taking no position which does not commend itself to the judgment of our consciences, our country, and of mankind. Of the wisdom of such a policy there need be no doubt: against it, there can be no successful resistance "

EDWARD WADE.

In his speech on the Slavery question, in the House of Representatives, August 2, 1856, Mr. Wade said:

" Inherent and fundamental right of freedom of speech and the press, does not and cannot exist in slaveholding communities. This is a necessity of despotic governments, it is more than a necessity of despotism, it is in itself, the essence of despotism. There is not a more morbidly suspicious, cruel, revengeful, or lawless despotism on the face of the earth, than the nightmare of slavery, which has settled down upon the people of the slaveholding States, with the exception of perhaps two or three of these States. There is more freedom of speech and of the press to-day, and more personal safety in the exercise of such freedom, at Vienna, St. Petersburg, Paris, or Rome, in an attack and exposure of the despotism which reigns supreme over those cities, than there is at Richmond, Charleston, Milledgeville, or Mobile, to attack and expose the slaveholding despotisms which rule over these cities with a rod of iron. There are probably more citizens, born and nurtured in the slave States, now in exile from their native States for the exercise of freedom of speech and the press, against the despotism of slaveholding, than there are from Austria, Russia, France, or the Two Sicilies, for the exercise of the same rights against the despotisms which crush those nations."

FRANCIS P. BLAIR, SEN.

In the course of an address to the Republicans of Maryland—his own State—in 1856, Mr. Blair said:

"In every aspect in which slavery among us can be considered, it is pregnant with difficulty. Its continuance in the States in which it has taken root has resulted in the monopoly of the soil, to a great extent, in the hands of the slaveholders, and the entire control of all departments of the State Government; and yet a majority of people in the slave States are not slaveowners. This produces an anomaly in the principle of our free institutions, which threatens in time to bring into subjugation to slaveowners the great body of the free white population."

FRANK P. BLAIR, JR.

In his speech at Concord, New Hampshire, February 2, 1859, Mr. Blair, of Missouri, of whom the non-slaveholders of the South have high hopes in the future, said :

"There is no other question before the country than that of slavery. It is the all-absorbing topic in every political circle. Upon this issue I have long since taken my ground against its extension and perpetuation. I believe that slavery should be restricted to its present limits, and that Congress should do all which lies in its power to prevent the perpetuation of this evil. I know that Congress has no power to interfere with it where it at present exists within the States ; and yet I doubt not that when the Republican party takes possession of the general government, and the corrupting patronage of the administration is diverted from its present channels, we shall be able to show the little oligarchy of slave-holders some things of which they little dream even within the States. . . . Although the institution of slavery is to be condemned, because it deprives the slave of everything except his bread and butter, and clothing, and shelter in winter, it merits more decided condemnation on another ground. It deprives the poor whites of the South of every aspiration which appertains to anything nobler than their bodies. It deprives them of the exercise of their intellects, of schools, education and culture, no less than of the bread of themselves and their children. I am more opposed to the institution on this ground than on any other, because it is our own race, the white race, which is here trampled upon —a race of working men and mechanics like yourselves. Slavery is the most odious institution ever known. It is essentially and vitally aristocratic. How dare these men stand up here and call themselves Democrats, while they have a race of whites pressed down under a twofold stratum of slaves and slave owners. I appeal to the people of New Hampshire to lend a helping hand to this oppressed race. Toward them the friends of slavery intrench themselves in exclusive rights of a twofold nature. The negro slave is instructed in all the mechanical arts for the benefit of his master, and the white non-slaveholder is thus excluded from all opportunities for elevating his family or providing for their wants."

GERRITT SMITH.

In his speech on the Nebraska bill, delivered in the House of Representatives, April 6, 1854, Mr. Smith said :

"The slavery question is up again—up again even in Congress ! It will not be kept down. At no bidding, however authoritative, will it keep down. The President of the United States commands it to keep down. Indeed he has, hitherto, seemed to make the keeping down of this question the great end of his great office. Members of Congress have so far humbled themselves, as to pledge themselves on this floor to keep it down. National political conventions promise to discountenance, and even to resist the agitation of slavery, both in and out of Congress. Commerce and politics are as afraid of this agitation, as Macbeth was of the ghost of Banquo ; and many titled divines, taking their cue from commerce and politics, and being no less servile than merchants and demagogues, do what they can to keep the slavery question out of sight. But all is of no avail. The saucy slavery question will not mind them. To repress it in one quarter, is only to have it burst forth more prominently in another quarter. If you hold it back here, it will break loose there, and rush forward with an accumulated force, that shall amply revenge for all its detention. And this is not strange, when we consider how great is the power of truth. It were madness for man to bid the grass not to grow, the waters not to run, the winds not to blow. it were madness for him to assume the mastery of the elements of the physical world. But more emphatically were it madness for him to attempt to hold in his puny fist the forces of the moral world. Canute's folly, in setting bounds to the sea, was wisdom itself, compared with the so much greater folly of attempting to subjugate the moral forces. Now, the power which is, ever and anon, throwing up the slavery question into our unwilling and affrighted faces, is Truth. The passion-blinded and the infatuated may not discern this mighty agent. Nevertheless, Truth lives and reigns forever ; and she will be, continually, tossing up unsettled questions. We must bear in mind, too, that every question, which has not been disposed of in conformity with her requirements, and which has not been laid to repose on her own blessed bosom, is an unsettled question. Hence, slavery is an unsettled question, and must continue such, until it shall have fled forever from the presence of liberty."

JOSHUA R. GIDDINGS.

In his speech on American Piracy, in Committee of the whole House, on the state of the Union, June 7, 1858, Mr. Giddings said :

"Every man who sells a slave thereby encourages the slave trade ; and no reflecting mind can regard the coastwise slave trade less criminal than that which is carried on upon the shores of Africa. In truth it was born of the African trade, and in its effects it is more atrocious, as its victims are more intelligent. It is thus that the African slave trade, the coastwise slave trade, the inter-State slave trade, the holding of slaves, the breeding of slaves, the selling and buying of slaves, are all connected and interwoven in one general network of moral turpitude, constituting an excrescence, a cancer upon the body politic of our nation. The African slave trade constitutes the germ, the root, from which our American slave trade, and all the various relations of that institution in this country, have sprung. If the tree be piracy, it is clear that its fruit can be nothing else than piracy ; and when the nation stamped that commerce as piratical, it proclaimed the guilt of every man who voluntarily connects himself with slavery."

ANSON BURLINGAME.

In his defence of Massachusetts, in the House of Representatives, June 21, 1856, Mr. Burlingame said :

"Freedom and slavery started together in the great race on this continent. In the very year the Pilgrim Fathers landed on Plymouth Rock, slaves landed in Virginia. Freedom has gone on trampling down barbarism, and planting States—building the symbols of its faith by every lake, and every river, until now the sons of the pilgrims stand by the shores of the Pacific. Slavery has also made its way toward the setting sun. It has reached the Rio Grande on the South ; and the groans of its victims, and the clank of its chains, may be heard as it slowly ascends the western tributaries of the Mississippi River. Freedom has left the land bespangled with free schools, and filled the whole heavens with the shining towers of religion and civilization. Slavery has left desolation, ignorance, and death, in its path. When we look at these things ; when we see what the country would have been had freedom been given to the territories ; when we think what it would have been but for this blight in the bosom of the country; that the whole South—that fair land God has blessed so much—would have been covered with cities, and villages, and railroads, and that in the country, in the place of twenty-five millions of people, thirty-five millions would have hailed the rising morn, exulting in republican liberty —when we think of these things, must every honest man—how must every man with brains in his head, or heart in his bosom—regret that the policy of old Virginia, in her better days, did not become the animating policy of this expanding Republic !"

GALUSHA A. GROW.

In his speech against the Lecompton Constitution, delivered in the House of Representatives, March 25, 1858, Mr. Grow said :

"Peace among a brave people is not the fruit of injustice, nor does agitation cease by the perpetration of wrong. For a third of a century, the advocates of slavery, while exercising unrestricted speech in its defence, have struggled to prevent all discussion against it—in the South, by penal statutes, mob law, and brute force ; in the North, by dispersing assemblages of peaceable citizens, pelting their lecturers, burning their halls, and destroying their presses ; in this forum of the people, by finality resolves on all laws for the benefit of slavery, not, however, to affect those in behalf of freedom, and by attempts to stifle the great constitutional right of the people at all times to petition their government. Yet, despite threats, mob law, and finality resolves, the discussion goes on, and will continue to, so long as right and wrong, justice and injustice, humanity and inhumanity, shall struggle for supremacy in the affairs of men."

RALPH WALDO EMERSON.

In his speech at Concord, Massachusetts, Aug. 1, 1844, celebrating the anniversary of the abolition of slavery in the West Indies, Mr. Emerson, the most practical and profound metaphysician in America, said :

" The crude element of good in human affairs must work and ripen, spite of whips, and plantation laws, and West Indian interests. Conscience rolled on its pillow, and could not sleep. We sympathize very tenderly here with the poor aggrieved planter, of whom so many unpleasant things are said ; but if we saw the whip applied to old men, to tender women ; and, undeniably, though I shrink to say so,—pregnant women set in the treadmill for refusing to work, when, not they, but the eternal law of animal nature refused to work ;—if we saw men's backs flayed with cowhides, and ' hot rum poured on, superinduced with brine or pickle, rubbed in with a corn-husk, in the scorching heat of the sun ;'—if we saw the runaways hunted with blood-hounds into swamps and hills ; and, in cases of passion, a planter throwing his negro into a copper of boiling cane juice,—if we saw these things with eyes, we too should wince. They are not pleasant sights. The blood is moral : the blood is anti-slavery : it runs cold in the veins : the stomach rises with disgust, and curses slavery. . . . . . .

" Unhappily, most unhappily, gentlemen, man is born with intellect, and love as with a love of sugar, and with a sense of justice, as well as a taste for strong drink. These ripened, as well as those. You could not educate him, you could not get any poetry, any wisdom, any beauty in woman, any strong and commanding character in man, but these absurdities would still come flashing out,—these absurdities of a demand for justice, a generosity for the weak and oppressed. Unhappily, too, for the planter, the laws of nature are in harmony with each other : that which the head and the heart demand, is found to be, in the long run, for what the grossest calculator calls his advantage. The moral sense is always supported by the permanent interest of the parties. Else, I know not how, in our world, any good would ever get done. It was shown to the planters that they, as well as the negroes, were slaves ; that though they paid no wages, they got very poor work ; that their estates were ruining them under the finest climate ; and that they needed the severest monopoly laws at home to keep them from bankruptcy. The oppression of the slave recoiled on them. They were full of vices ; their children were lumps of pride, sloth, sensuality and rottenness. The position of woman was nearly as bad as it could be, and, like other robbers, they could not sleep in security. Many planters have said, since the emancipation, that, before that day, they were the greatest slaves on the estate. Slavery is no scholar, no improver ; it does not love the whistle of the railroad ; it does not love the newspaper, the mail bag, a college, a book, or a preacher who has the absurd whim of saying what he thinks ; it does not increase the white population ; it does not improve the soil ; everything goes to decay."

THOMAS CORWIN.

In his speech against the Compromise Bill, delivered in the United States Senate, July 24, 1848, Mr. Corwin, once a Kentucky boy, now an Ohio man, said :

" I am the more confirmed in the course which I am determined to pursue, by some historical facts elicited in this very discussion. I remember what was said by the senator from Virginia the other day. It is a truth, that when the Constitution of the United States was made, South Carolina and Georgia refused to come into the Union unless the slave trade should be continued for twenty years ; and the North agreed that they would vote to continue the slave trade for twenty years ; yes,

voted that this new Republic should engage in piracy and murder at the will of two
States! So the history reads; and the condition of the agreement was, that those
two States should agree to some arrangement about navigation laws! I do not
blame South Carolina and Georgia for this transaction any more than I do those
Northern States who shared in it. But suppose the question were now presented here
by any one, whether we should adopt the foreign slave trade and continue it for
twenty years, would not the whole land turn pale with horror, that, in the middle
of the nineteenth century, a citizen of a free community, a senator of the United
States, should dare to propose the adoption of a system that has been denominated
piracy and murder, and is by law punished by death all over Christendom? What
did they do then? They had the power to prohibit it; but, at the command of
these two States, they allowed that to be introduced into the Constitution, to which
much of slavery now existing in our land is clearly to be traced. For who can
doubt that, but for that woeful bargain, slavery would by this time have disappeared
from all the States then in the Union, with one or two exceptions? The number
of slaves in the United States at this period was about six hundred thousand; it is
now three millions. And just as you extend the area of slavery, so you multiply
the difficulties which lie in the way of its extermination. It had been infinitely
better that day that South Carolina and Georgia had remained out of the Union for
a while, rather than that the Constitution should have been made to sanction the
slave trade for twenty years. The dissolution of the old Confederation would have
been nothing in comparison with that recognition of piracy and murder. I can
conceive of nothing in the dark record of man's enormities, from the death of Abel
down to this hour, so horrible as that of stealing people from their own home, and
making them and their posterity slaves forever. It is a crime which we know has
been visited with such signal punishment in the history of nations as to warrant the
belief that heaven itself had interfered to avenge the wrongs of earth."

B. GRATZ BROWN.

In the Missouri legislature, in January, 1857, Mr. Brown, of St.
Louis, proved himself a hero, a patriot and a statesman, in the following
words:

"I am a Free-Soiler, and I don't deny it. No word or vote of mine shall ever
inure to the benefit of such a monstrous doctrine as the extension of slavery over
the patrimony of the free white laborers of the country. I am for the greatest
good of the greatest number, and against the system which monopolizes the free
and fertile territory of our country for a few slaveholders, to the exclusion of thousands upon thousands of the sinewy sons of toil. The time will come, and perhaps
very soon. when the people will rule for their own benefit, and not for that of a
class which, numerically speaking, is insignificant. I stand here in the midst of the
assembled legislature of Missouri to avow myself a Free-Soiler. Let those who
are scared at names shrink from the position if they will. I shall take my stand in
favor of the white man. Here, in Missouri, I shall support the rights, the dignity
and the welfare of the eight hundred thousand non-slaveholders in preference to
upholding and perpetuating the dominancy of the thirty thousand slaveholders
who inhabit our State."

HENRY C. CAREY.

In his statesman-like Letters to the President, which Mr. Buchanan,
to whom they are most respectfully addressed, has not answered, for
the reason, we suppose, that it is absolutely impossible for him to
answer them with any credit to himself or to his party, Mr. Carey says,
assuring us that ten years ago conservative, patriotic men everywhere,
would have regarded as a false prophet the man who had predicted:

"That, at the close of a single decade, the regular expenditures of the federal
government, in a time of peace, would reach seventy millions of dollars—being five
times more than they had been but thirty years before.

"That the Executive would dictate to members of Congress what should be their
course, and publicly advertise the offices that were to be given, to those whose votes
should be in accordance with his desires.

"That the growing mental slavery thus indicated, would be attended by our responding growth in the belief, that 'one of the chief bulwarks of our institutions was to be found in the physical enslavement of the laborer.

" That the extension of the area of human slavery would have become the pri mary object of the government, and that, with that view, the great Ordinance of 1787, as carried out in the Missouri Compromise, would be repealed.

" That the reopening of the slave trade would be publicly advocated, and that the first step toward its accomplishment would be taken by a citizen of the United States—in rescinding all the prohibitions of the Central American government.

" That the prohibition of slavery in a Central American State would be considered sufficient reason for the rejection of a treaty.

" That the substitution, throughout all the minor employments of society, of slave labor for that of the freeman, would be publicly recommended by the Executive of a leading State.

" That, while always seeking territory in the South, the rights and interests of the people would be bartered away, for the sole and exclusive purpose of preventing annexation in the North.

" That Lynch-law would have found its way into the Senate chamber: that it would have superseded the provisions of the Constitution throughout the Southern States: that it would have superseded the civil authority, in one of the States of the Union: that the right of the States to prohibit slavery within their limits, would be so seriously questioned as to warrant the belief, that the day was near at hand when it would be totally denied : that all the decisions of the Supreme Court for sixty years, favorable to freedom, would by this time have been reversed : that the doctrine of constructive treason would be adopted in federal courts : and that the rights of the citizen would be thus in equal peril, from the extension of legal authority on one hand, and the substitution of the law of force on the other.

" That polygamy and slavery would go hand in hand with each other, and that the doctrine of a plurality of wives would be publicly proclaimed by men holding highly important offices under the Federal government."

WENDELL PHILLIPS.

In his speech at the City Hall, in Worcester, Mass., Jan. 15, 1857, Mr. Phillips, the Demosthenes of New England, whom certain Pro-Slavery fanatics of the South, in an insane effort to abuse, have highly complimented by describing him as " an infernal machine set to music," said :

" Slavery is so momentous an evil, that in its presence all others pale away. No thoughtful man can deem any sacrifice too great to secure its abolition. The safety of the people is the highest law. In this battle we demand a clear field and the use of every honorable weapon. Even the monuments of our fathers are no longer sacred, if the enemy are concealed behind them.

" This is my first claim upon every man who has an Anti-Slavery purpose. One of the greatest, if not the greatest question of the age, is that of Free Labor. I do not know—no man can prophecy—what sacrifices it will demand, no human sagacity divine what shape it will acquire in the kaleidoscope of the future. Nobody can foresee the combinations that will be necessary in order to secure liberty and turn law into justice. The pledge we make to each other, as Abolitionists, is, that to this slave question, embodying as it does the highest justice and the most perfect liberty, synonymous as it is with right, manhood, justice, with pure religion, a free press, an impartial judiciary and a true civilization, we will sacrifice everything. If any man dissents, he is not, in any just sense, an Abolitionist. If he has not studied the question enough to know that it binds up in itself all considerations of government, then he is not worthy of being called an Abolitionist."

Again, on the 17th of February, 1859, addressing a Committee of the Massachusetts legislature, in support of numerous petitions, asking for a law to prevent the recapture of fugitive slaves, he said :

" It is no answer to my request to say, that you will grant a jury trial—that you will hedge the citizen with such safeguards that none but a real fugitive can ever be de livered up. That is not the Massachusetts we want, and not the Massachusetts we have a right to claim. If the South has violated the Constitution repeatedly, palpably, avowedly, defiantly, atrociously, for her own purposes—to get power in the government, to perpetuate her system, to control the nation—we claim of you that you should exercise the privilege which that violation has given you. We claim of you that you should give us a Massachusetts worthy of its ancient name. Give us a State that is not disgraced by the trial, in the nineteenth century, in the midst of so-called Christian churches, of the issue, ' Is this man a chattel?' We will not rest until it is decided as the law of Massachusetts, that a human being, immortal, created by the hand of God, shall not be put upon trial in the Commonwealth, and required to prove that he is not property. It shall not be competent for the courts of Massachusetts to insult the civilization of the nineteenth century by asking that question, or making it the subject of evidence and proof."

THEODORE PARKER.

In his discourse at the Music Hall, in Boston, on Monday, February 12, 1854, Mr. Parker, who, bountifully supplied with brain, was born thinking, and whose abhorrence of slavery of the body is more than equalled by his abhorrence of slavery of the mind, said:

"Slavery hinders the education and the industry of the people ; it is fatal to their piety. Think of a religious kidnapper ! a Christian Slave-breeder ! a Slave-trader loving his neighbor as himself, receiving the 'sacraments' in some Protestant Church from the hand of a Christian apostle, then the next day selling babies by the dozen, and tearing young women from the arms of their husbands, to feed the lust of lecherous New Orleans ! Imagine a religious man selling his own children into eternal bondage ! Think of a Christian defending slavery out of the Bible and declaring there is no higher law, but Atheism is the first principle of Republican government. . . . . . . As soon as the North awakes to its ideas, and uses its vast strength of money, its vast strength of numbers, and its still more gigantic strength of educated intellect, we shall tread this monster underneath our feet. See how Spain has fallen—how poor and miserable is Spanish America. She stands there a perpetual warning to us. One day the North will rise in her majesty, and put Slavery under our feet, and then we shall extend the area of freedom. The blessing of Almighty God will come down upon the noblest people the world ever saw—who have triumphed over Theocracy, Monarchy, Aristocracy, Despotocracy, and have got a Democracy—a government of all, for all, and by all—a church without a bishop, a state without a king, a community without a lord, and a family without a slave."

WILLIAM LLOYD GARRISON.

In a recently published volume of his Writings and Speeches, Mr. Garrison, under whose most able counsel and convincing arguments organized opposition to slavery first became an important, and is destined soon to become a controlling, power in the government, says:

" It is the strength and glory of the Anti-Slavery cause, that its principles are so simple and elementary, and yet so vital to freedom, morality and religion, as to commend themselves to the understandings and consciences of men of every sect and party, every creed and persuasion, every caste and color. They are self-evident truths—fixed stars in the moral firmament—blazing suns in the great universe of mind, dispensing light and heat over the whole surface of humanity, and around which all social and moral affinities revolve in harmony. They are to be denied, only as the existence of a God, or the immortality of the soul, is denied. Unlike human theories, they can never lead astray ; unlike human devices, they can never be made subservient to ambition or selfishness. . . . . . . I will say, finally, that I tremble for the republic while slavery exists therein. If I look up to God for success, no smile of mercy or forgiveness dispels the gloom of futurity ; if to our resources, they are daily diminishing ; if to all history, our destruction is not only possible, but almost certain. Why should we slumber at this momentous crisis? If our hearts were dead to every throb of humanity ; if it were lawful to oppress, where power is ample ; still, if we had any regard for our safety and happiness, we should strive to crush the vampire which is feeding upon our life blood. All the selfishness of our nature cries aloud for a better security. Our own vices are too strong for us, and keep us in perpetual alarm ; how in addition to these, shall we be able to contend successfully with millions of armed and desperate men, as we must eventually, if slavery do not cease ?"

HENRY WARD BEECHER.

In his address before the American Tract Society of Boston, in the Church of the Puritans, New York, May 12, 1859, Mr. Beecher said:

" For more than thirty years the diapason of this country has not been the swell of the ocean. It has not been the sighing of the wind through our Western forests: the deep thunder-toned diapason that has rolled through this land, has been the sighing of the slave. Throughout all this time the Church has heard the voice, and scarcely knew what it was. But God has been rolling it upon her more and more. In my day a conflict has taken place. I remember the days of mobs. I remember when Birney's press was broken in pieces at Cincinnati and dragged into the Ohio River. I remember when Theodore Weld was driven by unvitalized eggs from place to place in the West. I remember the day when storehouses were sacked and houses pillaged in New York. I remember the day when a venerable man escaped from being murdered for a good cause, and because he escaped has never been engaged in it since. I remember when it was as much as a man's name was worth to be called an Abolitionist. I have within twenty years seen those parties which were the most tyrannic ground out of existence, and those churches which refused to discuss this question have been overrun by it and taken complete possession of. Synods, which have acted as dykes, have been overwhelmed and submerged. General Assemblies have been carried away captive by this good cause, and the public sentiment of the whole continent has been changed in this mighty work."

GEORGE B. CHEEVER.

In an address delivered in the Church of the Puritans, on Thursday, May 13, 1858, Dr. Cheever, speaking of the sin of slavery, said :

" We practise the iniquity upon children, innocent children, the natives of our own land, unbought, unsold, unpaid for, without consultation or consent of father or mother, or the shadow of a permission from the Almighty ; and they, the new-born babes of this system, are the compound interest year by year added to the sin and its capital, which thus doubles upon us in the next generation, and must treble in another. We make use of the most sacred domestic affections, of maternal, filial, and I was going to say, connubial love—but the system forbids, and I have to say *contubernal*—for such rapid and accumulating production of the iniquity, as shall be in some measure adequate to the demand. The whole family relation, the whole domestic state, is prostituted, poisoned, turned into a misery-making machine for the agent of all evil. What God meant should be the source and inspiration of happiness, becomes the fountain of sin and woe. The sacred names of husband, wife, father, mother, son, babe, become the exponents of various forces and values in the slave-breeding institute. And the whole perfection, completeness and concentration of this creative power in this manufacturing interest descends like a trip-hammer on the children, beating them from birth into marketable articles, and stamping and sealing them as chattels, foredoomed and fatalized to run till they wear out, as living spindles, wheels, activities of labor and productiveness, in the same horrible system.

" And each generation of immortal marketable stuff is as exactly fashioned in these grooves, molds, channels, wefted, netted and drawn through, to come out the invariable product, as the yards of carpeting are cut from the loom to be trodden on, or as the coins drop from the die for the circulation of society. This is the peculiarity of the sin of slavery in the foremost Christian country on the face of the earth. In this branch of native industry and manufacture we are self-reliant. Disavowing a protective policy in almost everything else, we are proudly patriotic for the security, superiority and abundance of this most sacred native product of domestic manufacture, and for neither the raw material nor the bleaching of it will depend on any other country in the world."

JOSEPH P. THOMPSON.

Trying the Fugitive Slave Law by the Old and New Testaments, Dr. Thompson, pastor of the Broadway Tabernacle, says:

" Whatever may be thought of the lawfulness or the expediency of introducing the general subject of slavery into the pulpit, there can be no question that the treatment due to fugitives from slavery is a legitimate topic for discussion there. That is a subject of which the Bible treats, and in making it a subject of discourse I am not preaching politics but am preaching the Gospel; applying the principles of the Bible to an important public interest. The subject legitimately belongs to the pulpit, and politicians should be careful how they tamper with it, lest they betray an ignorance of the principles of Biblical interpretation and of the spirit of Christianity, as gross as that ignorance of political affairs which they are prone to charge upon ministers of the Gospel. The treatment of fugitive slaves has indeed been made a political question ; but it was a Biblical question and a question of morality long before it was dragged into the arena of politics, and it was legislated upon by the King of heaven and earth ages before the Congress of the United States had an existence. . . . . . The laws of Moses were given in the wilderness, to a people just escaped from bondage, and who therefore had no slaves; they were given in anticipation of the introduction of slavery among that people when they should come to be settled as conquerors in Canaan ; they were given to restrain the lust of conquest and oppression, and to hedge in as much as possible the natural tendency of the emancipated to retaliate upon others the cruelties of their own bondage—to prevent the Israelites from becoming to each other and to the Canaanites what the Egyptians had been to the Israelites ; they were given in order, by a qualified and an onerous permission, to secure the overthrow of a system which, as the times and the people were, could not have been shut out by an absolute prohibition. And as the crowning act of legislation for the ultimate overthrow of an evil tolerated from necessity, it was decreed that no fugitive from slavery should ever be delivered up to his master. The slave was at liberty to escape from his master whenever he desired to better his condition, and in whatever part of Israel he should choose an asylum, there was he to be allowed to remain without molestation."

E. H. CHAPIN.

From two of Mr. Chapin's published works, one entitled " True Manliness," the other " City Life," we make the following extracts :

" I pass into the anti-slavery meeting. Here, I discover, is agitated a great truth —the natural equality of all men—the right of the poorest and lowest to be free, to breathe God's air upon what hill-top he will, to follow his sunshine around the earth if he list—the wrong of holding him in bondage, of putting him by force to do another's work. . . . . . . Intemperance, slavery, war, what are these but the flowering plants of interior sin? . . . . . . Activity and intelligence indicate a condition of material and individual freedom. A community which really thrives in all the departments of its industry, must be, essentially, a free community. Despotism prevails more where men do not feel that they have much at stake in the country, and where their faculties have not been aroused. But the toil of enterprise and the sense of possession, develop a consciousness of personality which resists encroachment and chafes under oppression."

HENRY W. BELLOWS.

Writing to his friend, the Rev. Thos. W. Higginson, under date of Jan. 6, 1857, Dr. Bellows says :

The last election has shown that the North is waking up in conscience, courage, and sensibility to her duty, not to herself alone, but to the Nation, the Union, and Humanity. The astonishing effect of the free press in arousing the people, indicates what will be the triumph of another election. The South sees for the first time that the North is in earnest, feels its power, and is determining to exercise it. And this is having an admirable effect upon the discussion of the subject. What I desire now and always to maintain is this : That our conscientious opposition to the extension of slavery is not to be abated or colored by fears for the Union ; and that, so far as it depends on the North, we are to stop its extension, let the consequences to the Union—to the North or the South—be what they will. This ground I believe to be the safe ground—the Christian, humane, patriotic, constitutional, unsectional, Union-saving ground, I take it as a lover of the North and a lover of the South; as a believer in the future of the United States. I take it as a hater of slavery, an undying foe to its extension, and a laborer for its overthrow and extinction in the speediest manner and time consistent with our whole duty as American citizens "

LEWIS TAPPAN.

In his thirteenth annual Report to the American and Foreign Anti-Slavery Society, Mr. Tappan says:

" Nature cries aloud against the inhumanities of slavery; Free Democracy abjures the hateful system ; and free Christianity recoils from its leprous touch. That it should exist, extend, and flourish in a nation planted by the excellent of the earth, and in opposition to the principles of republicanism and Christianity, excites the marvel and arouses the grief and indignation of good men throughout the world. . . . . . . American slavery is at war with the Declaration of Independence, the Constitution of the United States, natural justice, and Christianity. Agitation on the subject will not, therefore, cease while free discussion is allowed, while a free press exists, while Protestantism and Free Democracy are prized, while love to God and man prevail, until the curse is removed from the Church and Government of this country, and all its citizens are equal before the law. . . . . . . It is obvious to every intelligent and candid looker-on, that the anti-slavery cause, in spite of the sneers of opponents, the denunciations of men in power, and the designs of the crafty, is steadily pursuing its march to a glorious consummation."

JOSHUA LEAVITT.

In the course of an elaborate article on national politics, Dr. Leavitt, one of the able editors of the *Independent*—a New York weekly religious newspaper—says:

" The ascendency of the slave power in the councils of the nation, obtained through the ill-advised concessions of the federal constitution, and strengthened by a long series of usurpations on the one hand, and of surrenders on the other, is unjust, dangerous to the Union, and incompatible with the preservation of free government; and is the principal cause of the political and financial evils under which we groan ; and thus the only hope of relief is in a united determination of the friends of freedom, to employ all wise and lawful means for the extinction of slavery itself."

WILLIAM GOODELL.

In his careful and comprehensive "View of the Slavery Question," Mr. Goodell says:

" The inherent criminality of slavery and of slave holding, their utter repugnance to natural justice, to Christianity, to the law of nature, to the law of God, to the principles of democracy, to the liberties of the country—no longer present questions for serious discussion among the great body of intelligent citizens in the non-slaveholding States. Here and there a superanuated ecclesiastic (who has, perhaps, a son at the South, or in a college seeking Southern patronage) may thumb over his Polyglot, and pretend to find a justification of slavery. But nobody believes him. His disclaimers and self-contradictions prove that he does not, even in his dotage, believe it himself. . . . . . . Under the good providence of God, the dissensions among abolitionists, however humiliating to them, and however mischievous in some respects, have been over-ruled in other respects for good. Abolitionism, before the division, was a powerful elixir, in the phial of one anti-slavery organization, corked up tight, and carried about for exhibition. By the division, the phial was broken and the contents spilled over the whole surface of society, where it has been working as a leaven, ever since, till the mass is beginning to upheave."

SAMUEL J. MAY.

In his speech at Syracuse, New York, Oct. 14, 1851, Mr. May said:

" To urge that our Republic cannot be maintained, but upon principles diametrically opposite to those upon which it was so solemnly based, is as much as to proclaim to the world that our Declaration of Independence is found to be untrue ; and thus rejoice the hearts of tyrants throughout the world, and cast down forever the hopes of the oppressed everywhere. . . . . . Never have the principles on which the civil institutions of our country were founded been put to so severe a test, as at this day. The encroachments of the despotic power of a slaveholding oligarchy upon that liberty which our fathers thought they had bequeathed us, have been made to such an extent, that the champions of that oligarchy have, on the floor of our national Congress, pronounced the glorious declaration of '76, that all men have an inalienable right to liberty—a mere rhetorical flourish—and have dared to intimate that the poor and laboring people of the Northern States, ought not to be allowed to exercise the prerogatives of freemen, any more than the Southern slaves. And by the machinery of partyism, the leaders of the northern wings of the two political hosts, have been brought to acquiesce in the supremacy of the slaveholding power in our country, and to unite in requiring of us all, implicit obedience to its demands, though they violate, utterly, our highest sense of right, and outrage every feeling of humanity."

WILLIAM CULLEN BRYANT.

In his paper of Oct. 27th, 1858, Mr. Bryant, the venerable bard and unbending patriot, who has so long and so ably presided over the editorial columns of the New York *Evening Post*, says:

" By instigations to violence and threats of mob-law, the free expression of opinion in regard to slavery is put down in the Southern States. Freedom of speech in a community seems to depend on the recognition of personal freedom in all classes. Wherever slavery is introduced, a despotic oligarchy is created, which allows of no more liberty of speech than is permitted in Austria. . . . . . . The slaveholding aristocracy is the most cowardly of all aristocracies. It lives in constant fear of overthrow ; it knows that it has a bad name ; that the opinion of the world is against it, and, as those are apt to do who are conscious of standing in general discredit, it puts on a bold face and plays the bully where it has the opportunity, and the ruffian where it has the power."

HORACE GREELEY.

For the purpose of showing that Mr. Greeley is not, as he is generally represented by the oligarchy, an inveterate hater of the South, we introduce the following extracts from one of his editorial articles in a late number of the New York *Tribune*—a most faithful and efficient advocate of Free Labor, the circulation of which we are happy to be able to state, is greater than the aggregate circulation of a score or more of the principal pro-slavery sheets published south of the Potomac.

" Is it in vain that we pile fact upon fact, proof on proof, showing that slavery is a blight and a curse to the States which cherish it? These facts are multitudinous as the leaves of the forest ; conclusive as the demonstrations of geometry. Nobody attempts to refute them, but the champions of slavery extension seem determined to persist in ignoring them. Let it be understood, then, once for all. that we do not hate the South, war on the South, nor seek to ruin the South, in resisting the extension of slavery. We most earnestly believe human bondage a curse to the South, and to all whom it affects; but we do not labor for its overthrow otherwise than through the conviction of the South of its injustice and mischief. Its extension into new territories we determinedly resist, not by any means from ill will to the South, but under the impulse of good will to all mankind.

" Whenever we draw a parallel between Northern and Southern production, industry, thrift, wealth, the few who seek to parry the facts at all complain that the instances are unfairly selected—that the commercial ascendency of the North. with the profits and facilities thence accruing, accounts for the striking preponderance of the North. In vain we insist that slavery is the cause of this very commercial ascendency—that Norfolk and Richmond and Charleston might have been to this country what Boston, New York and Philadelphia now are, had not slavery spread its pall over and paralyzed the energies of the South."

HENRY J. RAYMOND.

In his paper of Sept. 3, 1856, Mr. Raymond, the enterprising and accomplished editor of the New York *Daily Times*, says·

"Here at the North everything is so free—men think and speak, and write and print, and teach so freely what they believe to be true, that it is hard to realize the actual tyranny which slavery has established over our Southern brethren. How thoroughly it rules all political action, we know from incidents of daily occurrence. But without careful study we cannot credit the absolutism of its sway over literature, the education, the social life, the religion even, of the Southern States. No man there dares to write, or print, or speak a word in reprobation of slavery. The editor in his chair, the writer at his desk, the clergyman in his pulpit, receive their orders from slavery, and must do its bidding. Whatever logic and reason may say, whatever lessons history may teach, whatever the principles of Christian brotherhood may require, all must be subordinate and secondary to the higher law of slavery."

THURLOW WEED.

In his paper of Dec. 8, 1858, Mr. Weed, who, with rare ability and success, has long conducted the Albany *Evening Journal*, says:

"It has always been the practice of doughface politicians to argue as if the prosperity of the North depended upon the degradation of the South, and to urge us to connive at the spread of slavery in order to drive a profitable trade with it. These arguments are as unphilosophical as they are unmanly. The States are so linked by commerce that whatever benefits one, benefits all, and whatever clogs the energies of one is a drag upon the prosperity of the united whole. The trade between the North and South is brisk, but it would be threefold as great, had no slave ever been imported from the Guinea Coast, and if each section now had the products of its own intelligent labor to exchange for those of the other. Let the New England or New York merchant or mechanic, who has been deceived by this doughface plea, ask himself whether his branch of business is the better or the worse for having in the Union such young, vigorous and Free States as Ohio, Indiana, Michigan, Illinois, Iowa, Wisconsin and Minnesota, and whether it would be worse or better for him, if they had come in slaveholding communities like Arkansas, Texas and Florida?"

J. WATSON WEBB.

In his paper of Oct. 1, 1856, Gen. Webb, the veteran editor of the New York *Courier and Enquirer*, says:

"It is idle, it is worse than idle, for Southern men or for ourselves, to blind the eyes to the fact that it is the sense of the civilized world that African slavery is a dishonor and a reproach to the American Republic. The fact that the principal nations of Europe have abolished it at a sacrifice, and set it down in the catalogue of crimes, is, in itself, irrefragable proof of the fact. And this sense weighs most heavily upon those Europeans who have the most adequate appreciation of the grandeur of our Republic, and the glorious principles upon which it is framed. The venerable Humboldt speaks as the representative of all that is most liberal and enlightened in the mind of Europe, when he says:

"'But there is one thing, sir, which grieves me more than I can describe, and that is the policy you have lately adopted in regard to slavery. I am not so unreasonable as to expect that you should instantly emancipate your slaves. I know well the formidable difficulties that you have to contend with in solving the problem of slavery. But what occasions deep sorrow and pain, believe me, to all lovers of your great country, is to find that, instead of adopting any means, however slow and gradual, to relieve yourselves of it, you are constantly trying to extend and consolidate a system which is not only opposed to all the principles of morality, but, as it appears to me, is pregnant with appalling and inevitable dangers to the future of the Republic itself. Tell your countrymen this from me.'

"Every man in the civilized world, who has a life to live in this nineteenth century, has an interest in this struggle. Whether they are on the immediate field or not, they all must more or less participate in its fortunes Human hearts have their affinities and mutual influences, which distance cannot dissipate, or difference in outward circumstances neutralize. Ideas, too, in these times, are winged; and whether good or evil, they find, fly where they may, principles and aims german to, if not identical with, those they serve in the land of their origin, or at least the conditions out of which such principles and aims may spring. They are as sure everywhere of the same human nature as of the same ambient atmosphere.'

GAMALIEL BAILEY.

As editor and proprietor of the *National Era*, Dr. Bailey, of Washington, D. C., whose very able and consistent management of the paper has entitled him to the high regard of every true lover of liberty, says:

" The tendency of slavery to diffuse itself, and to crowd out free labor, was early observed by American patriots, North and South ; and Mr. Jefferson, the great apostle of Republicanism, made an effort in 1784 to cut short the encroaching tide of barbaric despotism, by prohibiting slavery in all the Territories of the Union, down to thirty-one degrees of latitude, which was then our Southern boundary. His beneficent purpose failed, not for want of a decisive majority of votes present in the Congress of the Confederation, but in consequence of the absence of the delegates from one or two States, which were necessary to the constitutional majority. When the subject again came up, in 1787, Mr. Jefferson was minister to France, and the famous ordinance of that year was adopted, prohibiting slavery North and West of the Ohio River. Between 1784 and 1787, the strides of slavery westward into Tennessee and Kentucky, had become too considerable to admit of the policy of exclusion ; and besides those regions were then integral parts of Virginia and North Carolina, and of course they could not be touched without the consent of those States. In 1820, another effort was made to arrest the progress of slavery, which threatened to monopolize the whole Territory west of the Mississippi. In the meantime the South had apostatized from the faith of Jefferson. It had ceased to love universal liberty, and the growing importance of the cotton culture had caused the people to look with indifference upon the moral deformity of slavery ; and, as a matter of course, the politicians became its apologists and defenders. After a severe struggle a compromise was agreed upon, by which Missouri was to be admitted with slavery, which was the immediate point in controversy ; and slavery was to be excluded from all the territory north and west of that State.

" We have shown, from the most incontestable evidence, that there is in slave society a much greater tendency to diffuse itself into new regions, than belongs to freedom, for the reason that it has no internal vitality. It cannot live if circumscribed, and must, like a consumptive, be continually roving for a change of air to recuperate its wasting energies."

HARRIET BEECHER STOWE.

In her " Key to Uncle Tom's Cabin," Mrs. Stowe, whose name is everywhere wreathed and immortalized on the scrolls of liberty, says:

" Slavery is a simple retrogression of society to the worst abuses of the middle ages. We must not, therefore, be surprised to find the opinions and practices of the middle ages, as to civil and religious toleration, prevailing. . . . . . It is no child's play to attack an institution which has absorbed into itself so much of the political power and wealth of this nation. The very heart shrinks to think what the faithful Christian must endure who assails this institution on its own ground ; but it *must be done.* How was it at the North? There was a universal effort to put down the discussion of it here by mob-law. Printing-presses were broken, houses torn down, property destroyed. Brave men, however, stood firm : martyr blood was shed for the right of free opinion in speech ; and so the right of discussion was established. Nobody tries that sort of argument now—its day is past. In Kentucky, also, they tried to stop the discussion by similar means. Mob violence destroyed a printing press, and threatened the lives of individuals. But there were brave men there, who feared not violence or threats of death ; and emancipation is now open for discussion in Kentucky. The fact is the South *must* discuss the matter of slavery. She *cannot* shut it out, unless she lays an embargo on the literature of the whole civilized world ; if it be, indeed, divine and God-appointed, why does she so tremble to have it touched ? If it be of God, all the free inquiry in the world cannot overthrow it. Discussion must and will come. It only requires courageous men to lead the way."

MATTIE GRIFFITH.

In her very able and interesting " Autobiography of a Female Slave," a work of fiction which is fuller of fact than any book of the kind that we have ever read—a work which, for vivid, accurate delineation of indoor life in the South, and for terse, graphic portrayal of slaveholding manners and morals, has no equal—Miss Griffith, one of Kentucky's truest and noblest daughters, who, by the emancipation of her own slaves, has set a lofty example of pure patriotism and benevolence, says, writing pointedly to the people of her native State :

" By the oppression to which we were subjected under the yoke of Britain, and against which we wrestled so long, so patiently, so vigorously, in so many ways, and at last so triumphantly, I adjure you to put an end, at once, and forever, to the disreputable and despotic business of holding slaves. African slavery, as practised in America, is oppression indeed, in comparison with which, that which drew forth our angry and bitter complaints against England, was very freedom. Let us, instead of perpetuating the infamous system of slavery, be true to ourselves ; let us vindicate the pretensions we set up when we characterize ours as the ' land of liberty, the asylum of the oppressed,' by proclaiming to the nations of the earth that, so soon as a slave touches the soil of the United States, his manacles shall fall from him : let us verify the words engraven in enduring brass on the old bell which, from the tower of Independence Hall, rang out our glorious Declaration, and in deed and in truth proclaim ' Liberty to the captive, and the opening of the prison doors to them that are bound.' As you value truth, honor, justice, consistency— aye, humanity even, wipe out the black blot which defiles the border of our escutcheon, and the country will then be in reality what it is now only in name, a *free* country, loving liberty disinterestedly for its own sake, and for that of all peoples, and nations, and tribes, and tongues."

SARAH M. GRIMKÉ.

In her "Reasons for Action at the North," Miss Grimké, an estimable, right-minded lady, from South Carolina, says :

" Let Northerners respectfully ask for an alteration in that part of the Constitution by which they are bound to assist the South in quelling servile insurrections. Let them see to it that they send no man to Congress who would give his vote to the admission of another slave State into the national Union. Let them protest against the injustice and cruelty of delivering the fugitive slave back to his master as being a direct infringement of the Divine command, Let them petition their different Legislatures to grant a jury trial to the friendless, helpless runaway, and for the repeal of those laws which secure to the slaveholder his unjust claim to his slave, after he has voluntarily brought him within the verge of their jurisdiction, and for the enactment of such laws as will protect the colored man, woman, and child from the fangs of the kidnapper, who is constantly skulking about in the Northern States, seeking whom he may devour. Let the Northern churches refuse to receive slaveholders at their communion tables, or to permit slaveholding ministers to officiate in their pulpits."

ANGELINA E. WELD.

In her eloquent " Appeal to the Women of the Nominally Free States,' Mrs. Weld, of New Jersey, formerly Miss Grimké, of South Carolina, says :

" It is not the character alone of the mistress that is deeply injured by the possession and exercise of despotic power, nor is it the degradation and suffering to which the slave is continually subject ; but another important consideration is, that in consequence of the dreadful state of morals at the South, the wife and the daughter sometimes find their homes a scene of the most mortifying, heart-rending prefer-once of the degraded domestic, or the colored daughter of the head of the family. There are, alas, too many families, of which the contentions of Abraham's household is a fair example. But we forbear to lift the veil of private life any higher; let these few hints suffice to give you some idea of what is daily passing *behind* that curtain which has been so carefully drawn before the scenes of domestic life in slaveholding America."

JOHN C. UNDERWOOD.

Remonstrating against the consummate system of despotism which exiled him from his home and family in Virginia, in 1856, Mr. Underwood says:

" The history of the world, and especially of the States of this Union, shows most conclusively that public prosperity bears an almost mathematical proportion to the degree of freedom enjoyed by all the inhabitants of the State. Men will always work better for the cash than for the lash. The free laborer will produce and save as much, and consume and waste as little as he can. The slave, on the contrary, will produce and save as little, and consume and waste as much as possible. Hence States and countries filled with the former class must necessarily flourish and increase in population, arts, manufactures, wealth and education, because they are animated and incited by all the vigor of the will, while States and countries filled with the latter class, must exhibit comparative stagnation, because it is a universal law of nature that force and fear end in ruin and decay. We have an instructive example of the one class in the activity, enterprise, prosperity and intelligence of New England, and of the other in the pitiable condition of poor South Carolina, a State which, by neglecting the teachings of her Marions, and following her Butlers, her Brookses, her Keitts, and her Quattlebums, in the race of aristocracy and Africanization, is rapidly sinking into agricultural sterility, bloated egotism, and brutal barbarism, until she has most significantly adopted a cane for her emblem, which equally and strikingly typifies her military resources, and that imbecility and decrepitude which, without something to lean upon, must inevitably fall into speedy death and dissolution."

DANIEL R. GOODLOE.

As assistant editor of the *National Era*, the best centrally located Republican paper in the country, Mr. Goodloe, formerly of North Carolina, says:

" The history of the United States shows, that while the slave States increase in population less rapidly than the free, there is a tendency in slave society to diffusion, greater than is exhibited by free society. In fact, diffusion, or extension of area, is one of the necessities of slavery; the prevention of which is regarded as directly and immediately menacing to the existence of the institution. This arises from the almost exclusive application of slave labor to the one occupation of agriculture, and the difficulty, if not impossibility, of diversifying employments. Free society, on the contrary, has indefinite resources of development within a restricted area. It will far excel slave society in the cultivation of the ground—first, on account of the superior intelligence of the laborers; and secondly, in consequence of the greater and more various demands upon the earth's products, where commerce, manufactures, and the arts, abound. Then, these arts of life, by bringing men together in cities and towns, and employing them in the manufacture or transportation of the raw materials of the farmer, give rise to an indefinite increase of wealth and population. The confinement of a free people within narrow limits seems only to develop new resources of wealth, comfort and happiness; while slave society, pent up, withers and dies. It must continually be fed by new fields and forests, to be wasted and wilted under the poisonous tread of the slave."

BENJAMIN S. HEDRICK.

For daring to have political opinions of his own, and because he did not deem it his duty to conceal the fact that he loved liberty better than slavery, Prof. Hedrick, whose testimony we now offer, was peremptorily dismissed from his post as Analytical and Agricultural Chemist in the

University of North Carolina, ignominiously subjected to the indignities of a mob, and then savagely driven beyond the borders of his native State. His tyrannical persecutors, if not called to settle their accounts in another world within the next ten years, will probably survive to repent of the enormity of their pro-slavery folly.

In a letter vindicating his course at Chapil Hill—his only offence having been a mild expression of opinion in favor of Republicanism—Prof. H. says:

"Of my neighbors, friends and kindred, nearly one-half have left the State since I was old enough to remember. Many is the time I have stood by the loaded emigrant wagon, and given the parting hand to those whose faces I was never to look upon again. They were going to seek homes in the free West, knowing, as they did, that free and slave labor could not both exist and prosper in the same community. If any one thinks that I speak without knowledge, let him refer to the last census. He will there find that in 1850 there were fifty-eight thousand native North Carolinians living in the free States of the West—thirty-three thousand in Indiana alone. There were, at the same time, one hundred and eighty thousand Virginians living in the free States. Now, if these people were so much in love with the 'institution,' why did they not remain where they could enjoy its blessings?

"From my knowledge of the people of North Carolina, I believe that the majority of them who will go to Kansas during the next five years, would prefer that it should be a free State. I am sure that if I were to go there I should vote to exclude slavery."

MONCURE D. CONWAY.

In his volume entitled "Tracts for To-day," Mr. Conway, of Cincinnati, Ohio, formerly of Virginia, says:

"As a Virginian, with no ties of relationship northward of the remotest kind, past or present, I feel how easily I might slide into a justification of my dear mother, the South. But the soul knows no prejudices or sections, and must see all under the pure light of reason and conscience. . . . . I fear that, with the majority of us, the binding of a slave is not so horrible as the doubting of a miracle. . . . . The first error of the South has been an impatience in the discussion of the slavery question. reminding calm men of those unfortunate persons met with in lunatic asylums, who speak rationally on all topics until you touch that on which they are deranged, when their insanity bursts wildly forth. This has caused them to put themselves in an attitude before the world which has brought down its severest censure; and, feeling that this was not just what they deserved—since they were at least sincere—it has led them on to a still greater rage against a judgment which, however unfair, was the result of their own mistaken heat. It has precluded freedom of discussion even among themselves, a policy which no human brain or heart ever respected yet. The native sons of the South have again and again sought to discuss it in their own vicinities, and have as often been threatened and visited with angry processes, though the privilege is secured to them in the Bill of Rights of nearly every Southern State. The South has thus lost the confidence of many of her own children, who find that a freedom exercised by their lordly ancestors, Washington, Jefferson, Henry, and by them transmitted as an eternal inheritance, is now denied them by men who, beside those, are lilliputian."

J. E. SNODGRASS.

Vindicating his course, as editor of the *Baltimore Saturday Visitor*, against an unsuccessful attempt of certain members of the Maryland Legislature, in 1846, to suppress his paper and procure his imprison-ment, Dr. Snodgrass, of Virginia, more recently of Maryland, now of New York, said:

"There need be no fear of my arraying the slave against his master (as I have been charged with doing), however anxious I may be to array the sympathies of

the master in favor of his slave; in other words, to bring about the abolition of
slavery in Maryland by lawful as well as peaceful means, and with results which
shall convince my accusers that I have been the best friend of both master and
slave, and that the adoption of such views as I have been wont to promulge on all
suitable occasions, both in the *Visitor* and in my private intercourse with my
fellow-citizens, would be the surest guaranty of the glorious redemption of Maryland from the thralldom of an institution which has been her ever-present curse,
hanging, as it does, like an incubus upon the prosperity of the State, and utterly
crushing her every hope of future progress."

JOHN G. FEE.

In his "Anti-Slavery Manual," Mr. Fee, a noble, self-sacrificing
preacher of a free Gospel in Kentucky, says:

"Slavery causes the slaves to disregard the relation of marriage and practise the
consequent vice, concubinage. In our land, marriage, as a civil ordinance, they do
not enjoy. Our laws do not recognize this relation among them, nor defend it, nor
enforce its duties. This would interfere with the claims and interest of the master.
Hence, to use the language of the slaves themselves, they 'take up with one
another.' And this continues as long as their own convenience, and that of the
master, requires.

"Marriage is the great preservative against the abhorrent vices of concubinage
and adultery. It is the origin of those strong ties which cement and bind together
society. It is the fountain of the dearest earthly pleasures that man enjoys—
domestic bliss. Without it, the endearing relations of husband and wife, parent
and child, would be unknown. Without it, man and woman would wander forth,
selfish, shameless, and unrestrained, like one vast herd of brutes. And yet the
very tendency of our system of slavery is to abolish it. Christians! yea, all lovers
of virtue and order! what would you think, and how would you act, did these evils
exist to the same extent among the whites? And are they any the less ruinous to
society, and any the less criminal in the sight of God, in the black man than in the
white man? How many there are among us who are parents, and yet know no
one whom they can call husband or wife! And how many, even of those in whose
veins courses much of the blood of the white man, who know not their parents!
Oh! is it true that there is a single woman in the whole South who is opposed to
the abolition of slavery, when she remembers how many bosoms have been wrung
with anguish at the reflection that the husbands of their choice have been unfaith-
ful, in cases that never would have occurred had it not been for slavery? And I
will ask one more question. Is there in our State, even among Christians, as much
regard for the purity of the marriage relation of their slaves, and the proper descent
of slave children, as there is to have the best stock of sheep, hogs, cattle, to say
nothing of horses? May God pardon our shameful neglect of a relation which he
has so greatly honored."

JAMES D. PRETTYMAN.

As editor of the *Peninsular News and Advertiser*, published in Milford,
Del., Dr. Prettyman, who is there laboring manfully for the right, says:

"The great question to be settled by the people of this country in this the nineteenth century is, whether this boasted land of freedom shall become a nation of
masters and slaves, or whether it shall be made a land, the atmosphere of which no
slave can breathe and live a slave. . . . . . . We were born in a land of
slavery, have lived in a land of slavery, and are now writing in a land which is
deeply injured by slavery, and have had an opportunity to see and know something
of its inhumanity and wrong. We often wonder by what process of reasoning men
justify themselves in advocating the base, blighting institution. Slavery is bad
policy, it is an obstacle to the prosperity of the State, it has a demoralizing effect
on both master and slave, it is the origin of inhumanity, injustice and crime; but
far above all other arguments, objections, and sentiments of policy stands the un-
concealed truth, that it is wrong. It originated in wrong; it is the greatest wrong
of our age."

JOHN DIXON LONG.

In his "Pictures of Slavery," the painting of which aroused the mob
ocratic ire of his slaveholding neighbors, who forced him to leave the

State, Mr. Long, of Maryland, a minister of the Methodist Episcopal Church, says:

"It is contended that if the general conference should make slaveholding a test of membership, the preachers will not attempt to carry it out in slaveholding territory. Very well. Then the responsibility will rest on the preachers and members of that particular locality. The church at large and the discipline would be free from slaveholding taint; and brethren at the North and West would no longer have *their* cheeks mantled with shame, when infidels point to the discipline as it is, and prove that it allows men to hold human beings in ignorance and slavery, and will them at death to ungodly relatives, who may sell them as oxen. Let no man in the ministry or the laity of the M. E. Church leave her communion because her discipline is not yet perfect; but let him pray and labor, and lift up his voice against the abominations of chattel slavery, till a sound public opinion shall blow it away like chaff before the whirlwind."

WILLIAM S. BAILEY.

In his paper of May 13, 1859, in an article on the gubernatorial campaign, then progressing in his State, Mr. Bailey, the intrepid, mob-defying, persevering editor of the *Free South*, published in Newport, Kentucky, says:

"It must strike the mind of every reflecting man in Kentucky, as something strange and abnormal, to see the rank and file of the two political parties in the State engaged in a rivalry for extending over the domain of the Union the system of human chattelism which has been a blight and a curse to their own commonwealth. Such mad-cap zeal and transparent folly cannot long sway the minds of intelligent and honest men. There must be a reaction speedily, unless the propagandists succeed in carrying their measures, and in binding the white freemen of the country in fetters, before they become aroused to the impending danger.

"The present discussion, though of little moment in itself considered, may have some beneficial results. It may open the eyes of some men who have heretofore seemed half asleep, to the humiliating and disgraceful fact that our governments, State and National, are fast becoming mere engines for the perpetuation and propagation of slavery. In this direction, they are impelled by the slave-holding oligarchy, which aims at nothing short of the entire subjection of the whole country to the iron will of its despotism."

RICHARD HILDRETH.

In his "Despotism in America," Mr. Hildreth, the eminent historian, says:

"Slavery is a continuation of the state of war. It is true that one of the combatants is subdued and bound; but the war is not terminated. If I do not put the captive to death, this apparent clemency does not arise from any good will toward him, or any extinction on my part of hostile feelings and intentions. I spare his life merely because I expect to be able to put him to a use more advantageous to myself. And if the captive, on the other hand, feigns submission, still he is only watching for an opportunity to escape my grasp, and if possible to inflict upon me evils as great as those to which I have subjected him.

"War is justly regarded, and with the progress of civilization it comes every day more and more to be regarded, as the very greatest of social calamities. The introduction of slavery into a community, amounts to an eternal protraction of that calamity, and a universal diffusion of it through the whole mass of society, and that too, in its most ferocious form."

O. B. FROTHINGHAM.

In his speech before the American Anti-Slavery Society, in New York, May 8, 1856, Mr. Frothingham inquired:

"When shall we learn to speak plainly and sincerely against slavery, and to follow up our speech by our deeds? When shall we learn to throw our whole action unreservedly on the side of God? When will we believe that he who seeks first the kingdom of heaven shall have everything else added to him? They threaten us with war if we take this position. Useless threat! The war is already declared! The war has already begun! The war has been raging for half a century! Slavery itself is a condition of war. It had its origin in war, its first victims being captives of the spear. It lives by war—its agents being perpetually engaged in fomenting feuds between the native princes of Africa to gain material for their traffic. It protects itself by war—it hides behind walls and gates—it rings alarm bells; its barracks are guarded by armed patrols—it never walks abroad without bowie-knife and pistol—it appears in Boston, and the streets bristle with files of soldiery—the hall of justice is stunned by the din of arms—outcast ruffians and murderers stalk about insulting the citizens. It extends itself by war, riding into Kansas with rifle and halter, to conquer a territory it has stolen; substituting martial for civil law, and proclaiming the warrior's axiom that *might* is *right*. The very virtues incident to a state of slavery, the virtues of the dominant class, are warlike virtues such as belong to the soldier alone. The dashing recklessness, the hot-blooded chivalry, the lavish generosity, the fiery sense of honor, the careless gaiety, the frank, easy, good nature, the impetuous passion, whether of love or hate, the swaggering grace, the luxury, all mark the soldier. Such qualities are peculiar to feudal, which is military, society. Slavery is ever breathing menaces of war. On the least provocation it offers battle. For fifty years it has kept the country on the brink of civil broils. Only the greatest moderation on our part has saved us from bloodshed. It has submitted Boston to martial rule; it is waging war in Kansas. The North stands on the defensive with a pistol pointed at her breast. What is to be done? We must fight—in behalf of peace and order we must fight."

PARKE GODWIN.

In his volume entitled "Political Essays," Mr. Godwin, who always treats his subjects with remarkable elucidation and thoroughness, says:

"When the Constitution of the United States was formed, slavery existed in nearly all the States; but it existed as an acknowledged evil, which, it was hoped, the progress of events would, in the course of a few years, extinguish. With the exception of South Carolina, there was not a State in which some decided efforts had not been made toward its alleviation and ultimate removal. It was this feeling, that it was an evil, and that it would soon be abated, which excluded all mention of slavery by name from the Constitution, and which led to the adoption of such phraseology, in the parts referring to the subject, that they do not necessarily imply its existence. The Constitution was made for all time, while the makers of it supposed slavery to be but a transient fact, and the terms of it consequently were adapted to the larger purpose, and not to the temporary existence. A jurist from the interior of China, who knew nothing from the actual condition of our country, or Justinian, could he arise from the dead, would never learn, from the mere reading of that instrument, of the existence of slavery. He would read of 'persons held to service,' and of certain 'other persons,' who were to be counted only as three-fifths in the distribution of representative population; but he would never imagine them, unless expressly told, a species of property. The general sentiment was averse to slavery, and the men of the Revolution were unwilling to recognize it, except in an indirect and roundabout way, and then only, as they expected, for a limited period."

CHARLES W. ELLIOTT.

In the second volume of his excellent History of New England, Mr. Elliott says:

"A State is good or bad exactly in the degree in which it secures to each and all liberty to act out their individual natures according to the true principles of humanity and justice. Perfect society is complete individuality, acting in harmony with true law. The love of society is one of the strongest instincts of man's nature; it is a necessity. A hermit, therefore, is a monster, and anarchy impossible. It is also true that change and re-formation are a law of nature, opposed by stupidity, timidity, and selfish inaction. It is clear, too, that governments have, heretofore, been organized and upheld by the few for their own benefit, and the world has had only aristocracies and class legislation. The Republics of Greece and Rome were not republics, for they rested on a writhing people held in slavery. No such governments can or ought to continue long in peace, for revolt is the only remedy for the oppressed. . . . . . New England has done much to colonize and civilize the wide Western prairies, and wherever her men and women go, order, decency, industry, and education prevail over barbarism and violence. But she has more work to do ; we may hope that she will shake off that old man of the sea who hangs upon her—may more fully learn that principle is above profit, and a sound heart is better than a silver dollar—that she will lay her hand to the building up of galleries, and museums, and libraries, as well as of mills and workshops; and that she will not fear to meet and drive back the black brood of slavery to its own place, and assert, and maintain, and extend the rule of Right over Might; so that in the future, Democracy—the rights of all—may everywhere prevail over Aristocracy, which secures the privileges of the few, but perpetuates the wrongs of the many."

WILLIAM HENRY BURLEIGH.

In a volume of his fugitive poems, the reading of which has afforded us a high degree of pleasure, Mr. Burleigh says:

> " Now, tyrants ! look well to your path !
>   A cloud shall come over your fame,
> And the terrible storm of a free people's wrath,
>   Overwhelm you with anguish and shame !
> To years and to ages unborn,
>   Throughout every kindred and clime,
> Ye shall be as a by-word, a hissing and scorn,
>   To the pure and the good of all time !
> The curse of the slave and the taunt of the free
>   Henceforth and forever your portion shall be!

* * * * * * * *

> " Thank God ! that a limit is set
>   To the reach of the tyrant's control !
> That the down-trodden serf may not wholly forget
>   The right and the might of his soul !
> That though years of oppression may dim
>   The fire on the heart's altar laid,
> Yet, lit by the breath of Jehovah, like Him
>   It lives, and *shall* live, undecayed !
> Will the fires of the mountain grow feeble and die ?
>   Beware !—for the tread of the Earthquake is nigh !"

CHARLES C. BURLEIGH.

On the subject of " Slavery and the North," Mr. Burleigh says:

" The question of slavery is undeniably, for this country at least, the great question of the age. On the right decision of it depend interests too vast to be fitly set forth in words. Here are three millions of slaves in a land calling itself free ; three millions of human beings robbed of every right, and, by statute and custom, among a people self-styled Christian, held as brutes. Knowledge is forbidden, and religious worship, if allowed, is clogged with fetters ; the sanctity of marriage is denied ; and home and family and all the sacred names of kindred, which form the dialect of domestic love, are made unmeaning words. The soul is crushed, that the body may be safely coined into dollars. And not occasionally, by here and there a hardened villain, reckless alike of justice, law, and public sentiment ; fearing not God nor regarding man ; but on system, and by the combined strength of the whole nation. Most men at the North, and many even at the South, admit that this is wrong, all wrong—in morals, in policy every way wrong—that it is a gross injustice to the slave, a serious evil to the master, a great calamity to the country ; that it belies the nation's high professions, brings deep disgrace upon its character, and exposes it to unknown perils and disasters in the time to come."

J. MILLER M'KIM.

In his speech in the City Assembly Rooms, New York, May 11, 1859 Mr. McKim said:

"What the anti-slave trade agitation did incidentally for England, the anti-slaveholding agitation is doing collaterally for this country. It is rectifying public sentiment on all great questions of prerogative and duty. It is improving our politics, meliorating our religion, and raising the standard of public and social morals. The evidence of this is so palpable, that no one with eyes can fail to see it. . . . . . . In religion, the change, though less easily measured, is none the less striking. Ecclesiastically, as well as politically, anti-slavery has been a benefactor. It has stripped hypocrisy of its disguise, and divested priestcraft of much of its power for evil. Let me not be misunderstood ; I use this language in no sectarian sense. In what I say I allude to mere professional clergymen ; men who live by religion as demagogues do by politics ; Protestant as well as Catholic Tetzels, who peddle Christianity as a trade, and subsist on its profits. . . . . . The literature of the country has been revolutionized by our movement. Anti-slavery publications used to be burned in Charleston, and drowned in Philadelphia. Paulding and Park Benjamin, and the like, held sway in the republic of letters. Carey and Hart expurgated Longfellow's poems to increase their profits, and Hildreth and Whittier were only read by such as found their way into the anti-slavery office. How changed is everything now. The entire literature of the country—everything that is worthy of the name—is against slavery. Pro slavery booksellers grow rich on anti-slavery novels, and pandering theatrical managers put money in their purses from abolition dramas. All the best daily and weekly journals, and monthly and quarterly magazines are anti-slavery."

WILLIAM HENRY FURNESS.

In his " Derby Lecture," Dr. Furness, of Philadelphia, says :

" If we possessed the good that God hath showed us, were we obedient to his requisitions, were we to do justly, the fetters of the slave would disappear as if consumed by fire before the majestic and all-commanding sense of justice expressed in the action of the free Northern heart. Does any one ask at this late day, when the giant wrong which our country legalizes and fights for, threatens to strip us of the dearest attributes of freedom and humanity—does any one ask, what have we to do with the injustice that exists not here but in another part of the land? I answer freely, distinctly, emphatically, nothing. In simple justice we have no right to have anything to do with it. We have no right to stand guard over it as we do, with our unjust prejudices, more fatal than muskets or artillery. We have no right to surrender to it the sacred principle of freedom of speech, as we have done. We have no right to afford it the broad protection of our silence, as we do. We have no right to allow it to flourish in the capital of the nation as we do. We have no right to aid in extending and perpetuating and fighting for it, as, may God have mercy on us! we have done, and are doing. As we are doing all these unjust things, we are guilty of interfering most impertinently with things with which we have no right to interfere. We must turn over a new leaf, and learn, hard as the lesson may be, to mind every one his own business. And what is our business? Why, to do justly. It is what God specially requires of us, to cease from doing evil ; to maintain freedom of speech, that precious thing without which our civil security is but stubble, which the outbursting fires of violent passions may at any moment consume ; to guard the public liberties in the person of the meanest of the land ; to destroy injustice of all kinds, and let the voice of humanity, the swelling key-note of the world, be heard, pleading for the right."

A. D. MAYO.

In his new miscellaneous work, " Symbols of the Capital," a volume full of vigorous essays and fascinating delineations of life in the Empire State, Mr. Mayo says :

" The question of free labor is not to be argued so much from its economical results, though here the argument is triumphant, as from its spiritual aspects. Every true son of Adam will maintain that the happiest word that ever greeted his ears was his command to leave the Eden of childish innocence for a wilderness of manly toil. Free industry is for the elevation and education of the race. All human experience has demonstrated that the only way to greatness of any kind is the straight and narrow way of labor. And when man toils, in the exercise of his great attribute of freedom, he is in the way to gain his chief distinction. Creation is the grandest attribute of man, the point in which he approaches nearest his Maker. To create new combinations from the material universe; by the discipline of free industry to discover the creative laws of Omnipotence, and by obedience to them to express his best conceptions of existence ; to impress himself on the whole earth, and even fill the invisible elements with the finer energy of his victorious mind ; especially to create in the realm of spirit ; molding human nature into higher forms of individual and social life, and by a far-reaching insight, peopling the realms of imagination with new and glorious beings, which bear the seal of reality, and become the ideals of the generations. This is God-like, and only through Free Labor can man approach this throne of his power, and rise into the companionship of the creative love of the Father of all."

THOMAS DAVIS.

In the course of one of the best speeches ever made on the Kansas question—a speech replete with irrefutable facts and arguments—the delivery of which, in the House of Representatives, May 9, 1854, at once distinguished him in Congress and throughout the country, Mr. Davis, of Rhode Island, said :

"The despotism of slavery is not standing on its own basis, or defended by its own power, force, or ingenuity. It calls to its aid, and insists upon the obligation enforced by the doctrine that the Constitution of the United States requires of the general government to protect, maintain, and extend slavery. It is no longer an evil to be tolerated or endured, but, in the estimation of its fanatical advocates, it is to be extended and perpetuated.

"It is maintained by the combined power of monarchy, as represented in the Executive, wielding all the patronage of government by directly rewarding those who are subservient to its dictates, and proscribing all who dare to exercise with open manliness the right of American freemen, in condemnation of its rank injustice.

"Next, we have the slaveowners, who are an aristocracy not elected by or subject to any higher power, but firmly united by ties of common interest, ownership, and absolute control, amounting to a state of perpetual warfare where the weapons are all in the hands of one party. These combinations of power, monarchy, and oligarchy, might be deemed ample for the maintenance of their unholy ascendency ; but, sir, it seems it is not enough, for we have now a new proclamation in its defence. It finds itself incapable, with the weapons it has heretofore wielded, of accomplishing its purposes, and it now demands that the great and vital doctrine of the sovereignty of the people is peculiarly its own. Thus we have the combination of monarchy, or the powers of one man—oligarchy, or the favored few ; and democracy, or the powers of the whole people. Seizing upon this last principle, it profanes its holy name, using it for the purpose of sustaining a system destructive of all human rights ; for just in proportion as men feel the force and grandeur of their own nature and being, will they regard with sacred reverence the rights of others, which, in a republic, must be their highest security. Chattel slavery strikes at the root of this individual conviction, and is, to an alarming extent, destructive of the principles of self-government."

FREDERICK LAW OLMSTED.

In his "Seaboard Slave States," Mr. Olmsted, the eminently clever and competent superintendent of the great Central Park, in New York city—a traveller and author of exquisite discernment and indubitable veracity, writing from Norfolk, in Virginia, says :

"Incidents, trifling in themselves, constantly betray to a stranger the bad economy of using enslaved servants. The catastrophe of one such occurred since I began to write this letter. I ordered a fire to be made in my room, as I was going out this morning. On my return, I found a grand fire—the room door having been closed and locked upon it, and, by the way, I had to obtain assistance to open it, the lock being 'out of order.' Just now, while I was writing, down tumbled upon the floor, and rolled away close to the valance of the bed, half a hod-full of ignited coal, which had been so piled up on the diminutive grate, and left without a fender or any guard, that this result was almost inevitable. If I had not returned at the time I did, the house would have been fired, and probably an incendiary charged with it, while some Northern Insurance Company made good the loss to the owner. . . . . Such carelessness on the part of these enslaved servants you have momentarily to notice. The constantly-occurring delays, and the waste of time and labor that you encounter everywhere, are most annoying and provoking. The utter want of system and order, almost essential, as it would appear, where slaves are your instruments, is amazing. At a hotel, for instance, you go to your room and find no conveniences for washing; ring and ring again, and hear the office-keeper ring and ring again. At length two servants appear together at at your door, get orders, and go away. A quarter of an hour afterward, perhaps, one returns with a pitcher of water, but no towels; and so on. . . . . . It is impossible that the habits of the whole community should not be influenced by, and be made to accommodate to these habits of its laborers. It irresistibly affects the whole industrial character of the people. You may see it in the habits and manners of the free white mechanics and tradespeople. All of these must have dealings or be in competition with slaves, and so have their standard of excellence made low, and become accustomed to, until they are content with, slight, false, unsound workmanship."

THEODORE D. WELD.

Wielding a vigorous pen in behalf of a noble cause, the Pestalozzi of our country, Mr. Weld, founder and present principal of the famous eclectic school at Eagleswood, New Jersey, says:

"There is not a man on earth who does not believe that slavery is a curse. Human beings may be inconsistent, but human nature is true to herself. She has uttered her testimony against slavery with a shriek ever since the monster was begotten; and till it perishes amidst the execrations of the universe, she will traverse the world on its track, dealing her bolts upon its head, and dashing against it her condemning brand. We repeat it, every man knows that slavery is a curse. Whoever denies this, his lips libel his heart. Try him; clank the chains in his ears, and tell him they are for him; give him an hour to prepare his wife and children for a life of slavery; bid him make haste and get ready their necks for the yoke, and their wrists for the coffle-chains, then look at his pale lips and trembling knees, and you have Nature's testimony against slavery."

Thus, in the six last chapters inclusive, have we introduced a mass of anti-slavery arguments, human and divine, that will stand, irrefutable and convincing, as long as the earth itself shall continue to revolve in its orbit. Aside from unaffected truthfulness and candor, no merit is claimed for anything we have said on our own account. With the best of motives, and in the language of nature more than that of art, we have given utterance to the honest convictions of our heart—being impelled to it by a long-harbored and unmistakable sense of duty which grew stronger and deeper as the days passed away.

If half the time which has been spent in collecting and arranging these testimonies had been occupied in the composition of original matter, the weight of paper and binding and the number of pages would have been much greater ; but the value and effect of the contents would have been far less. From the first, our leading motive has been to convince our fellow-citizens of the South, non-slaveholders and slaveholders, that slavery, whether considered in all its bearings, or, setting aside the moral aspect of the question, and looking at it only in a pecuniary point of view, is impolitic, unprofitable, and degrading ; how well, thus far, we have succeeded in our undertaking, time will, perhaps, fully disclose.

In the words of a contemporaneous German writer, whose language we readily and heartily indorse, "It is the shame of our age that argument is needed against slavery." Taking things as they are, however, argument being needed, we have offered it; and we have offered it from such sources as will, in our honest opinion, confound the devil and his incarnate confederates.

These testimonies, culled from the accumulated wisdom of nearly sixty centuries, beginning with the great and good men of our own time, and running back through distant ages to Saint Paul, Saint John, and Saint Luke; to Cicero, Plato, and Socrates, to Solomon, David, and Moses, and even to the Deity himself, are the pillars of strength and beauty upon which the popularity of our work will, in all probability, be principally based. If the ablest writers of the Old Testament; if the eloquent prophets of old ; if the renowned philosophers of Greece and Rome ; if the heavenly minded authors and compilers of the New Testament; if the illustrious poets and prose-writers, heroes, statesmen, sages of all nations, ancient and modern; if God himself and the hosts of learned ministers whom he has commissioned to proclaim his word—if all these are wrong, then we are wrong ; on the other hand, however, if they are right, we are right; for, in effect, we only repeat and endeavor to enforce their precepts.

If we are in error, we desire to be corrected; and, if it is not asking too much, we respectfully request the advocates of slavery to favor us with an *exposé* of what they, in their one-sided view of things, conceive to be the advantages of their favorite and peculiar institution. Such an *exposé*, if skillfully executed, would doubtless be regarded as the funniest novel of the times—a fit production, if not too immoral in its tendencies, to be incorporated into the next edition of D'Israeli's Curiosities of Literature.

CHAPTER IX.

FREE FIGURES AND SLAVE.

God fix'd it certain, that, whatever day
Makes man a slave, takes half his worth away.
POPE'S HOMER.

UNDER this heading we propose to introduce the remainder of the more important statistics of the Free and of the Slave States;—especially those that relate to Commerce, Manufactures, Internal Improvements, Education and Religion. Originally it was our intention to devote a separate chapter to each of the industrial and moral interests above named; but other considerations have so greatly encroached on our space, that we are compelled to modify our design. To the thoughtful and discriminating reader, however, the chief statistics which follow will be none the less interesting for not being the subjects of annotation.

At present, all we ask of the pro-slavery men, no matter in what part of the world they may reside, is to look these figures fairly in the face. We wish them to do it, in the first instance, not on the platforms of public debate, where the exercise of eloquence is too often characterized by violent passion and subterfuge, but in their own private apartments, where no eye save that of the All-seeing One will rest upon them, and where, in considering the relations which they sustain to the past, the present, and the future, an opportunity will be afforded them of securing that most valuable of all possessions attainable on earth, a conscience void of offence toward God and man.

Each separate table or particular compilation of statistics will afford food for at least an hour's profitable reflection; indeed, the more these figures are studied, and the better they are understood, the sooner will the author's object be accomplished—the sooner will the genius of Universal Liberty dispel the dark clouds of slavery.

TABLE 13.

TONNAGE, EXPORTS AND IMPORTS OF THE FREE AND OF THE SLAVE STATES—1855.

Free States.	Tonnage.	Exports.	Imports.	Slave States.	Tonnage.	Exports.	Imports.
Cal.....	92,623	$8,224,066	$5,951,379	Ala. ...	36,274	$14,270,585	$619,964
Conn....	137,170	878,874	636,826	Ark....			
Illinois.	53,797	547,053	54,509	Del. ...	19,186	68,087	5,821
Indiana	8,698			Florida.	14,835	1,403,594	45,998
Iowa...				Georgia	29,505	7,543,519	273.716
Maine..	806,587	4,851,207	2,927,443	Ky.....	22,680		
Mass...	970,727	28,190,925	45,113,774	La.....	204,149	55,367,962	12,900,821
Mich...	69,490	568,091	281,379	Md.....	234,805	10,395,984	7,788,949
N. H. .	30,330	1,523	17,786	Miss....	2,475	....	1,661
N. J....	121,020	687	1,473	Mo.....	60,592		
N. Y...	1,404,221	113,731,238	164,776,511	N. C. ..	60,077	433,818	243,083
Ohio...	91,607	847,143	600,656	S. C....	60,935	12,700,250	1,588,542
Penn...	397,768	6,274,338	15,300,935	Tenn...	8,404		
R. I....	51,038	336,023	536,387	Texas..	8,812	916,961	262,568
Vt.	6,915	2,895,468	591.593	Va.....	92,788	4,379,928	855,405
Wis. ...	15,624	174,057	48,159				
	4,252,615	$167,520,693	$236,847,810		855,517	$107,480,688	$24,586,528

TABLE 14.

PRODUCT OF MANUFACTURES IN THE FREE AND IN THE SLAVE STATES—1850.

Free States.	Value of Annual products.	Capital invested.	Hands empl'ed	Slave States.	Value of Annual products.	Capital invested.	Hands empl'ed.
California	$12,862,522	$1,006,197	3,964	Alabama	$4,588,878	$3,450,606	4,936
Conn....	45,110,102	23,890,348	47,770	Arkansas	607,486	324,065	903
Illinois...	17,236,073	6,385,387	12,065	Delaware	4,649,296	2,978,945	3,888
Indiana..	18,922,651	7,941,002	14,342	Florida..	668,338	547,060	991
Iowa....	3,551,783	1,292,875	1,707	Georgia..	7,0·6,525	5,460,483	8,378
Maine....	24,664,185	14,700,452	28,078	Kentucky	24,588,483	12,350,734	24,385
Mass.....	151,137,145	83,357.642	165,938	Louisiana	7,320,948	5.318,074	6,437
Michigan.	10,976,894	6,534,250	9,290	Maryland	32,477,702	14,753,148	30,124
N. Hamp.	23,164,503	18,242,114	27,092	Miss.....	2,972,038	1,833,420	3,173
N. Jersey	39,713,586	22,184,730	37,311	Missouri.	23,749,265	9,079,695	16,850
New York	237,597,249	99,904,405	199,349	N. C.....	9,111,245	7,252,225	12,444
Ohio....	62,647,259	29,019,588	51,489	S. C.....	7,063,513	6,056,865	7,009
Penn.....	155,044,910	94,473,810	146,766	Tenn. ...	9,728,488	6,975,279	12,032
Rhode Is.	22,093,258	12,923,176	20,881	Texas...	1,165,538	539,290	1,066
Vermont.	8,570,920	5,001.377	8,445	Virginia.	29,705,387	18,109,993	29,109
Wisconsin	9,293,068	3,382,148	6,089				
	$842,586,058	$430,240,051	780,576		$165,413,027	$95,029,879	161,733

TABLE 15.

MILES OF CANALS AND RAILROADS IN THE FREE AND IN THE SLAVE STATES,
1854—1857.

Free States.	Canals, miles, 1854.	Railroads, miles, 1857.	Cost of Railroads, 1855.	Slave States.	Canals, miles, 1854.	Railroads, miles, 1857.	Cost of Railroads, 1855.
California	....	22	$25,224,191	Alabama .	51	484	$3,986,208
Conn.	61	600		Arkansas..			
Illinois...	100	2,524	55,663,656	Delaware.	14	120	600,000
Indiana..	367	1,806	29,585,923	Florida...	....	86	250,000
Iowa.....	....	253	2,300,000	Georgia ..	28	1,062	17,034,802
Maine ...	50	442	13,749.021	Kentucky..	486	306	6,179,072
Mass.....	100	1,285	59,167.781	Louisiana..	101	263	1,731,000
Michigan.	....	600	22,370,397	Maryland..	184	597	12,654,838
N. Hamp.	11	645	15,860,949	Mississippi.	....	410	4,520,000
N. Jersey	147	472	18,840,030	Missouri...	....	189	1,000,000
New York	989	2,700	111,882,503	N.Carolina	13	612	6,847,213
Ohio.....	921	2,869	67,798,202	S. Carolina	50	706	13,547,093
Penn.....	936	2,407	94,657,675	Tennessee.	....	508	10,436,610
Rhode Is.	....	85	2,614,484	Texas.....	....	57	16,466,250
Vermont..	....	515	17,998,835	Virginia...	189	1,479	
Wisconsin	....	629	5,600,000				
	8,682	17,855	$538,313,647		1,116	6,859	$95,252,581

TABLE 16.

BANK CAPITAL IN THE FREE AND IN THE SLAVE STATES—1855.

Free States.	Bank capital.	Slave States.	Bank capital.
California		Alabama	$2,296,400
Connecticut	$15,597,891	Arkansas..................	
Illinois	2,513,790	Delaware.................	1,393,175
Indiana	7,281,934	Florida............	
Iowa		Georgia	18,413,100
Maine......................	7,301,252	Kentucky	10,369,717
Massachusetts	54,492,660	Louisiana...	20,179,107
Michigan	980,416	Maryland	10,411,874
New Hampshire............	3,626,000	Mississippi, ...	240,165
New Jersey.................	5,314,885	Missouri..................	1,215,398
New York	83,773,288	North Carolina	5,205,073
Ohio	7,166,581	South Carolina............	16,603,253
Pennsylvania......	19,864,825	Tennessee	6,717,848
Rhode Island...............	17,511.162	Texas	
Vermont	3,275,656	Virginia	14,033,838
Wisconsin	1,400,000		
Total..................	$230,100,340	Total..............	$102,078,940

TABLE 17

MILITIA FORCE OF THE FREE AND OF THE SLAVE STATES—1852.

Free States.	Militia force.	Slave States.	Militia force.
California		Alabama	76,662
Connecticut	51,649	Arkansas................	17,137
Illinois	170,359	Delaware...............	9,229
Indiana	53,918	Florida	12,122
Iowa.......................		Georgia	57,312
Maine......................	62,588	Kentucky	81,840
Massachusetts	119,690	Louisiana	43,823
Michigan	63,938	Maryland	46,864
New Hampshire	32,151	Mississippi..............	36,084
New Jersey.......	39,171	Missouri................	61,000
New York..................	265,293	North Carolina	79,448
Ohio	176,455	South Carolina	55,209
Pennsylvania...............	276,070	Tennessee	71,252
Rhode Island...............	14,443	Texas	19,766
Vermont	23,915	Virginia	125,128
Wisconsin	32,203		
Total.................	1,381,843	Total.....	792,876

TABLE 18.

POST-OFFICE OPERATIONS IN THE FREE AND IN THE SLAVE STATES—1855.

Free States.	Stamps sold.	Total Postage collected.	Cost of Transport'g the mails.	Slave States.	Stamps sold.	Total Postage collected.	Cost of Transport'g the mails.
California..	$81,437	$234,591	$135,386	Alabama	$44,514	$104,514	$226,816
Connecticut	79,284	179,230	81,462	Arkansas	8,941	30,664	117,659
Illinois ...	105,252	279,887	280,083	Delaware	7,298	19,644	9,243
Indiana ..	60 578	180,405	190,480	Florida .	8,764	19,275	77,553
Iowa......	28,198	82,420	84,428	Georgia..	73,880	149,063	216,003
Maine.....	60,165	151,358	82,218	Kentucky	55,694	180,067	144,161
Mass...... .	259,062	532,184	153,091	Louisiana	50,778	133,753	133,810
Michigan ..	49,763	142,188	148,204	Maryland	77,743	191,485	192,743
New Hamp.	88,387	95,609	46,631	Miss.....	31,182	78,739	170,785
New Jersey	81,495	109,697	80,084	Missouri.	53,742	139,652	185,096
New York..	542,498	1,383,157	481,410	N. C.....	34,235	72,759	148,249
Ohio.......	167,958	452,643	421,870	S. C. ...	47,368	91,600	192,216
Penn......	217,293	583,013	251,833	Tenn. ...	48,377	103,686	116,091
Rhode Is...	30,291	58,624	13,891	Texas...	24,530	70,436	209,936
Vermont...	36,314	92,816	64,437	Virginia.	96,799	217,861	245,592
Wisconsin .	33,538	112,903	92,842				
	$1,719,513	$4,670,725	$2,608,295		$666,845	$1,553,198	$2,385,953

TABLE 19.

PUBLIC SCHOOLS OF THE FREE AND OF THE SLAVE STATES—1850.

Free States.	Number.	Teachers.	Pupils.	Slave States.	Number.	Teachers.	Pupils.
California	2	2	49	Alabama	1,152	1,195	28,380
Conn.....	1,656	1,787	71,269	Arkansas	353	355	8,493
Illinois...	4,052	4,248	125,725	Delaware	194	214	8,970
Indiana..	4,822	4,860	161,500	Florida..	69	73	1,878
Iowa	740	828	29,556	Georgia..	1,251	1,265	82,705
Maine....	4,042	5,540	192,815	Kentucky	2,234	2,306	71,429
Mass.....	3,679	4,443	176,475	Louisiana	664	822	25,046
Michigan.	2,714	3,231	110.455	Maryland	898	986	33,111
N. Hamp..	2,381	3,013	75,643	Mississippi	782	826	18,746
N. Jersey.	1,473	1,574	77,930	Missouri..	1,570	1,620	51,754
New York	11,580	13,965	675,221	N. C.....	2,657	2,730	104,095
Ohio	11,661	12,886	484,153	S. C......	724	739	17,838
Penn.....	9,061	10,024	413,706	Tennessee	2,680	2,819	104,117
Rhode Is..	416	518	23,180	Texas....	349	360	7,946
Vermont .	2,731	4,173	93,457	Virginia..	2,930	2,997	67,353
Wisconsin	1,423	1,529	58,817				
	62,433	72,621	2,769,901		18,507	19,307	581,861

TABLE 20.

LIBRARIES OTHER THAN PRIVATE IN THE FREE AND IN THE SLAVE STATES—1850.

Free States.	Number.	Volumes.	Slave States.	Number.	Volumes.
California			Alabama	56	20,623
Connecticut......	164	165,318	Arkansas	3	420
Illinois	152	62,486	Delaware	17	17,950
Indiana..........	151	68,403	Florida	7	2,660
Iowa	32	5,790	Georgia........	38	31,788
Maine	236	121,969	Kentucky	80	79,466
Massachusetts....	1,462	684,015	Louisiana.......	10	26,800
Michigan	417	107,943	Maryland.......	124	125,042
N. Hampshire.....	129	85,759	Mississippi	117	21,737
New Jersey	128	80,885	Missouri	97	75,056
New York........	11,013	1,760,820	North Carolina..	38	29,592
Ohio	352	186,826	South Carolina ..	26	107,472
Pennsylvania	393	363,400	Tennessee	34	22,896
Rhode Island.....	96	104,342	Texas	12	4,230
Vermont.........	96	64,641	Virginia	54	88,462
Wisconsin........	72	21,020			
	14,911	3,888,234		695	649,577

TABLE 21.

NEWSPAPERS AND PERIODICALS PUBLISHED IN THE FREE AND IN THE
SLAVE STATES—1850.

Free States.	Number.	Copies printed annually.	Slave States.	Number.	Copies printed annually.
California	7	161,208	Alabama........	60	2,662,741
Connecticut	46	4,267,932	Arkansas........	9	377,000
Illinois..........	107	5,102,276	Delaware	10	421,200
Indiana.	107	4,316,828	Florida	10	319,800
Iowa............ .	29	1,512,800	Georgia	51	4,070,868
Maine............	49	4,203,064	Kentucky	62	6,582,838
Massachusetts	202	64,820,564	Louisiana	55	12,416,224
Michigan........	58	3,247,736	Maryland	68	19,612,724
New Hampshire ..	38	3,067,552	Mississippi	50	1,752,504
New Jersey.......	51	4,098,678	Missouri........	61	6,195,560
New York........	428	115,385,473	North Carolina ..	51	2,020,564
Ohio	261	30,473,407	South Carolina ..	46	7,145,930
Pennsylvania.....	309	84,898,672	Tennessee.......	50	6,940,750
Rhode Island.....	19	2,756,950	Texas...........	34	1,296,924
Vermont	35	2,567,662	Virginia	87	9,223,068
Wisconsin........	46	2,665,487			
	1,790	334,146,261		704	81,038,698

TABLE 22.

ILLITERATE WHITE ADULTS IN THE FREE AND IN THE SLAVE STATES—1850.

Free States.	Native.	Foreign.	Total.	Slave States	Native.	Foreign.	Total.
California	2,201	2,917	5,118	Alabama	33,618	139	33,757
Conn. ...	826	4,013	4,739	Arkansas	16,792	27	16,819
Illinois ...	34,107	5,947	40,054	Delaware	4,132	404	4,536
Indiana..	67,275	3,265	70,540	Florida ..	3,564	295	3,859
Iowa.....	7,043	1,077	8,120	Georgia..	40,794	406	41,200
Maine ...	1,999	4,148	6,147	Kentucky	64,340	2,347	66,687
Mass.	1,055	26,484	27,539	Louisiana	14,950	6,271	21,221
Michigan.	4,903	3,009	7,912	Maryland	17,364	3,451	20,815
N. Hamp.	893	2,064	2,957	Mississippi	13,324	81	13,405
N. Jersey.	8,370	5,878	14,248	Missouri..	34,420	1,861	36,281
New York	23,241	68,052	91,293	N. C......	73,226	340	73,566
Ohio.....	51,968	9,062	61,030	S C.	15,580	104	15,684
Penn.	41,944	24,989	66,929	Tennessee	77,017	505	77,522
Rhode Is..	981	2,359	3,340	Texas....	8,337	2,488	10,825
Vermont..	565	5,624	6,189	Virginia..	75,868	1,137	77,005
Wisconsin	1,459	4,902	6,361				
	248,725	173,790	422,515		493,026	19,856	512,882

TABLE 23.

NATIONAL POLITICAL POWER OF THE FREE AND OF THE SLAVE STATES—
1859.

Free States.	Senators.	Reps. in lower H. of Cong.	Electoral votes.	Slave States.	Senators.	Reps. in lower H. of Cong.	Electoral votes.
California......	2	2	4	Alabama	2	7	9
Connecticut....	2	4	6	Arkansas	2	2	4
Illinois	2	9	11	Delaware.....	2	1	3
Indiana	2	11	13	Florida.......	2	1	3
Iowa	2	2	4	Georgia	2	8	10
Maine	2	6	8	Kentucky	2	10	12
Massachusetts..	2	11	13	Louisiana	2	4	6
Michigan	2	4	6	Maryland.....	2	6	8
Minnesota	2	2	4	Mississippi....	2	5	7
New Hampshire	2	3	5	Missouri......	2	7	9
New Jersey	2	5	7	N. Carolina...	2	8	10
New York......	2	33	35	S. Carolina ...	2	6	8
Ohio......... .	2	21	23	Tennessee	2	10	12
Pennsylvania ..	2	25	27	Texas	2	2	4
Rhode Island ...	2	2	4	Virginia	2	13	15
Vermont.......	2	3	5				
Wisconsin	2	3	5				
	34	146	180		30	90	120

TABLE 24.

POPULAR VOTE FOR PRESIDENT BY THE FREE AND BY THE SLAVE STATES
1856.

Free States.	Rep. Fremont.	Amer. Fillmore.	Dem. Buchanan.	Total.	Slave States.	Rep. Frem.	Amer. Fillmore.	Dem. Buch'n.	Total.
Cal....	20,339	35,113	51,925	107,377	Ala....		28,552	46,739	75,291
Conn..	42,715	2,615	34,995	80,325	Ark..		10,787	21,910	32,697
Illinois	96,189	37,444	105,348	238,981	Del....	308	6,175	8,004	14,487
Ind. ..	94,375	22,386	118,670	235,431	Florida		4,833	6,358	11,191
Iowa..	43,954	9,180	36,170	89,304	Ga....		42,228	56,578	98,806
Maine.	67,379	3,325	39,080	109,784	Ky....	314	67,416	74,642	142.372
Mass..	108,190	19,626	39,240	167,056	La....		20,709	22,164	42,873
Mich..	71,762	1,660	52,136	125,558	Md....	281	47,460	39,115	86,856
N. H...	38,345	422	32,789	71,556	Miss...		24,195	35,446	59,641
N. J...	28,338	24,115	46,943	99,396	Mo....		48,524	58,164	106,688
N. Y....	276.907	124,604	195,878	597,389	N. C...		36,886	48,246	85,132
Ohio..	187,497	28,126	170,874	386,497	S. C.*.				
Penn..	147,510	82,175	230,710	460,395	Tenn..		66,178	73,638	139,816
R. I...	11,467	1,675	6,580	19,722	Texas..		15,244	28,757	44,001
Vt.....	39,561	545	10,569	50,675	Va....	291	60,278	89,826	150,395
Wis. ..	66,090	579	52,843	119,512					
	1,340,618	393,590	1,224,750	2,958,958		1,194	479,465	609,587	1,090,246

No popular vote
8*

TABLE 25.

VALUE OF CHURCHES IN THE FREE AND IN THE SLAVE STATES—1850.

Free States.	Value.	Slave States.	Value.
California	$288,400	Alabama	$1,244,741
Connecticut	3,599,330	Arkansas...	149,686
Illinois.....	1,532,305	Delaware......	340,345
Indiana	1,568,906	Florida....................	192,600
Iowa	235,412	Georgia	1,327,112
Maine.........	1,794,209	Kentucky	2,295,353
Massachusetts	10,504,888	Louisiana	1,940,495
Michigan	793,180	Maryland	3,974,116
New Hampshire.............	1,433,266	Mississippi...........	832,622
New Jersey................	3,712,863	Missouri...................	1,730,135
New York	21,539,561	North Carolina	907,785
Ohio	5,860,059	South Carolina............	2,181,476
Pennsylvania..............	11,853,291	Tennessee	1,246,951
Rhode Island..............	1,293,600	Texas	408,944
Vermont	1,251,655	Virginia	2,902,220
Wisconsin	512,552		
Total	$67,773,477	Total................	$21,674,581

TABLE 26.

**PATENTS ISSUED ON NEW INVENTIONS IN THE FREE AND IN THE SLAVE
STATES—1856.**

Free States.	Patents.	Slave States.	Patents.
California	13	Alabama	11
Connecticut	142	Arkansas	
Illinois....................	93	Delaware..................	8
Indiana	67	Florida....................	8
Iowa	14	Georgia	13
Maine.........	42	Kentucky	26
Massachusetts	331	Louisiana	30
Michigan	22	Maryland	49
New Hampshire......	43	Mississippi...............	8
New Jersey................	78	Missouri...................	32
New York	592	North Carolina	9
Ohio ..:	139	South Carolina............	10
Pennsylvania..............	267	Tennessee	23
Rhode Island..............	18	Texas	4
Vermont	35	Virginia	42
Wisconsin	33		
Total.................	1,929	Total................	268

TABLE 27.

BIBLE CAUSE AND TRACT CAUSE IN THE FREE AND IN THE SLAVE STATES—1855.

Free States.	Contributions for the Bible Cause.	Contributions for the Tract Cause.	Slave States.	Contributions for the Bible Cause.	Contributions for the Tract Cause.
California........	$1,900	$ 5	Alabama	$3,351	$477
Connecticut......	24,528	15,872	Arkansas.......	2,950	110
Illinois...........	28,403	8,786	Delaware.......	1,037	163
Indiana..........	6,755	1,491	Florida.........	1,957	5
Iowa	4,216	2,005	Georgia	4,582	1,468
Maine......	5,449	2,981	Kentucky	5,956	1,366
Massachusetts....	43,444	11,492	Louisiana	1,810	1,099
Michigan	5,554	1,114	Maryland.......	8,909	5,365
New Hampshire ..	6,271	1,288	Mississippi......	1,067	267
New Jersey	15,475	8,546	Missouri........	4,711	936
New York........	123,386	61,233	N. Carolina....	6,197	1,419
Ohio.............	25,758	9,576	S. Carolina	3,984	3,222
Pennsylvania	25,360	12.121	Tennessee	8,383	1,807
Rhode Island.....	2,669	2,121	Texas	3,935	127
Vermont	5,709	2,867	Virginia	9,296	6,894
Wisconsin........	4,790	474			
	$319,667	$131,972		$68,125	$24,725

TABLE 28.

MISSIONARY CAUSE AND COLONIZATION * CAUSE IN THE FREE AND IN THE SLAVE STATES—1855-1856.

Free States.	Contributions for Missionary purposes, 1855.	Contributions for Colonization purposes, 1856.	Slave States.	Contributions for Missionary purposes, 1855.	Contributions for Colonization purposes, 1856.
California......	$ 192	$ 1	Alabama	$5,963	$1,113
Connecticut....	48,044	9,233	Arkansas	455	1
Illinois	10,040	543	Delaware	1,003	250
Indiana	4,705	34	Florida	340	13
Iowa	1,750	3	Georgia.......	9,846	5,323
Maine	13,929	1,719	Kentucky ...	6,953	4,436
Massachusetts..	128,505	1,422	Louisiana	334	871
Michigan	4,935	4	Maryland.....	20,677	406
New Hampshire	11,963	1,130	Mississippi	4,957	2,177
New Jersey	19,946	8,261	Missouri	2,712	313
New York......	172,115	24,371	North Carolina	6,010	969
Ohio......... .	19,890	2,687	South Carolina	15,248	129
Pennsylvania ..	43,412	4,287	Tennessee	4,971	1,611
Rhode Island ...	9,440	2,125	Texas	349	6
Vermont	11,094	304	Virginia	22,106	10,000
Wisconsin	2,216	806			
	$502,174	$51,930		$101,934	$27,613

* For colonizing free blacks in Liberia.

TABLE 29.

DEATHS IN THE FREE AND IN THE SLAVE STATES—1850.*

Free States.	Number of deaths.	Ratio to the Number living.	Slave States.	Number of deaths.	Ratio to the Number living.
California			Alabama........	9,084	84.94
Connecticut......	5,781	64.13	Arkansas........	2,987	70.18
Illinois	11,619	73.28	Delaware........	1,209	75.71
Indiana..........	12,728	77.65	Florida.....	963	93.67
Iowa	2,044	94.03	Georgia	9,920	91.93
Maine	7,545	77.29	Kentucky	15,206	64.60
Massachusetts....	19,414	51.23	Louisiana	11.948	42.85
Michigan	4,520	88.19	Maryland........	9,594	60.77
N. Hampshire.....	4,268	74.49	Mississippi.......	8,711	69.93
New Jersey	6,467	75.70	Missouri........	12,211	55.81
New York........	44,839	69.85	North Carolina ..	10,207	85.12
Ohio	28,949	68.41	South Carolina..	7,997	83.59
Pennsylvania	28,318	81.05	Tennessee	11,759	85.34
Rhode Island.....	2,241	65.83	Texas	3,046	69.79
Vermont.........	3,132	100.13	Virginia	19,053	74.61
Wisconsin........	2,884	105.82			
	184,249	72.91		133,865	71.82

TABLE 30.

FREE WHITE MALE PERSONS OVER FIFTEEN YEARS OF AGE ENGAGED IN AGRICULTURAL AND OTHER OUT-DOOR LABOR IN THE SLAVE STATES— 1850.

States.	Number engaged in Agriculture.	Number engaged in other out-door labor.	Total..
Alabama.............................	67,742	7,229	74,971
Arkansas........................ ..	28,436	5,596	84,082
Delaware.....................	6,225	4,184	10,409
Florida..........	5,472	2,598	8,070
Georgia	82,107	11,054	93,161
Kentucky	110,119	26,308	136,427
Louisiana...	11,524	13,827	25,351
Maryland............	24,672	17,146	41,818
Mississippi, ...	50,028	5,823	55,851
Missouri............................	64,292	19,900	84,192
North Carolina	76,338	21,876	98,214
South Carolina.......................	37,612	6,991	44,603
Tennessee	115,844	16,795	132,639
Texas ....:.....	24,987	22,713	47,700
Virginia	97,654	33,928	131,582
	803,052	215,968	1,019,020

* For an explanation of this Table see the next three pages

Too hot in the South, and too unhealthy there—white men "can't stand it"—negroes only can endure the heat of Southern climes! How often are our ears insulted with such wickedly false assertions as these! In what degree of latitude—pray tell us—in what degree of latitude do the rays of the sun become too calorific for white men? Certainly in no part of the United States, for in the extreme South we find a very large number of non-slaveholding whites over the age of fifteen, who derive their entire support from manual labor in the open fields. The sun, that brilliant bugbear of pro-slavery politicians, shone on more than one million of free white laborers—mostly agriculturists—in the slave States in 1850, exclusive of those engaged in commerce, trade, manufactures, the mechanic arts, and mining. Yet, notwithstanding all these instances of exposure to his wrath, we have had no intelligence whatever of a single case of *coup de soleil.* Alabama is not too hot; sixty-seven thousand white sons of toil till her soil. Mississippi is not too hot; fifty-five thousand free white laborers are hopeful devotees of her out-door pursuits. Texas is not too hot; forty-seven thousand free white persons, males, over the age of fifteen, daily perform their rural vocations amidst her unsheltered air.

It is stated on good authority that, in January, 1856, native ice, three inches thick, was found in Galveston Bay; we have seen it ten inches thick in North Carolina, with the mercury in the thermometer at two degrees below zero. In January, 1857, while the snow was from three to five feet deep in many parts of North Carolina, the thermometer indicated a degree of coldness seldom exceeded in any State in the Union—thirteen degrees below zero. The truth is, instead of its being too hot in the South for white men, it is too cold for negroes; and we long to see the day arrive when the latter shall have entirely receded from their uncongenial homes in America, and given full and undivided place to the former.

Too hot in the South for white men! It is not too hot for white women. Time and again, in different counties in North Carolina, have we seen the poor white wife of the poor white husband, following him in the harvest-field from morning till night, binding up the grain as it fell from his cradle. In the immediate neighborhood from which we hail, there are not less than thirty young women, non-slaveholding whites, between the ages of fifteen and twenty-five—some of whom are so well known to us that we could call them by name—who labor in the fields every summer; often hiring themselves out during harvest-time, the very hottest season of the year, to bind wheat and oats—each of them keeping up with the reaper; and this for the paltry consideration of twenty-five cents per day.

That any respectable man—any man with a heart or a soul in his composition—can look upon these poor toiling white women without feeling indignant at that accursed system of slavery which has entailed on them the miseries of poverty, ignorance, and degradation, we shall not do ourself the violence to believe. If they and their husbands, and their sons and daughters, and brothers and sisters, are not righted in some of the more important particulars in which they have been wronged, the fault shall lie at other doors than our own. In their behalf, chiefly, have we written and compiled this work ; and until our object shall have been accomplished, or until life shall have been extinguished, there shall be no abatement in our efforts to aid them in regaining the natural and inalienable prerogatives out of which they have been so craftily swindled. We want to see no more plowing, or hoeing, or raking, or grain-binding, by white women in the Southern States ; employment in cotton-mills and other factories would be far more profitable and congenial to them, and this they will have within a short period after slavery shall have been abolished.

Too hot in the South for white men ! What is the testimony of reliable Southrons themselves? Says Cassius M. Clay, of Kentucky :

" In the extreme South, at New Orleans, the laboring men—the stevedores and hackmen on the levee, where the heat is intensified by the proximity of the red brick buildings, are all white men, and they are in the full enjoyment of health. But how about cotton? I am informed by a friend of mine—himself a slaveholder, and therefore good authority—that in northwestern Texas, among the German settlements, who, true to their national instincts, will not employ the labor of a slave—they produce more cotton to the acre, and of a better quality, and selling at prices from a cent to a cent and a half a pound higher than that produced by slave labor."

Says Gov. Hammond, of South Carolina :

" The steady heat of our summers is not so prostrating as the short, but frequent and sudden, bursts of Northern summers."

In an extract, which may be found in our second chapter, and to which we respectfully refer the reader, it will be seen that this same South Carolinian, speaking of " not less than fifty thousand " non-slaveholding whites, says—' Most of these now follow agricultural pursuits."

Says Dr. Cartwright, of New Orleans :

" Here in New Orleans, the larger part of the drudgery—work requiring exposure to the sun, as railroad-making, street-paving, dray-driving, ditching, and building, is performed by white people."

To the statistical tables which show the number of deaths in the free and in the slave States in 1850, we would direct special attention. Those persons, particularly the propagandists of negro slavery, who, heretofore, have been so dreadfully exercised on account of what they have been pleased to term " the insalubrity of Southern climes," will there find something to allay their fearful apprehensions. A critical examination of said tables will disclose the fact that, in proportion to population, deaths occur more frequently in Massachusetts than in any Southern State except Louisiana ; more frequently in New York than in any of the Southern States, except Maryland, Missouri, Kentucky, Louisiana, and Texas ; more frequently in New Jersey, in Pennsylvania, and in Ohio, than in either Georgia, Florida, or Alabama. Leaving Wisconsin and Louisiana out of the account, and then comparing the bills of mortality in the remaining Northern States, with those in the remaining Southern States, we find the difference decidedly in favor of the latter : for, according to this calculation, while the ratio of deaths is as only one to 74.60 of the living population in the Southern States, it is as one to 72.39 in the Northern.

Says Dr. J. C. Nott, of Mobile :

" Heat, moisture, animal and vegetable matter, are said to be the elements which produce the diseases of the South, and yet tne testimony in proof of the health of the banks of the lower portion of the Mississippi River is too strong to be doubted,—not only the river itself, but also the numerous bayous which meander through Louisiana. Here is a perfectly flat alluvial country, covering several hundred miles, interspersed with interminable lakes, lagunes and jungles, and still we are informed by Dr. Cartwright, one of the most acute observers of the day, that this country is exempt from miasmatic disorders, and is extremely healthy. His assertion has been confirmed to me by hundreds of witnesses, and we know from our own observation, that the population present a robust and healthy appearance."

But the best part is yet to come. In spite of all the blatant assertions of the oligarchy, that the climate of the South was arranged expressly for the negroes, and that the negroes were created expressly to inhabit it as the healthful servitors of other men, a carefully kept register of all the deaths that occurred in Charleston, South Carolina, for the space of six years, shows that, even in that locality which is generally regarded as so unhealthy, the annual mortality was much greater among the blacks, in proportion to population, than among the whites. Dr. Nott himself shall state the facts. He says :

" The average mortality for the last six years in Charleston for all ages is 1 in 51, including all classes. Blacks alone 1 in 44 ; whites alone, 1 in 58—a very remarkable result, certainly. This mortality is perhaps not an unfair test, as the population during the last six years has been undisturbed by emigration and acclimated in a greater proportion than at any former period."

Numerous other authorities might be cited in proof of the general healthiness of the climate south of Mason and Dixon's line. Of 127 remarkable cases of American longevity, published in a recent edition of Blake's Biographical Dictionary, 68 deceased centenarians are credited to the Southern States, and 59 to the Northern—the list being headed with Betsey Trantham, of Tennessee—a white woman, who died in 1834, at the extraordinarily advanced age of 154 years.

TABLE 31.

NATIVES OF THE SLAVE STATES IN THE FREE STATES, AND NATIVES OF THE
FREE STATES IN THE SLAVE STATES.—1850.

Free States.	Natives of the Slave States.	Slave States.	Natives of the Free States.
California.........................	24,055	Alabama.....................	4,947
Connecticut	1,390	Arkansas....................	7,965
Illinois.......................	144,809	Delaware....	6,996
Indiana.......................	176,581	Florida.......................	1,718
Iowa	31,392	Georgia.....	4,249
Maine	458	Kentucky..........	31,340
Massachusetts	2,980	Louisiana...................	14,567
Michigan	3,634	Maryland....	23,815
New-Hampshire	215	Mississippi..................	4,517
New-Jersey	4,110	Missouri..........	55,664
New-York.....................	12,625	North Carolina.............	2,167
Ohio.........................	152,319	South Carolina.............	2,427
Pennsylvania	47,180	Tennessee..................	6,571
Rhode Island.................	982	Texas.......................	9,982
Vermont.....................	140	Virginia....................	28,999
Wisconsin....................	6,353		
Total............	609,223	Total..........	205,924

This last table, compiled from the 116th page of the Compendium of
the Seventh Census, shows, in a most lucid and startling manner, how
negroes, slavery and slaveholders are driving the native non-slaveholding whites away from their homes, and keeping at a distance other
decent people. From the South the tide of emigration still flows in a
westerly and northwesterly direction, and so it will continue to do
until slavery is abolished.

TABLE 32.

VALUE OF THE SLAVES AT $400 PER HEAD.—1850.*

States.	Value of the Slaves at $400 per head.	Value of Real and Personal Estate, less the value of slaves at $400 per head.
Alabama	$137,137,600	$81,066,732
Arkansas................................	18,840,000	21,001,025
Delaware............	916,000	17,989,863
Florida........	15,724,000	7,474,734
Georgia	152,672,800	182,752,914
Kentucky...............;..............	84,392,400	217,236,056
Louisiana...............................	97,923,600	136,075,164
Maryland	36,147,200	188,070,164
Mississippi	123,951,200	105,000,000
Missouri...	34,968,800	102,278,907
North Carolina........................	115,419,200	111,381,272
South Carolina........................	153,993,600	134,264,094
Tennessee................	95,783,600	111,671,104
Texas..................................	23,264,400	32,097,940
Virginia...	189,011,200	202,634,638
	$1,280,145,600	$1,655,945,137

* It is intended that this table shall be considered in connection with table No., 10.

To Dr. G. Bailey, editor of the *National Era*, Washington City, D. C., we are indebted for the following useful and interesting statistics, to which some of our readers will doubtless have frequent occasion to refer:

PRESIDENTS OF THE UNITED STATES.

March 4, 1789 " 3, 1797 } George Washington, Virginia.	March 4, 1837 " 3, 1841 } Martin Van Buren, New York.
March 4, 1797 " 3, 1801 } John Adams, Massachusetts.	March 4, 1841 " 3, 1845 } William H. Harrison, Ohio.
March 4, 1801 " 3, 1809 } Thomas Jefferson, Virginia.	March 4, 1845 " 3, 1849 } James K. Polk, Tennessee.
March 4, 1809 " 3, 1817 } James Madison, Virginia.	March 4, 1849 " 3, 1853 } Zachary Taylor, Louisiana.
March 4, 1817 " 3, 1825 } James Monroe, Virginia.	March 4, 1853 " 3, 1857 } Franklin Pierce, N. H.
March 4, 1825 " 3, 1829 } John Q. Adams, Mass.	March 4, 1857 " 3, 1861 } James Buchanan, Penn.
March 4, 1829 " 3, 1837 } Andrew Jackson, Tennessee.	

At the close of the term for which Mr. Buchanan is elected, it will have been seventy-two years since the organization of the present government.—

In that period, there have been eighteen elections for President, the candidates chosen in twelve of them being Southern men and slaveholders, in six of them Northern men and non-slaveholders.

No Northern man has ever been reëlected, but five Southern men have been thus honored.

Gen. Harrison, of Ohio, died one month after his inauguration. Gen. Taylor, of Louisiana, about four months after his inauguration. In the former case, John Tyler, of Virginia, became acting President, in the latter, Millard Fillmore of New York.

Of the seventy-two years, closing with Mr. Buchanan's term, should he live it out, Southern men and slaveholders have occupied the Presidential chair forty eight years and three months, or a little more than two-thirds of the time.

THE SUPREME COURT.

The judicial districts are organized so as to give five judges to the slave States, and four to the free, although the population, wealth and business of the latter are far in advance of those of the former. The arrangement affords, however, an excuse for constituting the Supreme Court, with a majority of judges from the slave holding States.

MEMBERS.

Chief Justice—R. B. Taney, Maryland.
Associate Justice—J. M. Wayne, Georgia.
"   "   John Catron, Tennessee.
"   "   P. V. Daniel, Virginia.
"   "   John A. Campbell, Ala.
"   "   John McLean, Ohio.

Associate Justice—S. Nelson, New York.
"   "   R. C. Grier, Pennsylvania.
"   "   Nathan Clifford, Maine.
Reporter, B. C. Howard, Maryland.
Clerk, W. T. Carroll, D. C.

SECRETARIES OF STATE.

The highest office in the Cabinet is that of Secretary of State, who has under his charge the foreign relations of the country. Since the year 1789, there have been twenty-three appointments to the office—fourteen from slave States, nine from free. Or, counting by years, the post has been filled by Southern men and slaveholders very nearly forty years out of sixty-nine as follows:

Appointed.
Sept. 26, 1789, Thomas Jefferson, Virginia.
Jan. 2, 1794, E. Randolph, Virginia
Dec. 10, 1795, T. Pickering, Massachusetts.
May 13, 1800, J. Marshall, Virginia.
March 5, 1801, James Madison, Virginia.
March 6, 1809, R. Smith, Maryland.
April 2, 1811, James Mon oe, Virginia.
Feb. 28, 1815, "   "   "
March 5, 1815, J. Q. Adams, Massachusetts.
March 7, 1825, Henry Clay, Kentucky.
March 6, 1829, Martin Van Buren, New York.
May 24, 1831, E. Livingston, Louisiana.

Appointed.
May 29. 1833, Louis McLane, Delaware.
June 27, 1834, J. Forsyth, Georgia.
March 5, 1841, Daniel Webster, Mass.
July 24, 1843, A. P. Upshur, Virginia.
March 6, 1844, J. C. Calhoun, South Carolina
March 5, 1845, James Buchanan, Penn.
March 7, 1849, J. M. Clayton, Delaware.
July 20, 1850, Daniel Webster, Mass.
Dec. 5, 1851, E. Everett, Massachusetts.
March 5, 1853, W. L. Marcy, New York.
March 6, 1857, Lewis Cass, Michigan.

PRESIDENTS PRO TEM. OF THE SENATE.

Since the year 1809, every President *pro tem.* of the Senate of the United States has been a Southern man and slaveholder, with the exception of Samuel L. Southard, of New Jersey, who held the office for a very short time, and Mr. Bright, of Indiana, who has held it for one or two sessions, we believe, having been elected, however, as a known adherent of the slave interest, believed to be interested in slave "property."

SPEAKERS OF THE HOUSE OF REPRESENTATIVES.

April, 1789 March 3, 1791	F. A. Muhlenberg, Penn.
Oct. 24, 1791 March 2, 1793	J. Trumbull, Connecticut.
Dec. 2, 1793 March 3, 1795	F. A. Muhlenberg, Penn.
Dec. 7, 1795 March 3, 1797	Jonathan Dayton, N. J.
May 15, 1797 March 3, 1799	" " "
Dec. 2, 1799 March 3, 1801	Theodore Sedgwick, Mass.
Dec. 7, 1801 March 3, 1807	Nathaniel Macon, N. C.
Oct. 26, 1807 March 3, 1811	J. B. Varnum, Massachusetts.
March 4, 1811 Jan. 19, 1814	Henry Clay, Kentucky.
Jan. 19, 1814 March 2, 1815	Langdon Cheves, S. C.
Dec. 4, 1815 Nov. 13, 1820	Henry Clay, Kentucky.
Nov. 15, 1820 March 3, 1821	J. W. Taylor, New York.
Dec. 3, 1821 March 3, 1823	P. B. Barbour, Virginia.
Dec. 1, 1823 March 3, 1825	Henry Clay, Kentucky.
Dec. 5, 1825 March 3, 1827	J. W. Taylor, New York.
Dec. 3, 1827 June 2, 1834	A. Stevenson, Virginia.
June 2, 1834 March 3, 1835	John Bell, Tennessee.
Dec. 7, 1835 March 3, 1839	James K. Polk, Tennessee.
Dec. 16, 1839 March 3, 1841	R. M. T. Hunter, Virginia.
May 31, 1841 March 3, 1843	John White, Tennessee.
Dec. 4, 1843 March 3, 1845	J. W. Jones, Virginia.
Dec. 1, 1845 March 3, 1847	J. W. Davis, Indiana.
Dec. 6, 1847 March 3, 1849	R. C. Winthrop, Mass.
Dec. 22, 1849 March 3, 1851	Howell Cobb, Georgia.
Dec. 1, 1851 March 3, 1853	Linn Boyd, Kentucky.
Dec. 1, 1853 March 3, 1855	" " "
Feb. 28, 1856 March 3, 1857	Nathaniel P. Banks, Mass.
Dec. 7. 1857 March 3, 1859	James L. Orr, S. C.

POSTMASTERS-GENERAL.

Appointed—
Sept. 26, 1789, S. Osgood, Massachusetts.
Aug. 12, 1791, T. Pickering, Massachusetts.
Feb. 25, 1795, J. Habersham, Georgia.
Nov. 28, 1801, G. Granger, Connecticut.
March 17, 1814, R J. Meigs, Ohio.
June 25, 1823, John McLean, Ohio.
March 9, 1829, W. T. Barry, Kentucky.
May 1, 1835, A. Kendall, Kentucky.
May 18, 1840, J. M. Niles, Connecticut.

Appointed—
March 6, 1841, F. Granger, New York.
Sept. 13, 1841, C. A. Wickliffe, Kentucky.
March 5, 1845, C. Johnson, Tennessee.
March 7, 1849, J. Collamer, Vermont.
July 20, 1850, N. K. Hall, New York.
Aug. 31, 1852, S. D. Hubbard, Connecticut.
March 5, 1853, J. Campbell, Pennsylvania.
March 6, 1857, Aaron V. Brown, Tennessee.

Sectionalism does not seem to have had much to do with this department or with that of the interior, created in 1848-'49.

SECRETARIES OF THE INTERIOR.

Appointed—
March 7, 1849, T. Ewing, Ohio.
July 20, 1850, J. A. Pearce, Maryland.
Aug. 15, 1850, T. M. T. McKennon, Pa.

Appointed—
Sept. 12, 1850, A. H. H. Stuart, Virginia.
March 5, 1853, R. McClelland, Michigan.
March 6, 1857, Jacob Thompson, Mississippi

ATTORNEYS-GENERAL.

Appointed—
Sept. 26, 1789, E. Randolph, Virginia.
June 27, 1794, W Bradford, Pennsylvania.
Dec. 10, 1795, C. Lee, Virginia.
Feb. 20, 1800, T. Parsons, Massachusetts.
March 5, 1801, L. Lincoln, Massachusetts.
March 2, 1805, R. Smith, Maryland.
Dec. 23, 1805, J. Breckinridge, Kentucky.
Jan. 20, 1807, C. A. Rodney, Pennsylvania.
Dec. 11, 1811, W. Pinkney, Maryland.
Feb. 10, 1814, R. Rush, Pennsylvania.
Nov. 13, 1817, W. Wirt, Virginia.
March 9, 1829, J. McPherson Berrien, Georgia.
July 20, 1831, Roger B. Taney, Maryland.

Appointed—
Nov. 15, 1833, B. F. Butler, New York.
July 7, 1838, F. Grundy, Tennessee.
Jan. 10, 1840, H. D. Gilpin, Pennsylvania.
March 5, 1841, J. J. Crittenden, Kentucky.
Sept. 13, 1841, H. S. Legare, South Carolina.
July 1, 1843, John Nelson, Maryland.
March 5, 1845, J. Y. Mason, Virginia.
Oct. 17, 1846, N. Clifford, Maine.
June 21, 1848, Isaac Toucey, Connecticut.
March 7, 1849, R. Johnson, Maryland.
July 20, 1850, J. J. Crittenden, Kentucky.
March 5, 1853, C. Cushing, Massachusetts.
March 6, 1857, Jeremiah S. Black, Pa.

SECRETARIES OF THE TREASURY.

The post of Secretary of the Treasury, although one of great importance, requires financial abilities of a high order, which are more frequently found in the North than in the South, and affords little opportunity for influencing general politics, or the questions springing out of slavery. We need not, therefore, be surprised to learn that Northern men have been allowed to discharge its duties some forty-eight years out of sixty-nine, as follows :

Appointed—

Sept. 11, 1789, A. Hamilton, New York.	Sept. 23, 1833, Roger B. Taney, Maryland.
Feb. 3, 1795, O. Wolcott, Connecticut.	June 27, 1834, L. Woodbury, New Hampshire.
Dec. 31, 1800, S. Dexter, Massachusetts.	March 5, 1841, Thomas Ewing, Ohio.
May 14, 1801, A. Gallatin, Pennsylvania.	Sept. 13, 1841, W. Forward, Pennsylvania.
Feb. 9, 1814, G. W. Campbell, Tennessee.	March 3, 1843, J. C. Spencer, New York.
Oct. 6, 1814, A. J. Dallas, Pennsylvania.	June 15, 1844, G. M. Bibb, Kentucky.
Oct. 22, 1816, W. H. Crawford, Georgia.	March 5, 1845, R. J. Walker. Mississippi.
March 7, 1825, R. Rush, Pennsylvania.	March 7, 1849, W. M. Meredith, Pennsylvania.
March 6, 1829, S. D. Ingham, Pennsylvania.	June 20, 1850, Thomas Corwin, Ohio.
Aug. 8, 1831, L. McLane, Delaware.	March 5. 1853, James Guthrie, Kentucky.
May 29, 1833, W. J. Duane, Pennsylvania.	March 6, 1857, Howell Cobb, Georgia.

SECRETARIES OF WAR AND THE NAVY.

The slaveholders, since March 8th, 1841, a period of nearly eighteen years, have taken almost exclusive supervision of the navy, Northern men having occupied the Secretaryship only six years. Nor has any Northern man been Secretary of War since 1849. Considering that nearly all the shipping belongs to the free States, which also supply the seamen, it does seem remarkable that slaveholders should have monopolized for the last eighteen years the control of the navy.

SECRETARIES OF WAR.

Appointed—

Sept. 12, 1789, Henry Knox, Massachusetts.	March 9, 1829, J. H. Eaton, Tennessee.
Jan. 2, 1795, T. Pickering, Massachusetts.	Aug. 1, 1831, Lewis Cass, Ohio.
Jan. 27, 1796, J. McHenry, Maryland.	March 3, 1837, B. F. Butler, New York.
May 7, 1800, J. Marshall, Virginia.	March 7, 1837, J. R. Poinsett, South Carolina.
May 13, 1800, S. Dexter, Massachusetts.	March 5, 1841, James Bell, Tennessee.
Feb. 3, 1801, R. Griswold, Connecticut.	Sept. 13, 1841, John McLean, Ohio.
March 5, 1801, H. Dearborn, Massachusetts.	Oct. 12, 1841, J. C. Spencer, New York.
March 7, 1802, W. Eustis, Massachusetts.	March 8, 1843, J. W. Porter, Pennsylvania.
Jan. 13, 1813, J. Armstrong, New York.	Feb. 15, 1844, W. Wilkins, Pennsylvania.
Sept. 27, 1814, James Monroe, Virginia.	March 5, 1845, William L. Marcy, New York.
March 3, 1815, W. H. Crawford, Georgia.	March 7, 1849, G. W. Crawford, Georgia.
March 5, 1817, J. Shelby, Kentucky.	July 20, 1850, E. Bates, Missouri.
April 7, 1817, G. Graham, Virginia.	Aug. 15, 1850, C. M. Conrad, Louisiana.
Oct. 8, 1817, J. C. Calhoun, South Carolina.	March 5, 1853, Jefferson Davis, Mississippi.
March 7, 1825, J. Barbour, Virginia.	March 6, 1857, John B. Floyd, Virginia.
May 26, 1828 P. B. Porter, Pennsylvania.	

SECRETARIES OF THE NAVY.

Appointed—

May 3, 1798, G. Cabot, Massachusetts.	June 20, 1838, J. K. Paulding, New York.
May 21, 1798, B. Stoddart, Maryland.	March 5, 1841, G. F. Badger, North Carolina.
July 15, 1801, R. Smith, Maryland.	Sept. 13, 1841, A. P. Upshur, Virginia.
May 3, 1805, J. Crowninshield, Mass.	July 24, 1843, D. Henshaw, Massachusetts.
March 7, 1809, P. Hamilton, South Carolina.	Feb. 12, 1844, T. W. Gilmer, Virginia.
Jan. 12, 1813, W. Jones, Pennsylvania.	March 14, 1844, James Y. Mason, Virginia.
Dec. 17, 1814, B. W. Crowninshield, Mass.	March 10, 1845, G. Bancroft, Massachusetts.
Nov. 9, 1818, Smith Thompson, New York.	Sept. 9, 1846, James Y. Mason, Virginia.
Sept. 1, 1823, John Rogers, Massachusetts.	March 7, 1849, W. B. Preston, Virginia.
Sept. 16, 1823, S. L. Southard, New Jersey.	July 20, 1850, W. A. Graham, N. Carolina.
March 9, 1829, John Branch, North Carolina.	July 22, 1852, J. P. Kennedy, Maryland.
May 23, 1831, L. Woodbury, New Hampshire.	March 3, 1853, J. C. Dobbin, N. Carolina.
June 30, 1834, M. Dickerson, New Jersey.	March 6, 1857, Isaac Toucey, Connecticut.

RECAPITULATION.

Presidency.—Southern men and slaveholders, 48 years 3 months ; Northern men, 23 years 9 months.

Pro Tem. Presidency of the Senate.—Since 1809, held by Southern men and slaveholders, except for three or four sessions by Northern men.

Speakership of the House.—Filled by Southern men and slaveholers forty-five years, Northern men, twenty-five.

Supreme Court.—A majority of the Judges, including Chief-Justice, southern men and slaveholders.

Secretaryship of State.—Filled by southern men and slaveholders forty years; northern, twenty-nine.

Attorney Generalship.—Filled by southern men and slaveholders forty-two years; northern men, twenty-seven.

War and Navy.—Secretaryship of the Navy, southern men and slaveholders, the last eighteen years, with an interval of six years.

WILLIAM HENRY HURLBUT,

Of South Carolina, a gentleman of enviable literary attainments, and one from whom we may expect a continuation of good service in the eminently holy crusade now going on against slavery and the devil, furnished not long since, to the *Edinburgh Review*, in the course of a long and highly interesting article, the following summary of oligarchal usurpations—showing that slaveholders have occupied the principal posts of the government nearly two-thirds of the time:

```
Presidents.............................................. 11 out of  16
Judges of the Supreme Court........................... 17 out of  28
Attorneys-General..................................... 14 out of  19
Presidents of the Senate.............................. 61 out of  77
Speakers of the House................................. 21 out of  33
Foreign Ministers..................................... 80 out of 134
```

As a matter of general interest, and as showing that, while there have been but eleven non-slaveholders directly before the people as candidates for the Presidency, there have been *at least* sixteen slaveholders who were willing to serve their country in the capacity of chief magistrate the following table may be here introduced:

RESULT OF THE PRESIDENTIAL ELECTIONS IN THE UNITED STATES FROM 1796 TO 1856.

Year.	Name of Candidate.	Elect'l vote.	Year.	Name of Candidate.	Elect'l vote.
1796	John Adams................	71	1832	Andrew Jackson..........	219
	Thomas Jefferson.........	68		Henry Clay..............	49
1800	Thomas Jefferson.........	73		John Floyd..............	11
	John Adams..............	64		William Wirt............	7
1804	Thomas Jefferson.........	162		Martin Van Buren........	170
	Charles C. Pinckney.....	14		William H. Harrison......	73
1808	James Madison...........	128	1836	Hugh L. White...........	26
	Charles C. Pinckney......	45		Willie P. Mangum........	11
1812	James Madison...........	122		Daniel Webster..........	14
	De Witt Clinton.........	89		William H. Harrison......	234
1816	James Monroe...........	183	1840	Martin Van Buren........	60
	Rufus King..............	34		James K. Polk...........	170
1820	James Monroe.	218	1844	Henry Clay..............	105
	No opposition but one vote			Zachary Taylor..........	163
	Andrew Jackson*........	99	1848	Lewis Cass..............	127
1824	John Q. Adams..........	84		Franklin Pierce..........	254
	W. H. Crawford..........	41	1852	General Winfield Scott....	42
	Henry Clay..............	37		James Buchanan.........	174
1828	Andrew Jackson........	178	1856	John C. Fremont........	114
	John Q. Adams..........	83		Millard Fillmore..........	8

AID FOR KANSAS.

As a sort of accompaniment to many of the preceding tables, we will

---

* No choice by the people· John Q. Adams elected by the House of Representatives.

here introduce a few items which will more fully illustrate the liberality of freedom and the niggardliness of slave·y.

From an editorial article that appeared in the Richmond (Va.,) *Dispatch*, in July, 1856, bewailing the close-fistedness of slavery, we make the following extract:

" Gerrit Smith, the Abolitionist, has just pledged himself to give $1,500 a month for the next twelve months to aid in establishing freedom in Kansas. He gave, but a short time since, at the Kansas relief meeting in Albany, $3,000. Prior to that, he had sent about $1,000 to the Boston Emigrant Committee. Out of his own funds, he subsequently equipped a Madison county company, of one hundred picked men, and paid their expenses to Kansas. At Syracuse he subscribed $10.000 for Abolition purposes, so that his entire contributions amount to at least $40,000."

Under date of August 9, 1856, an Eastern paper informs us that

" The sum of $500 was contributed at a meeting at New Bedford on Monday evening, to make Kansas free. The following sums have been contributed for the same purpose: $2,000 in Taunton; $600 in Raynham; $800 in Clinton; $300 in Danbury, Ct. In Wisconsin, $2,500 at Janesville; $500 at Dalton; $500 at the Women's Aid Meeting in Chicago; $2,000 in Rockford, Ill."

A telegraphic dispatch, dated Boston, January 2, 1857, says:

" The Secretary of the Kansas Aid Committee acknowledges the receipt of $42,678."

Exclusive of the amounts above, the readers of the New York *Tribune* contributed at least $30,000 for the purpose of securing Kansas to Freedom; and with the same object in view, other individuals and societies, as occasion required, made large contributions, of which we failed to keep a memorandum. The Legislature of Vermont appropriated $20,000; and other free state legislatures were prepared to appropriate millions, if necessary. Free men had determined that Kansas should be free, and free it is, and will ever so remain. All honor to the immortal patriots who saved her from the death-grasp of slavery!

Now let us see how Slavery rewarded the poor, ignorant, deluded, and degraded mortals—swaggering lickspittles—who labored so hard to gain for it a " local habitation and a name " in the disputed territory. One D. B. Atchison, chairman of the Executive Committee of Border Ruffians, shall tell us all about it. Over date of October 13th, 1856, he says:

" Up to this moment, from all the States except Missouri, we have only received the following sums, and through the following persons:

A. W. Jones, Houston, Miss.	$152
H. D. Clayton, Eufala, Ala.	500
Capt. Deedrick, South Carolina	500
	$1,152 "

On this subject further comment is unnecessary.

Numerous other contrasts, equally disproportionate, might be drawn between the vigor and munificence of Freedom and the impotence and stinginess of Slavery. We will, however, in addition to the above, advert to only a single instance. During the latter part of the summer of 1855, the citizens of the despicable little slave-towns of Norfolk and Portsmouth, in Virginia, were sorely plagued with yellow fever. Many of them fell victims to the disease, and most of those who survived, and who were not too unwell to travel, left their homes horror-stricken and dejected. To the honor of mankind in general, and to the glory of freemen in particular, contributions in money, provisions, clothing, and other valuable supplies, poured in from all parts of the country for the relief of the sufferers. Portsmouth alone, according to the report of her relief association, received $42,547 in cash from the free States, and only $12,182 in cash from all the slave States, exclusive of Virginia, within whose borders the malady prevailed. Including Virginia, the sum total of all the slave State contributions amounted to only $33,398. Well did the Richmond *Examiner* remark at the time—" we fear that generosity of Virginians is but a figure of speech." Slavery! thy name is shame!

The following statistics of Congressional representation, which we transcribe from " Reynolds' Political Map of the United States," published in 1856, deserve to be carefully studied :

UNITED STATES SENATE.

Sixteen free States, with a white population of 13,238,670 have thirty-two Senators.
Fifteen slave States, with a white population of 6,186,477, have thirty Senators.
So that 413,708 free men of the North enjoy but the same political privileges in the United States Senate as is given to 206,215 slave propagandists.

HOUSE OF REPRESENTATIVES.

The free States have a total of 144 members.
The slave States have a total of 90 members.
One free State Representative represents 91,935 white men and women.
One slave State Representative represents 68,725 white men and women.
Slave Representation gives to slavery an advantage over freedom of thirty votes in the House of Representatives.

CUSTOM HOUSE RECEIPTS—1854.

Free States...$60,010,489
Slave States... 5,136,969

Balance in favor of the Free States.......................$54,873,520

A contrast quite distinguishable !

That the apologists of slavery cannot excuse the shame and the shabbiness of themselves and their country, as we have frequently heard them attempt to do, by falsely asserting that the North has enjoyed over the South the advantages of priority of settlement, will fully appear from the following table:

FREE STATES.	SLAVE STATES.
1614 New York first settled by the Dutch.	1607 Virginia first settled by the English.
1620 Massachusetts settled by the Puritans.	1627 Delaware settled by the Swedes and Fins
1623 New Hampshire settled by the Puritans.	1635 Maryland settled by Irish Catholics.
1624 New Jersey settled by the Dutch.	1650 North Carolina settled by the English.
1635 Connecticut settled by the Puritans.	1670 South Carolina settled by the Huguenots.
1636 Rhode Island settled by Roger Williams.	1733 Georgia settled by Gen. Oglethorpe.
1682 Pennsylvania settled by William Penn.	1782 Kentucky admitted into the Union.
1791 Vermont admitted into the Union.	1796 Tennessee admitted into the Union.
1802 Ohio admitted into the Union.	1811 Louisiana admitted into the Union.
1816 Indiana admitted into the Union.	1817 Mississippi admitted into the Union.
1818 Illinois admitted into the Union.	1819 Alabama admitted into the Union.
1820 Maine admitted into the Union.	1821 Missouri admitted into the Union.
1836 Michigan admitted into the Union.	1836 Arkansas admitted into the Union.
1846 Iowa admitted into the Union.	1845 Florida admitted into the Union.
1848 Wisconsin admitted into the Union.	1846 Texas admitted into the Union.
1850 California admitted into the Union.	

In the course of an exceedingly interesting article on the early settlements in America, R. K. Browne, formerly editor and proprietor of the San Francisco *Evening Journal*, says:

"Many people seem to think that the Pilgrim Fathers were the first who settled upon our shores, and therefore that they ought to be entitled, in a particular manner, to our remembrance and esteem.

"This is not the case, and we herewith present to our readers a list of settlements made in the present United States, prior to that of Plymouth:

1564. A Colony of French Protestants under Ribault, settled in Florida.

1565. St. Augustine* founded by Pedro Melendez.

1584. Sir Walter Raleigh obtains a patent and sends two vessels to the American coast, which receives the name of Virginia.

1607. The first effectual settlement made at Jamestown, Va., by the London Company.

1614. A fort erected by the Dutch upon the site of New York.

1615. Fort Orange built near the site of Albany, N. Y.

1619. The first General Assembly called in Virginia.

1620. The Pilgrims land on Plymouth Rock."

FREEDOM AND SLAVERY AT THE FAIR.

WHAT FREEDOM DID.

At an Agricultural Fair held at Watertown, in the State of New York, on the 2d day of October, 1856, two hundred and twenty premiums, ranging from three to fifty dollars each, were awarded to successful competitors—the aggregate amount of said premiums being $2,396, or an average of $10 89 each. From the proceedings of the Awarding Committee we make the following extracts:

Best Team of Oxen,	Hiram Converse	$50 00
Best Horse Colt,	George Parish	25 00
Best Filly,	J. Staplin	20 00
Best Brood Mare,	A. Blunt	25 00
Best Bull,	Wm. Johnson	25 00
Best Heifer,	A. M. Rogers	20 00
Best Cow,	C. Baker	25 00
Best Stall-fed Beef,	J. W. Taylor	10 00
Best sample Wheat,	Wm. Ottley	5 00
Best sample Flaxseed,	H. Weir	3 00
Best sample Timothy Seed,	E. S. Hayward	3 00
Best sample Sweet Corn,	L. Marshall	3 00

Aggregate amount of twelve premiums....................$214 00
An average of $17 83 each.

* The oldest town in the United States.

WHAT SLAVERY DID.

At the Rowan County Agricultural Fair, held at Mineral Springs, in North Carolina, on 13th day of November, 1856, thirty premiums ranging from twenty-five cents to two dollars each, were awarded to successful competitors—the aggregate amount of said premiums being $42 00, or an average of $1 40 each. From the proceedings of the Awarding Committee we make the following extracts:

Best pair Match Horses,	R. W. Griffith	$2 00
Best Horse Colt,	T. A. Burke	2 00
Best Filly,	James Cowan	2 00
Best Brood Mare,	M. W. Goodman	2 00
Best Bull,	J. F. McCorkle	2 00
Best Heifer,	J. F. McCorkle	2 00
Best Cow,	T. A. Burke	2 00
Best Stall-fed Beef,	S. D. Rankin	1 00
Best Sample Wheat,	M W. Goodman	50
Best Lot Beets,	J. J. Summerell	25
Best Lot Turnips,	Thomas Barber	25
Best Lot Cabbage,	Thomas Hyde	25

Aggregate amount of twelve premiums...........................$16 25
An average of $1 36 each.

Besides the two hundred and twenty premiums, amounting in the aggregate to $2,396, Freedom granted several diplomas and silver medals; besides the thirty premiums amounting in the aggregate to $42, Slavery granted none—nothing. While examining these figures, it should be recollected that agriculture is the peculiar province of the slave States. If commerce or manufactures had been the subject of the fair, the result might have shown even a greater disproportion in favor of Freedom, and yet there would have been some excuse for Slavery, for it makes no pretensions to either the one or the other; but as agriculture was the subject, Slavery can have no excuse whatever, but must bear all the shame of its niggardly and revolting impotence; this it must do for the reason that agriculture is its special and almost only pursuit.

The Reports of the Comptrollers of the States of New York and North Carolina, for the year 1856, are now before us. From each report we have gleaned a single item, which, when compared, the one with the other, speaks volumes in favor of Freedom and against Slavery. We refer to the average value per acre of lands in the two States; let slaveholders read, reflect, and repent.

In 1856, there were assessed for taxation in the State of

NEW YORK,

Acres of land........................:............................30,080,000
Valued at..$1,112,133,136
Average value per acre......................................$36 97

In 1856, there were assessed for taxation in the State of

NORTH CAROLINA,

Acres of land............................ 32,450,560
Valued at...$98,800.636
Average value per acre................................ .. ..$3 06

It is difficult for us to make any remarks on the official facts above. Our indignation is struck almost dumb at this astounding and revolting display of the awful wreck that slavery is leaving behind it in the South. We will, however, go into a calculation for the purpose of ascertaining as nearly as possible, in this one particular, how much North Carolina has lost by the retention of slavery. As we have already seen, the average value per acre of land in the State of New York is $36 97 ; in North Carolina it is only $3 06 ; why is it so much less, or even any less, in the latter than in the former ? The answer is, *Slavery*. In soil, in climate, in minerals, in water-power for manufactural purposes, and in area of territory, North Carolina has the advantage of New York, and, with the exception of slavery, no plausible reason can possibly be assigned why land should not be *at least* as valuable in the valley of the Yadkin as it is along the banks of the Genesee.

The difference between $36 97 and $3 06 is $33 91, which, multiplied by the whole number of acres of land in North Carolina, will show, in this one particular, the enormous loss that freedom has sustained on account of slavery in the Old North State. Thus :

32,450,560 acres *a* $33 91 ..... $1,100,398,489.

Let it be indelibly impressed on the mind, however, that this amount, large as it is, is only a moiety of the sum that it has cost to maintain slavery in North Carolina. From time to time, hundreds upon hundreds of millions of dollars have left the State, either in search of profitable, permanent investment abroad, or in the shape of profits to Northern merchants and manufacturers, who have become the moneyed aristocracy of the country by supplying to the South such articles of necessity, utility, and adornment, as would have been produced at home but for the pernicious presence of the peculiar institution.

A reward of eleven hundred million of dollars is offered for the conversion of the lands of North Carolina into free soil. The lands themselves, desolate and impoverished under the fatal foot of slavery, offer the reward. How, then, can it be made to appear that the abolition of slavery in North Carolina, and, indeed, throughout all the Southern States—for slavery is exceedingly inimical to them all—is not demanded by every consideration of justice, prudence, and good sense ? In 1850, the total value of all the slaves of the State at the rate of four hundred dollars per head, amounted to less than one hundred and sixteen million of dollars. Is the sum of one hundred and sixteen million of dollars more desirable than the sum of eleven hundred million of dollars ? When a man has land for sale, does he reject thirty-six dollars per acre and take three ? Non-slaveholding whites ! look well to your interests ! Many of you have lands ; comparatively speaking, you have nothing else. Abolish slavery, and you will enhance the value of every league, your own and your neighbors', from three to thirty-six dollars per acre. Your little tract containing two hundred acres, now valued at the pitiful sum of only six hundred dollars, will then be worth seven thousand. Your children, now deprived of even the meagre advantages of common schools, will then reap the benefits of a collegiate education. Your rivers and smaller streams, now wasting their waters in idleness, will then turn the wheels of multitudinous mills. Your bays and harbors, now unknown to commerce, will then swarm with ships from every enlightened quarter of the globe. Non-slaveholding whites! look well to your interests!

Would the slaveholders of North Carolina lose anything by the abolition of slavery? Let us see. According to their own estimate, their slaves are worth, in round numbers, say, one hundred and twenty millions of dollars. There are in the State twenty-eight thousand slaveholders, owning, it may be safely assumed, an average of at least five hundred acres of land each—fourteen million of acres in all. This number of acres, multiplied by thirty-three dollars and ninety-one cents, the difference in value between free soil and slave soil, makes the enormous sum of four hundred and seventy-four million of dollars—showing that by the abolition of slavery, the slaveholders themselves would realize a net profit of not less than three hundred and fifty-four million of dollars.

Not long since, a gentleman in Baltimore, a native of Maryland, remarked in our presence that he was an abolitionist because he felt that it was right and proper to be one; "but," inquired he, " are there not, in some of the States, many widows and orphans who would be left in destitute circumstances, if their negroes were taken from them?" We replied that slavery had already reduced thousands and tens of thousands of non-slaveholding widows and orphans to the lowest depths of poverty and ignorance, and that we did not believe one slaveholding widow and three orphans were of more, or even of as much consequence as five non-slaveholding widows and fifteen orphans. "You are right," exclaimed the gentleman, "you are right, I had not viewed the subject in that light before; I perceive you go in for the greatest good to the greatest number." Of course we were right—we do go in for the greatest good to the greatest number.

The fact is, every slave in the South costs the State in which he resides at least three times as much as he, in the whole course of his life, is worth to his master. Slavery benefits no one but its immediate, individual owners, and them only in a pecuniary point of view, and at the sacrifice of the dearest rights and interests of the whole mass of non-slaveholders, white and black. Even the masters themselves, as we have already shown, would have been far better off without it than with it. To all classes of society the institution is a curse; an especial curse is it to those who own it not. Non-slaveholding whites! look well to your interests!

CHAPTER X.

IF great improvements are seldom to be expected from great proprietors, they are least of all to be expected when they employ slaves for their workmen. The experience of all ages and nations, I believe, demonstrates that the work done by slaves, though it appears to cost only their maintenance, is in the end the dearest of any. A person who can acquire no property, can have no interest but to eat as much, and to labor as little as possible. Whatever work he does beyond what is sufficient to purchase his own maintenance, can be squeezed out of him by violence only, and not by any interest of his own.—ADAM SMITH.

OUR theme is a city—a great Southern importing, exporting and manufacturing city, to be located at some point or port on the coast of the Carolinas, Georgia or Virginia, where we can carry on active commerce, buy, sell, fabricate, receive the profits which accrue from the exchange of our own commodities, open facilities for direct communication with foreign countries, and establish all those collateral sources of wealth, utility and adornment, which are the usual concomitants of a metropolis, and which add so very materially to the interest and importance of a nation. Without a city of this kind, the South can never develop her commercial resources nor attain to that eminent position to which those vast resources would otherwise exalt her. According to calculations based upon reasonable estimates, it is owing to the lack of a great commercial city in the South, that we are now *annually* drained of more than One Hundred and Twenty Millions of Dollars! We should, however, take into consideration the negative loss as well as the positive. Especially should we think of the influx of emigrants, of the visits of strangers and cosmopolites, of the patronage to hotels and public halls, of the profits of travel and transportation, of the emoluments of foreign and domestic trade, and of numerous other advantages which have their origin exclusively in wealthy, enterprising and densely populated cities.

Nothing is more evident than the fact, that our people have never entertained a proper opinion of the importance of home cities. Blindly, and greatly to our own injury, we have contributed hundreds of millions of dollars toward the erection of mammoth cities at the North, while our own magnificent bays and harbors have been most shamefully disregarded and neglected. Now, instead of carrying all our money to New York, Philadelphia, Boston and Cincinnati, suppose we had kept it on the south side of Mason and Dixon's line—as we would have done, had it not been for slavery—and had disbursed it in the upbuilding of Norfolk, Beaufort, Charleston or Savannah, how much richer, better, greater would the South have been to-day? How much larger and more intelligent would have been our population? How many hundred thousand natives of the South would now be thriving at home, instead of adding to the wealth and political power of other parts of the Union? How much greater would be the number and length of our railroads, canals, turnpikes and telegraphs? How much greater would be the extent and diversity of our manufactures? How much greater would be the grandeur, and how much larger would be the number of our churches, theatres, schools, colleges, lyceums, banks, hotels, stores and private dwellings? How many more clippers and steamships would we have sailing on the ocean, how vastly more reputable would we be abroad, how infinitely more respectable, progressive and happy would we be at home?

That we may learn something of the importance of cities in general, let us look for a moment at the great capitals of the world. What would England be without London? What would France be without Paris? What would Turkey be without Constantinople? Or, to come nearer home, what would Maryland be without Baltimore? What would Louisiana be without New Orleans? What would South Carolina be without Charleston? Do we ever think of these countries or States without thinking of their cities also? If we want to learn the news of the country, do we not go to the city, or to the city papers? Every metropolis may be regarded as the nucleus or epitome of the country in which it is situated; and the more prominent features and characteristics of a country, particularly of the people of a country, are almost always to be seen within the limits of its capital city. Almost invariably do we find the bulk of the floating funds, the best talent, and the most vigorous energies of a nation concentrated in its chief cities; and does not this concentration of wealth, energy and talent conduce, in an extraordinary degree, to the growth and prosperity of a nation? Unquestionably. Wealth develops wealth, energy develops energy, talent develops talent. What, then, must be the condition of those countries which do not possess the means or facilities of centralizing their material forces, their energies and their talents? Are they not destined to occupy an inferior rank among the nations of the earth? Let the South answer.

And now let us ask, and we would put the question particularly to Southern merchants, what do we so much need as a great Southern metropolis? Merchants of the South, slaveholders! you are the avaricious assassinators of your country! You are the channels through which more than one hundred and twenty millions of dollars—

$120,000,000—are annually drained from the South and conveyed to the North. You are daily engaged in the unmanly and unpatriotic work of impoverishing the land of your birth. You are constantly enfeebling our resources and rendering us more and more tributary to distant parts of the nation. Your conduct is reprehensible, base, criminal.

Whether Southern merchants ever think of the numerous ways in which they contribute to the aggrandizement of the North, while, at the same time, they enervate and dishonor the South, has for many years, with us, been a matter of more than ordinary conjecture. If, as it would seem, they have never yet thought of the subject, it is certainly desirable that they should exercise their minds upon it at once. Let them scrutinize the workings of Southern money after it passes north of Mason and Dixon's line. Let them consider how much they pay to Northern railroads and hotels, how much to Northern merchants and shopkeepers, how much to Northern shippers and insurers, how much to Northern theatres, newspapers, and periodicals. Let them also consider what disposition is made of it after it is lodged in the hands of the North. Is not the greater part of it paid out to Northern manufacturers, merchants, and laborers, for the very articles which are purchased at the North—and to the extent that this is done, are not Northern manufacturers, mechanics, and laborers directly countenanced and encouraged, while, at the same time, Southern manufacturers, mechanics, and laborers, are indirectly abased, depressed, and disabled? It is, however, a matter of impossibility, on these small pages, to notice or enumerate all the methods in which the money we deposit in the North is made to operate against us; suffice it to say that it is circulated and expended there, among all classes of the people, to the injury and impoverishment of all almost every individual in the South. And yet, our cousins of the North are not, by any means, blameworthy for availing themselves of the advantages which we have voluntarily yielded to them. They have shown their wisdom in growing great at our expense, and we have shown our folly in allowing them to do so. In this respect, Southern merchants, slaveholders, and slavebreeders, should be the special objects of our censure; they have desolated and impoverished the South ; they are now making merchandise of the vitals of their country ; patriotism is a word nowhere recorded in their vocabulary; town, city, country—they care for neither; with them, self is always paramount to every other consideration.

From letters received in 1857, from the mayors of eighteen of our great commercial cities, nine free, and nine slave, which letters have been published in all the book editions of this work, we present the following important particulars:

NINE FREE CITIES.

Name.	Population.	Wealth.	Wealth per capita.
New York....	700,000	$511,740,492	$731
Philadelphia	500,000	325,000,000	650
Boston	165,000	249,162,500	1,510
Brooklyn...........	225,000	95,800,440	425
Cincinnati........................	210,000	88,810,734	422
Chicago......................	112,000	171,000,000	1,527
Providence..............	60,000	58,064,516	967
Buffalo..........................	90,000	45,474,476	505
New Bedford...	21,000	27,047,000	1,288
	2,083,000	$1,572,100,158	$754

NINE SLAVE CITIES.

Name.	Population.	Wealth.	Wealth per capita.
Baltimore	250,000	$102,053,839	$408
New Orleans.....................	175,000	91,188,195	521
St. Louis	140,000	63,000,000	450
Charleston......................	60,000	36,127,751	602
Louisville.......................	70,000	31,500,000	450
Richmond	40,000	20,143,520	503
Norfolk.......	17,000	12,000,000	705
Savannah	25,000	11,999,015	480
Wilmington........	10,000	7,850,000	785
	787,000	$375 862,320	$477

Let it not be forgotten that the slaves themselves are valued at so much per head, and counted as part of the wealth of slave cities; and yet, though we assent, as we have done, to the inclusion of all this fictitious wealth, it will be observed that the residents of free cities are far wealthier, *per capita*, than the residents of slave cities. The reader, we trust, will not fail to examine the figures with great care.

In this age of the world, commerce is an indispensable element of national greatness. Without commerce we can have no great cities, and without great cities we can have no reliable tenure of distinct nationality. Commerce is the forerunner of wealth and population; and it is mainly these that make invincible the power of undying states.

How it is, in this enlightened age, that men of ordinary intelligence can be so far led into error as to suppose that commerce, or any other noble enterprise, can be established and successfully prosecuted under the dominion of slavery, is, to us, one of the most inexplicable of mysteries. Southern Conventions, composed of the self-titled lordlings of slavery, Generals, Colonels, Majors, Captains, and Squires—may act out their annual programmes of farcical nonsense from now until doomsday; but they will never add one iota to the material, moral, or mental interests of the South—never can, until their ebony idol shall have been utterly demolished.

It is a remarkable fact, but one not at all surprising to those whose philosophy leads them to think aright, that Baltimore and St. Louis, the two most prosperous cities in the slave States, have fewer slaves in proportion to the aggregate population than any other city or cities in the South. While the entire population of the former is now estimated at 250,000, and that of the latter at 140,000—making a grand total of 890,000 in the two cities, less than 6,000 of this latter number are slaves; indeed, neither city is cursed with half the number of 6,000.

In 1850, there were only 2,946 slaves in Baltimore, and 2,656 in St. Louis—total in the two cities, 5,602; and in both places, thank heaven, th.s heathenish class of the population was rapidly decreasing. The census of 1860 will, in all probability, show that the two cities are entirely exempt from slaves and slavery; and that of 1880 will, we prayerfully hope, show that the United States at large, at that time, will have been wholly redeemed from the unspeakable curse of human bondage.

What about Southern commerce? Is it not almost entirely tributary to the commerce of the North? Are we not dependent on New York, Philadelphia, Boston, and Cincinnati, for nearly every article of merchandise, whether foreign or domestic? Where are our ships, our mariners, our naval architects? Alas! echo answers where?

Reader! would you understand how abjectly slaveholders themselves are enslaved to the products of Northern industry? If you would, fix your mind on a Virginia gentleman—a breeder, buyer, and seller of bipedal black cattle—who, withal, professes to be a Christian! Observe the routine of his daily life. See him rise in the morning from a Northern bed, and clothe himself in Northern apparel; see him walk across the floor on a Northern carpet, and perform his ablutions out of a Northern ewer and basin. See him uncover a box of Northern powders, and cleanse his teeth with a Northern brush; see him reflecting his physiognomy in a Northern mirror, and arranging his hair with a Northern comb. See him dosing himself with the medicaments of Northern quacks, and perfuming his handkerchief with Northern cologne. See him referring to the time in a Northern watch, and glancing at the news in a Northern gazette. See him and his family sitting in Northern chairs, and singing and praying out of Northern books. See him at the breakfast table, saying grace over a Northern plate, eating with Northern cutlery, and drinking from Northern utensils. See him charmed with the melody of a Northern piano, or musing over the pages of a Northern novel. See him riding to his neighbor's in a Northern carriage, or furrowing his lands with a Northern plough. See him lighting his cigar with a Northern match, and flogging his negroes with a Northern lash. See him with Northern pen and ink, writing letters on Northern paper, and sending them away in Northern envelopes, sealed with Northern wax, and impressed with a Northern stamp. Perhaps our Virginia gentleman is a merchant; if so, see him at his store, making an unpatriotic

use of his time in the miserable traffic of Northern gimcracks and haber-
dashery ; see him when you will, where you will, he is ever surrounded
with the industrial products of those whom, in the strange inconsistency
of his heart, he execrates as enemies, yet treats as friends. His labors,
his talents, his influence, are all for the North, and not for the South.
For the stability of slavery, and for the sake of his own personal aggrandizement, he is willing to sacrifice, and does sacrifice, the dearest interests of his country.

As we see our ruinous system of commerce exemplified in the family
of our Virginia gentleman—a branch of one of the *first* families, of
course !—so we may see it exemplified, to a greater or lesser degree, in
almost every other family throughout the length and breadth of the
slaveholding States. We are all constantly buying, and selling, and
wearing, and using Northern merchandise, at a double expense to both
ourselves and our neighbors. If we but look at ourselves attentively,
we shall find that we are all clothed *cap-à-pie* in Northern habiliments.
Our hats, our caps, our cravats, our coats, our vests, our pants, our
gloves, our boots, our shoes, our under-garments—all come from the
North ; whence, too, Southern ladies procure all their bonnets, plumes,
and flowers ; dresses, shawls, and scarfs ; frills, ribbons, and ruffles ; cuffs,
capes, and collars.

True it is that the South has wonderful powers of endurance and recuper-
ation ; but she cannot forever support the reckless prodigality of her sons.
We are all spendthrifts ; some of us should become financiers. We must
learn to take care of our money ; we should withhold it from the North,
and open avenues for its circulation at home. We should not run to
New York, to Philadelphia, to Boston, to Cincinnati, or to any other
Northern city, every time we want a shoe-string, or a bedstead, a fish-
hook or a hand-saw, a tooth-pick or a cotton-gin. In ease and luxury
we have been lolling long enough ; we should now bestir ourselves, and
keep pace with the progress of the age. We must expand our energies,
and acquire habits of enterprise and industry ; we should arouse ourselves from the couch of lassitude, and inure our minds to thought and
our bodies to action. We must begin to feed on a more substantial diet
than that of pro-slavery politics ; we should leave off our siestas and
post-meridian naps, and employ our time in profitable vocations.
Before us there is a vast work to be accomplished—a work which has
been accumulating on our hands for many years. It is no less a work
than that of infusing the spirit of liberty into all our systems of commerce, agriculture, manufactures, government, literature, and religion.
Oligarchal despotism must be overthrown ; slavery must be abolished.

9*

CHAPTER XI.

FACTS AND ARGUMENTS BY THE WAYSIDE.

Slavery is the infringement of all laws. A law having a tendency to preserve slavery would be the grossest sacrilege. Man to be possessed by his fellow-man!—man to be made property of! The image of the Deity to be put under the yoke! Let these usurpers show us their title-deeds!—BOLIVAR.

FINDING that we shall have to leave unsaid a great many things which we intended to say, and that we shall have to omit much valuable matter, the product of other pens than our own, but which, having collected at considerable labor and expense, we had hoped to be able to introduce, we have concluded to present, under the above heading, only a few of the more important particulars.

In the first place, we will give an explanation of the reason

WHY THE PRESENT VOLUME WAS NOT PUBLISHED IN BALTIMORE.

A considerable portion of this work was written in Baltimore; and the whole of it would have been written and published there, but for the following odious clause, which we extract from the Statutes of Maryland :

" Be it enacted by the General Assembly of Maryland, That after the passage of this act, it shall not be lawful for any citizen of this State, knowingly to make, print, or engrave, or aid in the making, printing, or engraving, within this State, any pictorial representation, or to write or print, or to aid in the writing or printing any pamphlet, newspaper, handbill or other paper of an inflammatory character, and having a tendency to excite discontent, or stir up insurrection amongst the people of color of this State, or of either of the other States or Territories of the United States, or knowingly to carry or send, or to aid in the carrying or sending the same for circulation amongst the inhabitants of either of the other States or Territories of the United States, and any person so offending shall be guilty of a felony, and shall on conviction be sentenced to confinement in the penitentiary of this State, for a period not less than ten nor more than twenty years, from the time of sentence pronounced on such person."—*Act passed Dec.* 1831. *See 2d Dorsey, page* 1218.

Now, so long as slaveholders are clothed with the mantle of office, so long will they continue to make laws, like the above, expressly calculated to bring the non-slaveholding whites under a system of vassalage little less onerous and debasing than that to which the negroes themselves are accustomed. What wonder is it that there is no native literature in the South? The South can never have a literature of her own until after slavery shall have been abolished. Slaveholders are either too lazy or too ignorant to write it, and the non-slaveholders—even the few whose minds are cultivated at all—are not permitted even to make the attempt. Down with the oligarchy! Ineligibility of slaveholders—never another vote to the trafficker in human flesh!

SLAVERY THOUGHTFUL—SIGNS OF CONTRITION.

The real condition of the South is most graphically described in the following doleful admissions from the Charleston *Standard :*

"In its every aspect, our present condition is provincial. We have within our limits no solitary metropolis of interest or ideas—no marts of exchange—no radiating centres of opinion. Whatever we have of genius and productive energy, goes freely in to swell the importance of the North. Possessing the material which constitutes two-thirds of the commerce of the whole country, it might have been supposed that we could have influence upon the councils of foreign States; but we are never taken into contemplation. It might have been supposed that England, bound to us by the cords upon which depend the existence of four millions of her subjects, would be considerate of our feelings; but receiving her cotton from the North, it is for them she has concern, and it is her interest and her pleasure to reproach us. It might have been supposed, that, producing the material which is sent abroad, to us would come the articles that are taken in exchange for it; but to the North they go for distribution, and to us are parcelled out the fabrics that are suited to so remote a section.

Instead, therefore, of New York being tributary to Norfolk, Charleston, Savannah or New Orleans, these cities are tributary to New York. Instead of the merchants of New York standing cap in hand to the merchants of Charleston, the merchants of Charleston stand cap in hand to the merchants of New York. Instead of receiving foreign ships in Southern waters, and calling up the merchants of the country to a distribution of the cargo, the merchants of the South are hurried off to make a distribution elsewhere. In virtue of our relations to a greater system, we have little development of internal interests; receiving supplies from the great centre, we have made little effort to supply ourselves. We support the makers of boots, shoes, hats, coats, shirts, flannels, blankets, carpets, chairs, tables, mantels, mats, carriages, jewelry, cradles, couches, coffins, by the thousand and hundreds of thousands; but they scorn to live amongst us. They must have the gaieties and splendors of a great metropolis, and are not content to vegetate upon the dim verge of this remote frontier.

As it is in material interests, so it is in arts and letters—our pictures are painted at the North, our books are published at the North, our periodicals and papers are printed at the North. We are even fed on police reports and villainy from the North. The papers published at the South which ignore the questions at issue between the sections are generally well sustained; the books which expose the evils of our institution are even read with avidity beyond our limits, but the ideas that are turned to the condition of the South are intensely provincial. If, as things now are, a man should rise with all the genius of Shakspeare, or Dickens, or Fielding, or of all the three combined, and speak from the South, he would not receive enough to pay the costs of publication. If published at the South, his book would never be seen or heard of, and published at the North it would not be read. So perfect is our provincialism, therefore, that enterprise is forced to the North for a sphere—talent for a market—genius for the ideas upon which to work —indolence for ease, and the tourist for attractions."

This extract exhibits in bold relief, and in small space, a large number of the present evils of past errors. It is charmingly frank and truthful. De Quincey's "Confessions of an Opium Eater," are nothing to it. A distinguished writer on medical jurisprudence informs us that "the knowledge of the disease is half the cure;" and if it be true, as perhaps it is, we think the *Standard* is in a fair way to be reclaimed from the enormous vices of pro-slavery statism.

FREE LABOR MOVEMENTS IN THE SOUTH.

Those of our readers who share with us the conviction that one of the very best means of ridding the South of the great crime and curse of slavery, is, by a system of thorough organization on the part of a considerable number of individuals, to bring Free Labor into direct competition with Forced Labor, will also share with us the profound satisfaction of learning, from the following communication, that the united efforts of gentlemen of noble instincts and purposes have been eminently successful in this regard; and that the future is glowing with promises of grand results which are destined soon to be brought about through the energy and patriotism of such companies and corporations as the one in question:

"OFFICE OF THE AMERICAN EMIGRANT AID AND HOMESTEAD COMPANY,
No. 146 BROADWAY, NEW YORK, June 9th, 1859.

"H. R. HELPER, ESQ.:

"DEAR SIR: In fulfillment of my promise, I will try to give you an outline of the object and operations of the American Emigrant Aid and Homestead Company. Your 'Impending Crisis' has abundantly demonstrated the fact, that land in the slave States is valued, purchased and sold at prices many times less than the same quality of land will command in the free States. It is likewise easy to show that, in the border slave States, counties comparatively free are worth many times as much per acre as land of the same quality in counties cursed with the incubus of slavery.

"In the little State of Delaware, containing only three counties, nearly all the slaves are found in the Southern county of Sussex, which by the last census was appraised at $8 per acre, while the Northern county of Newcastle, without slaves, was, by the same census, appraised at over $28 per acre. The fact above stated is also very clearly shown by the statistics of the following counties in Virginia:

Name.	Acres.	Valuation.	Val. per acre.	Freemen.	Slaves.
Hancock..............	49,7 9	$1,181,512	$23 75	4,047	8
Brooke....	52,441	1,316,591	25 10	5,023	31
Ohio.............. ...	59,731	2,025,951	34 00	17,842	164
Southampton.......	3 5,691	1,068,103	3 01	7,766	5,755
Greenville..........	1 6 988	427,173	2 70	1,854	3,785

"It is worthy of note that the comparatively free counties here given, are very hilly, far from tide water, and settled within the last fifty or sixty years, while the slave counties have a beautiful, gently rolling surface, lie near tide water, and the unequalled harbor of Norfolk, and have had the advantage of cultivation for nearly two hundred years. The Homestead Company, looking at these facts, proposes Christian colonization in the border slave States, not by single or separate settlement, but by *organized emigration*, carrying with it all the schools, churches, habits of industry, social institutions, and elements of a high civilization; and thus, settling large tracts by united and sympathizing companies of liberty and Union-loving men, their investments are quadrupled in value by the mere act of settlement. We believe there is no department of human enterprise more benefited by system and coöperation, than that of emigration. Our experience has amply proved that this plan is not only profitable to all parties concerned as a financial operation, but that it furnish s the most feasible means of extending the Empire of Freedom and genuine Christianity, and is, in fact, one of the most inviting and beneficent enterprises of the age. We feel confident that our movement of concerted emigration has already demontrated the truth of the proposition, that freedom, like godliness, 'is profitable for the life that now is, as well as that which is to come;' and that it has opened an easy, practicable, and profitable way to establish free institutions in all the border slave States.

"Our operations have been thus far confined principally to the State of Virginia, and the results, to myself have been highly gratifying. One of the outgrowths of our enterprise, has been the establishment of freedom of speech. During the last year I have been allowed a liberty of discussion on the subject of slavery, which, in 1856, would have demanded my blood or banishment. Indeed, in the towns of Western Virginia I have been serenaded, and invited to public entertainments and to make addresses upon that subject so lately proscribed, and scarcely breathed without incurring the penalty of exile or ostracism. We have now, in Western Virginia, three excellent weekly Republican papers, and one daily and tri-weekly, and we expect shortly to welcome several others to the ranks of free dom. These are but a few of the many encouraging results of our experiment.

"In the cause of liberty and humanity,

"Yours truly,

"JOHN C. UNDERWOOD."

As well might the Oligarchy attempt to stay the flux and reflux of the tides, as to attempt to stay the progress of Freedom in the South. Approved of God, the edict of the genius of Universal Emancipation has been proclaimed to the world, and nothing, save Deity himself, can possibly reverse it. To connive at the perpetuation of slavery is to disobey the commands of heaven. Not to be an Abolitionist, is to be a willful and diabolical instrument of the devil. The South needs to be free, the South wants to be free, the South *shall* be free!

To all our readers, especially to our Southern readers, we cordially commend the following list of

REPUBLICAN NEWSPAPERS PUBLISHED IN THE SLAVE STATES.

ENGLISH.

The Missouri Democrat	St. Louis, Missouri.
The Free South	Newport, Kentucky.
The Wheeling Intelligencer	Wheeling, Virginia.
The Wellsburg Herald	Wellsburg, "
The Ceredo Crescent	Ceredo, "
The National Era	Washington, D. C.
The Republic	" "
The News and Advertiser	Milford, Delaware.

GERMAN.

Der Anzeiger des Westens	St. Louis, Missouri.
Die Westliche Post	" "
Das Hermann Wochenblatt	Hermann, "
Der St. Charles Demokrat	St. Charles, "
Die Deutsche Zeitung	St. Joseph, "
Die Missouri Post	Kansas City, "
Der Louisviller Anzeiger	Louisville, Kentucky.
Der Baltimore Wecker	Baltimore, Maryland.

Non-slaveholders of the South! it is of the highest importance to you that these papers should be well sustained, and that ample encourage ment should be given for the establishment of others. Patronize as many of them as you can, consistently with your other duties and interests—subscribe for one at least—and lose no opportunity to extend their circulation among your neighbors. Just in proportion as the masses are enlightened will they love liberty and abhor slavery.

THE ILLITERATE POOR WHITES OF THE SOUTH.

Had we the power to sketch a true picture of life among the non-slaveholding whites of the South, every intelligent man who has a spark of philanthropy in his breast, and who should happen to gaze upon the picture, would burn with unquenchable indignation at that system of

African slavery, which entails unutterable stupidity, shiftlessness and degradation on the superior race. It is quite impossible, however, to describe accurately the miserable condition of the class to which we refer. Their poverty, their ignorance and their comparative nothingness, as a power in the State, are deplorable in the extreme. The serfs of Russia have reason to congratulate themselves that they are neither the negroes nor the non-slaveholding whites of the South. Than the latter there can be no people in Christendom more unhappily situated. Below will be found a few extracts which will throw some light on the subject now under consideration.

In an address which he delivered before the South Carolina Institute. in 1851, William Gregg says:

" From the best estimates that I have been able to make, I put down the white people who ought to work, and who do not, or who are so employed as to be wholly unproductive to the State, at one hundred and twenty-five thousand. Any man who is an observer of things could hardly pass through our country without being struck with the fact, that all the capital, enterprise and intelligence, is employed in directing slave labor; and the consequence is, that a large portion of our poor white people are wholly neglected, and are suffered to while away an existence in a state but one step in advance of the Indian of the forest. It is an evil of vast magnitude, and nothing but a change in public sentiment will effect its cure. These people must be brought into daily contact with the rich and intelligent—they must be stimulated to mental action, and taught to appreciate education and the comforts of civilized life; and this, we believe, may be effected only by the introduction of manufactures. My experience at Graniteville has satisfied me that unless our poor people can be brought together in villages, and some means of employment afforded them, it will be an utterly hopeless effort to undertake to educate them. We have collected at that place about eight hundred people, and as likely looking a set of country girls as may be found—industrious and orderly people—but deplorably ignorant, three-fourths of the adults not being able to read or to write their own names.

" It is only necessary to build a manufacturing village of shanties, in a healthy location, in any part of the State, to have crowds of these people around you, seeking employment at half the compensation given to operatives at the North. It is indeed painful to be brought in contact with such ignorance and degradation."

Again, he asks:

" Shall we pass unnoticed the thousands of poor, ignorant, degraded white people among us, who, in this land of plenty, live in comparative nakedness and starvation? Many a one is reared in *proud* South Carolina, from birth to manhood, who has never passed a month in which he has not, some part of the time, been stinted for meat. Many a mother is there who will tell you that her children are but scantily provided with bread, and much more scantily with meat; and, if they be clad with comfortable raiment, it is at the expense of these scanty allowances of food. These may be startling statements, but they are nevertheless true; and if not believed in Charleston, the members of our legislature who have traversed the State in electioneering campaigns, can attest the truth."

Black slave labor, though far less valuable, is almost invariably better paid than free white labor. The reason is this: the fiat of the oligarchy has made it fashionable to " have negroes around," and there are, we are grieved to say, many non-slaveholding white sycophants, who, in order to retain on their premises a hired slave whom they falsely imagine secures to them not only the appearance of wealth, but also a position of high social standing in the community, keep themselves in a perpetual strait.

In the spring of 1856, we made it our special business to ascertain the ruling rates of wages paid for labor, free and slave, in North Carolina. We found sober, energetic white men, between twenty and forty years of age, engaged in agricultural pursuits at a salary of $7 per month— including board only ; negro men, slaves, who performed little more than half the amount of labor, and who were exceedingly sluggish, awkward, and careless in all their movements, were hired out on adjoining farms at an average of about $10 per month, including board, clothing, and medical attendance. Free white men and slaves were in the employ of the North Carolina Railroad Company ; the former, whose services, in our opinion, were at least twice as valuable as the latter, received only $12 per month each ; the masters of the latter received $16 per month for every slave so employed. Industrious, tidy white girls, from sixteen to twenty years of age, had much difficulty in hiring themselves out as domestics in private families for $40 per annum— board only included ; negro wenches, slaves, of corresponding ages, so ungraceful, stupid and filthy that no decent man would ever permit one of them to cross the threshold of his dwelling, were in brisk demand at from $65 to $70 per annum, including victuals, clothes, and medical attendance. These are facts, and in considering them, the students of political and social economy will not fail to arrive at conclusions of their own.

Notwithstanding the greater density of population in the free States, labor of every kind is, on an average, about one hundred per cent. higher there than it is in the slave States. This is another important fact, and one that every non-slaveholding white should keep registered in his mind.

Poverty, ignorance, and superstition, are the three leading characteristics of the non-slaveholding whites of the South. Many of them grow up to the age of maturity, and pass through life without ever owning as much as five dollars at a time. Thousands of them die at an advanced age, as ignorant of the common alphabet as if it had never been invented. All are more or less impressed with a belief in witches, ghosts, and supernatural signs. Few are exempt from habits of sensuality and intemperance. None have anything like adequate ideas of the duties which they owe either to their God, to themselves, or to their fellow-men. Pitiable, indeed, in the fullest sense of the term, is their condition.

It is the almost utter lack of an education that has reduced them to their present unenviable situation. They are now completely under the domination of the oligarchy, and it is madness to suppose that they will ever be able to rise to a position of true manhood, until after the slave power shall have been utterly overthrown.

CHAPTER XII.

SOUTHERN LITERATURE.

Meanwhile a change was proceeding, infinitely more momentous than the acquisition or loss of any province, than the rise or fall of any dynasty. Slavery, and the evils by which slavery is everywhere accompanied, were fast disappearing.—MACAULAY.

> My voice is still for war.
> Gods! can a Roman Senate long debate
> Which of the two to choose, slavery or death?
> *　*　*　*　*　*
> A day—an hour of virtuous Liberty
> Is worth a whole eternity of bondage!
> ADDISON.

> Write, speak, avenge, for ancient sufferings feel,
> Impale each tyrant on their pens of steel,
> Declare how freemen can a world create,
> And slaves and masters ruin every State.
> BARLOW.

IT is with some degree of hesitation that we add a chapter on Southern Literature—not that the theme is inappropriate to this work; still less, that it is an unfruitful one; but our hesitation results from our conscious inability, in the limited time and space at our command, to do the subject justice. Few, except those whose experience has taught them, have any adequate idea of the amount of preparatory labor requisite to the production of a work into which the statistical element largely enters; especially is this so, when the statistics desired are not readily accessible through public and official documents. The author who honestly aims at entire accuracy in his statements, may find himself baffled for weeks in his pursuit of a single item of information, not of much importance in itself perhaps, when separately considered, but necessary in its connection with others, to the completion of a harmonious whole. Not unfrequently, during the preparation of the preceding pages, have we been subjected to this delay and annoyance.

What is the actual condition of Literature at the South? Our question includes more than simple authorship in the various departments of letters, from the compilation of a primary reader to the production of a Scientific or Theological Treatise. We comprehend in it all the activities engaged in the creation, publication, and sale of books and period icals, from the penny primer to the heavy folio, and from the dingy, coarse-typed weekly paper, to the large, well-filled daily.

Turning our attention to the periodical literature of the South, we obtain these results: By the census of 1850, we ascertain that the entire number of periodicals, daily, semi-weekly, weekly, semi-monthly, monthly and quarterly, published in the slave States, including the District of Columbia, were seven hundred and twenty-two. These had an aggregate *yearly* circulation of ninety-two million one hundred and sixty-seven thousand one hundred and twenty-nine (92,167,129). The number of periodicals, of every class, published in the non-slaveholding States (exclusive of California) was one thousand eight hundred and ninety-three, with an aggregate yearly circulation of three hundred and thirty-three million three hundred and eighty-six thousand and eighty-one (333,386,081).

Nearly nine years have elapsed since these statistics were taken, and these nine years have wrought an immense change in the journalism of the North, without any corresponding change in that of the South. It is noteworthy that, as a general thing, the principal journals of the free States are more comprehensive in their scope, more complete in every department, and enlist, if not a higher order of talent, at least *more* talent, than they did nine years ago. This improvement extends not only to the metropolitan, but to the country papers also. In fact, the very highest literary ability, in finance, in political economy, in science, in statism, in law, in theology, in medicine, in belles-lettres, is laid under contribution by the journals of the non-slaveholding States. This is true only to a very limited degree of Southern journals. Their position, with but few exceptions, is substantially the same that it was ten years ago. They are neither worse nor better—the imbecility and inertia which attaches to everything which slavery touches, clings to them now as tenaciously as it did when Henry A. Wise thanked God for the paucity of newspapers in the Old Dominion, and the platitudes of Father Ritchie were recognized as the political gospel of the South. They have not, so far as we can learn, increased materially in number, nor in the aggregate of their yearly circulation. In the free States no week passes that does not add to the number of their journals, and extend the circle of their readers and their influence. Since the census tables to which we have referred were prepared, two of the many excellent weekly journals of which the city of New York can boast, have sprung into being, and attained an aggregate circulation more than twice as large as that of the entire newspaper press of Virginia in 1850—and exceeding, by some thousands, the aggregate circulation of the two hundred and fifty journals of which Alabama, Arkansas, Kentucky, Georgia, North Carolina and Florida, could boast at the time above-mentioned.

Facts of great interest and importance appertaining to the two most widely circulated and influential journals in America--perhaps we might, with propriety, say in the world—will be found in the following carefully-prepared tabular statement:

TABLE 33.

AGGREGATE CIRCULATION OF THE DAILY, SEMI-WEEKLY, AND WEEKLY NEW YORK TRIBUNE,* APRIL 25, 1859, AND OF THE DAILY NEW YORK HERALD,† AUGUST 2, 1856.

Free States.	Tribune.	Herald.	Slave States.	Tribune.	Herald.
California	2,431		Alabama	51	80
Connecticut	8,638	2,146	Arkansas	10	
Illinois	12,769	858	Delaware	253	235
Indiana	10,098	36	Florida	41	45
Iowa	7,523	49	Georgia	78	170
Maine	7,677	58	Kentucky	548	68
Massachusetts	8,154	1,058	Louisiana	108	85
Michigan	9,264	256	Maryland	457	1,153
New Hampshire	6,239	189	Mississippi	15	11
New Jersey	5,477	8,330	Missouri	633	41
New York	65,186	47,275	North Carolina	57	44
Ohio	19,740	200	South Carolina	45	139
Pennsylvania	15,292	2,510	Tennessee	307	42
Rhode Island	2,151	322	Texas	132	5
Vermont	8,242	135	Virginia	375	176
Wisconsin	8,042	38	District of Columbia	130	817
Totals	196,923	58,410	Totals	3,240	2,611

Throughout the non-slaveholding States, the newspaper or magazine that has *not* improved during the last decade of years, is an exception to the general rule. Throughout the entire slaveholding States, the newspaper or magazine that *has* improved during that time, is no less an exception to the general rule that there obtains. Outside of the larger cities of the South, there are not, probably, half a dozen newspapers in the whole slaveholding region that can safely challenge a comparison with the country press of the North. What that country press was twenty years ago, the country press of the South is now.

The self-stultification of folly, was never more evident than it is in the current gabble of the Oligarchs about a Southern literature. They do not mean by it a healthy, manly, moral utterance of unfettered minds, without which there can be no proper literature; but an emasculated substitute therefor, from which the element of freedom is eliminated; husks, from which the kernel has escaped—a body, from which the vitalizing spirit has fled—a literature which ignores manhood by confounding if with brutehood; or, at best, deals with all similes of freedom as treason against the "peculiar institution." There is not a single great name in the literary annals of the old or new world that could dwarf itself to the stature requisite to gain admission into the

---

* See THE TRIBUNE of April 25th and 27th, 1859.
† See THE HERALD of August 6th, 1856.

Pantheon erected by these devotees of the Inane for their Lilliputian deities. Thank God, a Southern literature, in the sense intended by the champions of slavery, is a simple impossibility, rendered such by that exility of mind which they demand in its producers as a prerequisite to admission into the guild of Southern authorship. The tenuous thoughts of such authorlings could not survive a single breath of manly criticism. The history of the rise, progress and decline of their literature could be easily written on a child's smooth palm, and leave space enough for its funeral oration and epitaph. The latter might appropriately be that which, in one of our rural districts, marks the grave of a still-born infant:

"If so early I am done for,
I wonder what I was begun for."

We desire to see the South bear its just proportion in the literary activities and achievements of our common country. It has never yet done so, and it never will until its own manhood is vindicated in the abolition of slavery. The impulse which such a measure would give to all industrial pursuits that deal with the elements of material prosperity, would be imparted also to the no less valuable but more intangible creations of the mind. Take from the intellect of the South the incubus which now oppresses it, and its rebound would be glorious; the era of its diviner inspirations would begin; and its triumphs would be a perpetual vindication of the superiority of free institutions over those of slavery.

The people of the South are not a reading people. Many of the adult population never learned to read; still more, do not care to read. We have been impressed, during a temporary sojourn in the North, with the difference between the middle and laboring classes in the free States, and the same classes in the slave States, in this respect. Passing along the great routes of travel in the former, or taking our seat in the comfortable cars that pass up and down the avenues of our great commercial metropolis, we have not failed to contrast the employment of our fellow-passengers with that which occupies the attention of the corresponding classes on our various Southern routes of travel. In the one case, a large proportion of the passengers seem intent upon mastering the contents of the newspaper, or some recently published book. The merchant, the mechanic, the artisan, the professional man, and even the common laborer, going to or returning from their daily avocations, are busy with their morning and evening paper, or engaged in an intelligent discussion of some topic of public interest. This is their leisure hour, and it is given to the acquisition of such information as may be of immediate or ultimate use, or to the cultivation of a taste for elegant literature. In the other case, newspapers and books seem generally ignored, and noisy discussions of village and State politics, the tobacco and cotton crops, filibusterism in Cuba, Nicaragua, or Sonora, the price of negroes generally, and especially of "fine-looking wenches," the beauties of lynch-law, the delights of horse-racing, the excitement of street fights with bowie-knives and revolvers, the "manifest destiny" theory that justifies the stealing of all territory contiguous to our own, and kindred topics, constitute the warp and woof of conversation.

What follows, our readers will, we think, agree with us, is of great significance in this connection :

TABLE 34.

NUMBER OF PUBLIC DOCUMENTS FRANKED BY UNITED STATES SENATORS*—1858.

FREE STATE SENATORS.				SLAVE STATE SENATORS.			
State.	Name.	Documents.	Total	State.	Name.	Documents.	Total.
California.....	Broderick 18,000 Gwin..... 19,000		37,500	Alabama	Fitzpatrick 1,500 Clay....... 11,500		18,000
Connecticut...	Foster .... 7,000 Dixon		7,000	Arkansas.....	Sebastian.. 2,000 Johnson... 8,000		10,000
Illinois	Douglas... 345,000 Trumbull. 40,000		385,000	Delaware. ...	Bates...... ..... Bayard.		......
Indiana. ...	Fitch..... 11,000 Bright ... 15,000		26,000	Florida.......	Mallory ... 6,000 Yulee 2,000		8,000
Iowa.... ...	Jones.. .. 4,000 Harlan... 10,000		14,000	Georgia.......	Iverson.... 3,000 Toombs.... 2,000		5,000
Maine........	Fessenden 14,000 Hamlin .. 10,000		24,000	Kentucky... .	Thompson. ..... Crittenden. 10,000		10,000
Massachusetts.	Wilson ... . Sumner... 1,000		1,000	Louisiana. ..	Benjamin.. 11,000 Slidell..... 8,000		19,000
Michigan	Stuart ... 49,000 Chandler . 214,000		263,000	Maryland.....	Pearce .... 6,000 Kennedy.. 5,000		11,000
N. Hampshire.	Hale ..... 14,000 Clark..... 51,000		65,000	Mississippi....	Brown..... 18,000 Davis...... 6,000		24,000
New Jersey...	Wright ... 7,000 Thompson 1,000		8,000	Missouri......	Green..... 12,000 Polk....... 15,000		27,000
New York.....	Seward... 81,000 King 19,000		100,000	N. Carolina...	Reid....... 1,000 Clingman.. 21,500		22,500
Ohio.........	Pugh..... 4,000 Wade 2,000		6,000	S. Carolina. ..	Evans.... ..... Hammond.		......
Pennsylvania.	Bigler .... 54,000 Cameron . 10,000		64,000	Tennessee	Bell . ..... 7,000 Johnson... 11,000		18,000
Rhode Island.	Allen..... 300 Simmons.. 2,500		2,800	Texas	Houston... 5,000 Henderson.		5,000
Vermont......	Collamer . 3,000 Foot..... 2,000		5,000	Virginia	Mason..... 2,000 Hunter.... 2,000		4,000
Wisconsin	Durkee... 6,500 Doolittle.. 4,000		10,000		Total.........176,500		
	Total.........1,019,800						

Thus we perceive by the above table, that, while thirty-two Free State Senators send 1,019,800 documents—an average of 31,869 each, thirty Slave State Senators send only 176,500 documents—an average of but 5,883 each, showing an average balance of 25,986 in favor of every

* See debate on the proposed amendment to the Post-office bill, to increase the rates of postage, in the United States Senate, February 24, 1859. Senators from the slave States strongly, but unsuccessfully, advocated the passage of the amendment. Thanks to the free State Senators, who opposed and defeated it ! On account of the pitiable poverty and ignorance of slavery, as is shown in a preceding table, the mails were transported throughout the Southern States, during the year 1855, at an extra cost to the General Government of more than six hundred thousand dollars ! In the free States, during the same period, postages were received to the amount of more than two million of dollars over and above the cost of transportation !

Free State Senator! Thus do the lazy pro-slavery officials of the South perpetuate the ignorance and degradation of their constituents, by withholding from them—especially from their miserably-duped non-slaveholding constituents—the means of information to which they are justly entitled, and which they would receive, if represented by men whose sense of duty and honor was not irremediably debased by social contact with slaves and slavery.

The proportion of white adults over twenty years of age, in each State, who cannot read and write, to the *whole* white population, is as follows:

Connecticut	1 to every 568	Louisiana	1 to every 33½
Vermont	1 " 473	Maryland	1 " 27
New Hampshire	1 " 310	Mississippi	1 " 20
Massachusetts	1 " 166	Delaware	1 " 18
Maine	1 " 108	South Carolina	1 " 17
Michigan	1 " 97	Missouri	1 " 16
Rhode Island	1 " 67	Alabama	1 " 15
New Jersey	1 " 58	Kentucky	1 " 13½
New York	1 " 56	Georgia	1 " 13
Pennsylvania	1 " 50	Virginia	1 " 12½
Ohio	1 " 43	Arkansas	1 " 11½
Indiana	1 " 18	Tennessee	1 " 11
Illinois	1 " 17	North Carolina	1 " 7

In the slave States the proportion of free white children, between the ages of five and twenty, who are found at any school or college, is not quite *one-fifth* of the whole; in the free States, the proportion is more than *three-fifths.*

We could fill our pages with facts like these to an almost indefinite extent, but it cannot be necessary. No truth is more demonstrable, nay, no truth has been more abundantly demonstrated, than this: that slavery is hostile to general education; its strength, its very life, is in the ignorance and stolidity of the masses; it naturally and necessarily represses general literary culture. A free press is an institution almost unknown at the South. Free speech is considered as treason against slavery: and when people dare neither speak nor print their thoughts, free thought itself is well-nigh extinguished. All that can be said in *defence* of human bondage may be spoken freely, but question either its morality or its policy, and the terrors of Lynch-law are at once invoked to put down the pestilent heresy. The legislation of the slave States for the suppression of the freedom of speech and the press, is disgraceful and cowardly to the last degree, and can find its parallel only in the meanest and bloodiest despotisms of the old world. No institution that could bear the light would thus sneakingly seek to burrow itself in utter darkness. Look, too, at the mobbings, lynchings, robberies, social and political proscriptions, and all manner of nameless outrages, to which men in the South have been subjected, simply upon the suspicion that they were the enemies of slavery. We could fill page after page of this volume with the record of such atrocities. But a simple reference to them is enough. Our countrymen have not yet forgotten why John C. Underwood was, but a short while since, banished from his home in Virginia, and the accomplished Hedrick driven from his college professorship in North Carolina. They believed slavery inimical to the best interest of the South, and for daring to give expression to this belief in moderate yet manly language, they were ostracized by the despotic slave power, and compelled to seek a refuge from its vengeance in States where the principles of freedom are better understood. Pending the last Presidential election, there were thousands, nay, tens of thousands of voters in the slave States, who desired to give their suffrages for the Republican nominee, John C. Fremont, himself a Southron, but a non-slaveholder. The Constitution of the United States guaranteed to these men an expression of their preference at the ballot-box. But were they permitted such an expression? Not at all. They were denounced, threatened, overawed, by the slave power—and it is not too much to say, that there was really no *Constitutional election*—that is, no such free expression of political preferences as the Constitution aims to secure —in a majority of the slave States.

From a multiplicity of facts like these, the inference is unavoidable, that slavery tolerates no freedom of the press, no freedom of speech, no freedom of opinion. To expect that a whole-souled, manly literature can flourish under such conditions, is as absurd as it would be to look for health amid the pestilential vapors of a dungeon.

The truth is, slavery destroys, or vitiates, or pollutes, whatever it touches. No interest of society escapes the influence of its clinging curse. It makes Southern religion a stench in the nostrils of Christendom—it makes Southern politics a libel upon all the principles of Republicanism—it makes Southern literature a travesty upon the honorable profession of letters. Than the better class of Southern authors themselves, none will feel more keenly the truth of our remarks. They write books, but can find for them neither publishers nor remunerative sales at the South. The executors of Calhoun seek, for his works, a Northern publisher. Benton writes history and prepares voluminous compilations, which are given to the world through a Northern publisher. Simms writes novels and poems, and they are scattered abroad from the presses of Northern publishers. Eighty per cent. of all the copies sold are probably bought by Northern readers.

Our limits, not our materials, are exhausted. We would gladly say more, but can only, in conclusion, add as the result of our investigations in this department of our subject, that Literature and Liberty are inseparable ; the one can never have a vigorous existence without being wedded to the other.

Our work is done. It is the voice of the non-slaveholding whites of the South, through one identified with them by interest, by feeling, by position. That voice, by whomsoever spoken, must yet be heard and heeded. The time hastens—the doom of slavery is written—the redemption of the South draws nigh.

In taking leave of our readers, we know not how we can give more forcible expression to our thoughts and intentions than by saying that, in concert with the intelligent free voters of the North, we, the non-slaveholding whites of the South, desire and expect to elevate to the Presidency, in 1860, an able and worthy representative of the great principles enunciated in the Republican platform adopted at Philadelphia in 1856; and that, forever thereafter, we will, if we can, by our suffrages, hold the Presidential chair, and other high official positions in the Federal Government, sacredly intact from the occupancy and pollution of Pro-Slavery demagogues, whether from the North or from the South; and furthermore, that if, in any case, the Oligarchs do not quietly submit to the will of a constitutional majority of the people, as expressed at the ballot-box, the first battle between Freedom and Slavery will be fought at home—and may God defend the Right!

THE END.